THE CHURCH
IN FRANCE

THE CHURCH IN FRANCE

1848—1907

BY

C. S. PHILLIPS, M.A., D.D.

*Formerly Fellow and Lecturer of Selwyn College and
Foundation Scholar of King's College, Cambridge*

The reason why moderate men fail is
not because they are moderate, but because
they are few.

NEW YORK / RUSSELL & RUSSELL

FIRST PUBLISHED IN 1936
REISSUED, 1967, BY RUSSELL & RUSSELL
A DIVISION OF ATHENEUM HOUSE, INC.
L.C. CATALOG CARD NO: 66–24749

PRINTED IN THE UNITED STATES OF AMERICA

2 2 4 4 0

CONTENTS

INTRODUCTORY CHAPTER

THE RISE AND GROWTH OF ULTRAMONTANISM IN FRANCE

In a letter dated Sept. 10th, 1853, Archbishop Sibour of Paris wrote to the Comte de Montalembert as follows :

" When twenty-five years ago you, like myself, made fearless profession of ' Ultramontanism ' . . . the Ultramontane school was the school of liberty. We defended against the pretensions and aggressions of the temporal power the independence of the spiritual : but we respected the constitution of the State and the constitution of the Church. . . . The Pope and the Emperor were not respectively the whole of the Church and the whole of the State. On the one hand, there were bishops and councils with a real authority : on the other, there were elements both aristocratic and democratic which had their place and their right.

" Without doubt there are times when the Pope may raise himself above all rules . . . and when his power is as wide as the necessities of the Church—just as there are cases in which in civil societies (as we have recently seen) the political power may free itself from the laws and save the country in their despite. . . . The earlier Ultramontanes recognised this : but they did not turn the exception into the rule. The new Ultramontanes have rushed to extremes in both directions, and in reckless exaggeration of the principle of authority have argued *à outrance* against all liberties—those of the State and those of the Church alike."

To which Montalembert replied :

" You are right a thousand times. When we Ultramontanes of former days defended the rights of the Holy See, of justice and liberty, against the Gallicanism of the lawyers and *universitaires,* the Ultramontane school was a school of liberty. The attempt is now made to turn it into a school of slavery—and with only too much success." [1]

This fragment of correspondence may fitly serve as prelude to a work which will be largely concerned with the triumph, in the Church of France as elsewhere, of the principles and tendencies labelled " Ultramontane." For it indicates, in

[1] Both letters are printed in Lecanuet, *Montalembert* iii. 104—6. 1902. This excellent work has been extensively used in the preparation of the earlier chapters of the present book.

authoritative fashion, the important fact that about the middle of the nineteenth century the name " Ultramontane " underwent a change of meaning which made it henceforth inapplicable to many of the most distinguished of those who had formerly been proud to bear it.   In the earlier sense of the word both Sibour and Montalembert, by their own admission, had served under the banner of " Ultramontanism."   In its later sense they were among its most determined opponents, and a principal target of attack to those who sought to secure its triumph.   The " Ultramontanism " of 1870, in short, is in many ways quite a different thing from the "Ultramontanism" of 1830 : and we shall fail entirely to get the history of the Church of France in the last century in its right perspective unless we bear this fact carefully in mind.

Wherein then does this change of meaning consist?   And what were the forces and influences that brought it about?

The answer to the first part of this question (as we shall see) is that suggested in Sibour's letter.   We may ignore for the moment the attitude in regard to secular politics of those whom he denounces.   This attitude was indeed no more than an opportunist concession to the exigencies of the time, and was to be cruelly falsified by the event.   We confine ourselves to the ecclesiastical aspect of the change of front to which the Archbishop alludes.

It is neither possible nor necessary here to trace at length the rise and progress within the Catholic Church of the ideas connoted by " Ultramontanism " in the sense in which the word is generally accepted to-day.   The policy of the Papacy has always been a policy of centralization.   It has never abated its efforts to win for itself the supreme and exclusive authority in the Church in matters of both faith and practice.   But before its final triumph in 1870 it had a long road to travel and many opposing forces to defeat—forces with which it contended at different times with widely varying degrees of success.   The ideal of a spiritual autocracy had two arch-enemies in particular lying across its path—the General Council, and the claim of kings and nations to settle, at least in a large measure, their own ecclesiastical affairs.   The former was within an ace of winning a final victory in the first half of the fifteenth century : and it needed all the adroitness and good fortune of the Popes to avert this and to postpone, without deciding, the issue. For more than three centuries longer Council and Papacy were to be set up against one another by their respective champions as rival claimants to the supreme authority in the Church, without any obligation on the part of the faithful to accept the claim of one or the other. As regards the other obstacle to papal ambition—the recalcitrance of the civil power—this, already pronounced in the Middle Ages, was to become more pronounced still with the decay of medieval aspirations after unity and the emergence, in their place, of the nationalist ideals embodied in the great autocratic monarchies of Europe. In England and in a large part of Germany it resulted in a repudiation of papal authority altogether : " The Bishop of Rome hath no jurisdiction in this realm of England." In France, Spain and the rest of Germany, the Pope was still recognised as the divinely appointed Head of the Church : but any attempt on his part to settle the affairs of religion by his own exclusive authority was stoutly resisted, and the Church was held in a strong grip by the civil power.

In the maintenance of both kinds of opposition France played the leading part. The sufficient proof of this is the existence of the word " Gallicanism "—a term that is used to cover both the view that a General Council is above the Pope and the view that the civil authority has the right to interfere in ecclesiastical matters even in the Pope's despite. The mainspring and focus of the great Conciliar movement which at Constance and Basle nearly spiked the guns of the Popes for ever were supplied by French divines, with the famous Gerson at their head : and towards the close of the seventeenth century its aims were once more emphatically asserted in France and found a mouthpiece in the still more famous Bossuet. [2] Under the later French monarchy the Church was

[2] The classic formulation of Gallicanism is found in the " Gallican Articles " issued by the Assembly of the Clergy in 1682, during the struggle between Louis XIV. and Innocent XI. They are here given in an abbreviated form :

largely enslaved to the State: and in the reign of Louis XIV. the opposition of Pope and King only just fell short of precipitating a schism.

The fortunes of the Papacy in the eighteenth century were at a very low ebb. The expansive power of the Counter-Reformation movement had exhausted itself; the Popes were personally undistinguished; in every country the forces of irreligion and scepticism gathered a strength and audacity unknown before. The governments of the Catholic nations were thoroughly materialistic in their outlook : their statesmen, even when they were not openly or secretly infidels, regarded religion chiefly as an instrument of government and, for this and other reasons, were intensely jealous of outside interference. Nor was there in the national Churches themselves any force of spiritual independence or enthusiasm to counteract the Erastianism of the civil power. As the century wore on, the Papacy found itself more and more helpless and defenceless. The rulers of Europe were increasingly dominated by the *esprit philosophique* and the idea of the omnipotent State. It was these that inspired the ecclesiastical reforms of Joseph II., which the Pope of the time (Pius VI.) found himself powerless to resist. At a slightly earlier period (1773) the same influences led to the extinction, at the unwilling hands of the Pope himself, of the great Jesuit Order—always the most fervent and persistent champion of papal autocracy.

Bad though the situation was before 1789, the revolutionary

1. S. Peter and his successors, vicars of Christ, and likewise the Church itself have received from God power in things spiritual—but not in things temporal and civil. . . . Consequently kings and princes are not by the law of God subject to any ecclesiastical power . . . with respect to their temporal government.

2. The plenitude of power in things spiritual which resides in the Apostolic see . . . is such that at the same time the decrees of the Œcumenical Council of Constance . . . remain in full force and perpetual obligation.

3. Hence the exercise of the Apostolic authority must be regulated by the canons enacted by the Spirit of God. . . . The ancient rules, customs and institutions received by the realm and Church of France likewise remain inviolable.

4. The Pope has the principal place in deciding questions of faith and his decrees extend to . . . all Churches: but nevertheless his judgment is not irreversible unless confirmed by consent of the Church.

and Napoleonic period that followed made it infinitely worse. The *Constitution Civile du Clergé* of 1790 was an expression of the Gallican spirit in its extremest form and made the Church in France a mere department of the State. The tie that linked it with the Pope was attenuated to vanishing point : and his condemnation of the Constitution was not merely defied but made a ground for the bitter persecution of those who on the strength of that condemnation refused to accept it. With the advent of Bonaparte to power the situation temporarily improved. The Concordat of 1801 restored to the Pope some part of the position in regard to the Church in France that he had formerly enjoyed. Further, the clause by which Pius VII. undertook to wipe out, as by a stroke of the pen, the whole of the existing body of bishops involved a recognition of the subordination of the episcopate to the Holy See in its most extreme form. No doubt Bonaparte did not mean it as such—his aim was merely to clear the ground. But the Holy See knew perfectly well what it was doing and was to make abundant capital out of its action later on. On the other hand, the bargain driven was a bitterly hard one, and was made harder still by the so-called " Organic Articles " [3] appended to the Concordat in the decree of the Corps Législatif that gave it legal force the following year. When a few years later the Pope dared to refuse certain demands of Napoleon that his conscience forbade him to concede, he was deprived of his Temporal Power and virtually imprisoned.

The fall of the Empire restored to him his liberty and his States. But the Gallicanism of the old Bourbon regime in France persisted under the new. The Concordat of 1801

---

[3] As these will be mentioned frequently in the course of this work, it may be well to indicate some of their more important provisions : (1) No written communications from the Pope of any kind might be received in France without the authorization of the Government. (2) His legates and representatives must receive the same authorization. (3) The decrees of foreign synods, and even of General Councils, might not be published in France until the government had examined and approved them. (4) No Council—national, metropolitan or diocesan—might assemble without the Government's permission. (5) In the case of any abuse of their powers by ecclesiastical persons, recourse was to be had to the Council of State. (6) Professors of seminaries were to teach the " Gallican Articles " of 1682.

remained in force, even if interpreted in a somewhat more liberal manner. Under the Restoration, the Pope was treated with becoming respect : but his authority was watched with a jealous eye. As for the Church itself, it certainly enjoyed the patronage of the civil power. But this patronage was by no means purely disinterested in its motives, and the Church enjoyed little freedom of independent action. The restriction of its liberty was particularly marked in the sphere of education. An important part of Napoleon's work of reconstruction after the Revolution had been the foundation of the Université —an organization of all grades of the teaching profession exercising in the name of the State a virtual monopoly of the national education. This system was maintained after 1815 : and though under the Restoration its administration was largely placed in the hands of ecclesiastics and a certain number of Catholic schools were exempted from its control altogether, yet the general spirit of the Université as a body was unsympathetic to the Church, and its virtual monopoly was deeply resented by the more ardent Catholics, who called it the " eldest daughter of the Revolution " and " la fille de Buonaparte."[4]

The story of the process by which the Church succeeded in winning at least a measure of freedom from its bondage to the State has been told by the present writer in a previous volume[5] and need not be retold here. We content ourselves with pointing out the general character of the movement and the principles that inspired it. Its inception was the work of the wayward and brilliant genius Lamennais,[6] who in the closing years of the Restoration attacked in words of burning eloquence the subjugation of the Church to the State and declared that only under a regime of freedom could it carry out the work of saving society with which it was entrusted.

---

[4] Weill : *Histoire du Catholicisme Libéral en France*, 9.
[5] Phillips : *The Church in France, 1789—1848: a Study in Revival.* 1929.
[6] The story of Lamennais' career has been told in admirable and sympathetic fashion by Boutard, *Lamennais: sa vie et ses doctrines*, 3 vols., 1905—13. See also the brilliant study by R. Vallery-Radot, *Lamennais, ou le prêtre malgré lui.* 1931. On Lamennais as the founder of Liberal Catholicism, see Weill, *op. cit.*, 13ff.

There was indeed small chance of such ideas being given practical effect so long as the elder Bourbon line sat on the throne. The clergy themselves cared as little for them as the statesmen. But the revolution of 1830 altered the whole situation. The alliance between the Altar and the Throne was at an end. Henceforth the Church must depend more on its own resources and less on the interested support of the civil power, with the inevitable price that must be paid for this in the shape of continual interference in its affairs. In the pages of his newspaper, the *Avenir,* Lamennais urged it to do so without fear or scruple; to rely no more on the arm of the flesh but to take its stand boldly on the ground of freedom to do its own work in its own way—no less and no more.

For the moment the appeal fell on deaf ears. The Government opposed the movement; the hierarchy frowned on it; finally the Pope himself publicly condemned it. Lamennais in rage and despair quitted the Church for ever. But his friends were more tenacious. If circumstances forbade the realisation of the ideals of the *Avenir* in their fullness, yet its watchword—" Liberty for the Church "—might still serve as the basis of constructive and aggressive action—and the more hopefully in that the new political regime, unlike the old, was founded (at least in theory) on the principle that liberty is a thing desirable in itself. It was along these lines that the notable revival of Church life under the July monarchy, associated especially with the names of Lacordaire and Montalembert, was carried into effect. In particular, a vigorous offensive was directed against the educational monopoly of the Université, which since 1830 had steadily grown more and more ill-disposed to the Church. The struggle was not to be finally crowned with success until 1850 : but throughout the 'forties the cause of freedom of education gathered momentum and taught Catholics to act together in defence of their interests.

In the pursuit of this policy of securing a greater freedom for the Church it was necessary that there should be some *point d'appui* which might serve to rally enthusiasm and to supply a moral support, in face of the determination of the government not to relax the grip upon the Church that it had inherited from its predecessor. There was no chance of finding anything of the sort within France itself. Time was when the great Gallican Church had been proudly self-sufficient and needed neither support nor direction from outside. If she allowed herself to be unduly deferential to the civil power, it was largely because she chose to have it so and because it suited her purposes. Her clergy formed the First Estate of the Realm; she had her own diocesan, provincial and national assemblies; in the Sorbonne she possessed the most famous school of theological thought and learning in the world, before which even Rome itself might tremble. But all that had passed with the *ancien régime*. Her servitude to the State remained, but none of the prestige and resources that had made that servitude tolerable. In such circumstances only one refuge remained—the Holy See.

It is true that, with such a Pope as Gregory XVI. on the throne, Rome was not always in practice as helpful as she might have been. Yet none the less the Pope was the Head of the Church, the Vice-gerent of Jesus Christ, the supreme symbol and depositary of spiritual authority as opposed to the powers of the world : and his name was a name before which all faithful hearts must bow. The old splendour that had surrounded his office in days gone by had recently glowed into new life in the pages of Joseph de Maistre :[7] and if many of those who now called on the name of Rome would hardly have subscribed to the theories of that great reactionary in their entirety, they could not fail to feel the thrill of the dream he had evoked. The great problem was to assert, in face of the Erastianism of the civil power, the nature of the Church as a world-wide spiritual society, endued with the right to settle its affairs for itself without reference to any authority save its own. Looked at in this way, Ultramontanism stands for a principle which is the very life-blood of the Church and can never be ignored without fatal results to its vitality and effectiveness. It was in this sense (as Sibour's letter suggests) that the French Ultramontanes of the first half of the nine-

[7] Joseph de Maistre : *Du Pape.* 1819.

teenth century understood and made proud boast of the name. The cause of spiritual freedom was the cause of the Pope : and the cause of the Pope was the cause of spiritual freedom.

In the period we are considering the " Ultramontane " movement was essentially a movement of the rank and file of the Catholic body. It could hardly be otherwise. The Concordat of 1801 gave the nomination of the bishops into the hand of the Government, subject to a confirmation by the Pope which (after 1814) was hardly ever refused : and both under the Restoration and under Louis Philippe the Government was careful to see that its nominees were of its own way of thinking as to the relations between Church and State. It is true that on one occasion at least (in 1844) the bishops were induced to assert themselves as a body in the cause of freedom of education—but only under strong pressure from the lower clergy and the laity.

The former, in particular, had good reason for lifting up their eyes to the Seven Hills of Rome. [8] In the Church of France as it was before 1789 the parochial clergy had enjoyed a certain amount of independence in regard to their bishops. True, their stipends were for the most part beggarly enough; the vast wealth of the Church being almost exclusively concentrated in the hands of the bishops and the monastic orders. But by the provisions of the canon law they could not be removed from office except on the ground of delinquency juridically proved in courts appointed for the purpose : and they enjoyed the right of representation in their provincial and diocesan assemblies. But the Concordat, with the Organic Articles accompanying it, handed the lower clergy over, bound hand and foot, to the bishops. Napoleon's idea was that this was the best way to keep them in order. The bishops would control the clergy, while he would control the bishops. This military conception of the episcopal office was well summed up many years later under the Second Empire when a Cardinal Archbishop, addressing the generals who were his colleagues in the Senate, said : " Every bishop has, like you,

[8] On what follows, see especially E. Ollivier: *"L'Église et l'État au Concile du Vatican,* i. 282ff. Also Weill, *op. cit.,* 61f.

sirs, a regiment to command : and when he says ' March,' it marches." [9]

The bishops entered *con amore* into the rôle assigned to them. In the new delimitation of parochial boundaries (made by the bishops themselves immediately after the Concordat, as delegates of the Cardinal-Legate Caprara) the rural curés were in the great majority of cases turned into mere *desservants* removable from their office at the will and pleasure of their diocesan. Neither the *Officialités* (or Consistory Courts, as we might call them) nor the diocesan synods were revived. The provisions of the Canon Law were simply ignored. As Émile Ollivier observes of the bishops, " the zeal of the Lord's house only devoured them where they themselves were concerned." One of them is reported to have said, " The Canon Law in my diocese is—myself." [10]

The parish priest was thus at the mercy of his bishop, who might change his sphere of work or deprive him of one altogether without having to give a reason to anybody— whether to gratify the prejudice or spite of some local person- age or for whatever other cause. Nor did it avail him if, feeling himself unjustly treated, he had recourse by way of *appel comme d'abus* to the civil power—though the Organic Articles ostensibly enjoined this in cases of defect of justice.[11] The Council of State simply declined cognizance, maintaining that it was the bishop's business and nobody else's. In the case of a minority of *curés inamovibles* the position was less easy to maintain : but no real satisfaction was given. The poor rural priest had thus no alternative but either to grin and bear his lot in silence—or to revolt openly and take the consequences.

It is easy to imagine how, to men set in this way like toads under the harrow, the glowing accents in which Lamennais and his friends exalted the authority, the equity, the beneficence of the Pope, the Father of all the faithful, supplied

---

[9] The speaker was Cardinal de Bonnechose, Archbishop of Rouen, in the course of a debate on the speech from the throne, March 11th, 1865. See Maurain : *La politique ecclésiastique du 2nd Empire*, 730.
[10] Ollivier : *op. cit.*, i. 283.
[11] Articles 6 and 8.

a consolation and a hope unknown before. Unfortunately, in this as in other matters, Gregory XVI. was unequal to the rôle for which he was cast. In 1839 two priests, the brothers Allignol, published a pamphlet depicting the wretched state to which the Concordatist regime had reduced the lower clergy and declaring that the only remedy lay in a return to the safe-guards provided by the canon law—*l'inamovibilité* in par-ticular. The bishops at once took alarm, and ominous charges of " presbyterianism " were bandied about—not perhaps wholly without cause. The Bishop of Viviers, Mgr. Guibert, with the cordial approval of his fellow-bishops, pronounced a censure on the two brothers, who appealed to the Pope. Gregory supported the bishop, if only in a private letter ad-dressed to the latter.[12] A few years later a general petition of *desservants* to the Pope against the episcopal absolutism, organised by the *Voix de la Vérité* (the organ of the Abbé Migne, celebrated as the editor of the *Patrologia*), was condemned by Archbishop Affre of Paris (1847).[13] In but one quarter in the episcopate did the woes of the lower clergy find sympathy. Sibour, then Bishop of Digne, outlined a scheme which, while emphatically asserting the authority of the bishop, went at least some way towards re-erecting the canonical machinery that might guard against its abuse. But his example was neither welcomed nor followed by his brethren, so that his initiative bore no fruit.

With the accession of a new Pope, however, the situation underwent an important change. Pius IX. was of a very different calibre from his predecessor. Generous and impulsive, intensely conscious of the rights and claims of his great office and never afraid to assert them in the face of all the world, he lent a willing—sometimes a too willing—ear to the complaints of the victims of episcopal " tyranny." Nor (we may assume) was he unready to put a spoke in the wheel of prelates who in many cases were inclined to assume what seemed to him an unduly independent attitude towards the Holy See. A new champion, too, of the rights of the lower clergy now arose who

[12] See Paguelle de Follenay: *Vie du Cardinal Guibert*, ii., 41ff.
[13] Weill: *op. cit.*, 62.

was careful to avoid the mistakes that had contributed to the failure of the brothers Allignol. The Abbé St. André was deeply versed in the Canon Law and kept his demands strictly within the limits of the decrees of the Council of Trent, the validity of which no one dared to dispute. The Pope showed himself sympathetic. Henceforth appeals to Rome from clerics who had been deprived and displaced were received and judged in accordance with regulations drawn up for the purpose by the Roman congregations.

Such generous condescension to the lowly could not fail to win clerical hearts and disposed them to lend a willing ear to those whose aim it was to exalt the papal prerogatives in theory and to make them increasingly effective in practice. Among these, the most striking figure was not an ecclesiastic, but a layman—the famous Catholic journalist, LouisVeuillot.[14] His paper, the *Univers,* was the oracle of the Ultramontane party and was read with avidity in the presbyteries all over the country. It was under his guidance and that of the ecclesiastics and laymen associated with him that "Ultramontanism" underwent the change of meaning to which Sibour's letter alludes. No longer does it represent merely an attempt to " defend against the pretensions and aggressions of the temporal power the independence of the spiritual." Rather is it a vindication of the claims of the Church (and particularly of the Papacy) in their extremest form—a form far more extreme (be it noted) than any that has received permanently authoritative sanction from Rome itself.

It has been already recalled how in the earlier years of the Restoration Joseph de Maistre set himself to regild the tarnished glories of the Papacy. His inspiring motive was even more political than religious.[15] For him the Revolution was " Satanic in its essence "—an evil spirit destructive of all

[14] See E. and F. Veuillot: *Louis Veuillot,* 4 vols. 1899—1913. This work (by Veuillot's brother and nephew) is very favourable to its subject. Lecanuet, *Montalembert,* and Lagrange, *Dupanloup,* provide a less flattering portrait.

[15] On de Maistre and the origins of Neo-Ultramontanism generally, see Wilfred Ward: *William George Ward and the Catholic Revival,* 1893, chapter v.

authority and order and therefore fatal to that " unity " which was the eternal purpose of God for mankind. Only in one way could this spirit be exorcised and the ruin it had wrought be made good—by a return to the doctrines of Christianity as enshrined in the infallible teaching of the Catholic Church. Of this teaching the Pope was the divinely-accredited mouthpiece. Just as the Papacy had built up Christian civilization in the past, so it alone could rebuild it in the future. The Pope is the apex of the pyramid of human society : even kings and nations must bow before his decrees. To Holy Church is committed by God the ultimate control of human life in all its departments : and its voice is the voice of the Pope. Being as he is the infallible organ of divine truth and of the divine will, his authority is final : and when he has spoken, *causa finita est.*

Such were the views which now, in the hands of Veuillot and his fellow-champions of the " new Ultramontanism," were to become no longer a theory and a dream but an effective force in ecclesiastical politics. For them, as for de Maistre, liberty was anathema, the parent of every human ill. The freedom of thought and action upon which the modern social order rests is contrary to the will of God, and the Church must wage unceasing war against it. The exercise of man's reasoning faculties must be strictly controlled by the decisions of the Vicar of Christ : and the more numerous and frequent these are the better. The claim of science to form its own conclusions independently of ecclesiastical authority and the claim of peoples to settle their own destinies for themselves are alike condemned. Man's glory is not to be free but to obey. Even the successors of the Apostles must be strictly subordinated to the Pope. He is *episcopus episcoporum :* the bishops are merely his delegates and are subject to his control.

It was in reference to this wholesale condemnation of modern ideas that the split took place which drove many of the most eminent " Ultramontanes " of an earlier day into an attitude of passionate opposition to " Ultramontanism " in its later sense. Montalembert, Dupanloup, Lacordaire, Falloux and the rest of the so-called " Liberal Catholics " had fairly earned the right to be regarded as faithful sons of the Church. But they declined to believe that the forces and ideas that govern modern society are wholly evil, and that the only means of salvation lies in a return to such a theocracy as the Middle Ages dreamed of but never realized. In particular, they were convinced that Catholicism may consist with a whole-hearted belief in political freedom and the " principles of 1789." Nor would they accept the extreme claims made on behalf of the Pope by the Ultramontane fanatics in the ecclesiastical sphere. The Pope (to quote Sibour again) is not " the whole of the Church." Such views were hotly resented by Veuillot and his friends, and subjected their holders to a ceaseless fire of abuse and denunciation in the *Univers* and elsewhere.

As Veuillot will figure largely in the pages of this work as the standard-bearer of " Ultramontanism " (in the later sense) in all its aspects, it may be well to attempt a portrait of his personality. Born in 1813 at Boynes in the Gâtinais, the child of humble parents, he became a journalist at an early age. Brought up apart from religious influences, he was converted during a visit to Rome in 1838; and during a retreat in Switzerland that followed dedicated himself henceforth to advancing the cause of Catholicism by all the means in his power. Soon afterwards he received a minor administrative post in Paris, but continued to ply his pen in his leisure hours. At first a contributor to the *Univers,* he assumed its direction in 1843. His force of character and amazing ability soon raised what had been an obscure religious journal to the position of a potent force in the ecclesiastical world. Through all the vicissitudes of journal and editor the connection between the two was to last till Veuillot's death in 1883.

The fanaticism of Veuillot's views and the unbridled virulence of his invective must not blind us to his good qualities. Affectionate and warm-hearted, he was an admirable husband and father, a man of genuine piety and capable of intense devotion to the persons and causes he loved. Even in his most bitter attacks on those who opposed his views he seems to have honestly striven to avoid personal animosity (though perhaps he was not quite so entirely innocent of this as he believed himself to be) and to keep his controversies on the objective level. In his will he declared that he had " never hated anyone knowingly or willingly." He had loved those he fought—" *surtout Montalembert.*" [16] He contrived to be supremely offensive : but it is doubtful if he realised how offensive he was. He was one of those people who say the most abominable things to or about an opponent, and then are genuinely surprised and even hurt that he should resent them. Moreover, he was a Frenchman : and we more phlegmatic English find it hard to realise how supremely offensive Frenchmen can be to one another when they disagree. It must be added that if he was virulent and aggressive, his adversaries were often the same. The complaints of the anticlericals concerning his " want of charity " strike one as somewhat Pecksniffian : and as for the Liberal Catholics—if they received many hard knocks, they also did their best to provoke them. In the ceaseless conflict between their respective parties, Montalembert and Dupanloup could be quite as violent and aggressive in their way as Veuillot : and they never lost an opportunity of attacking the *Univers* with every weapon at their disposal. In fact, of the two sides, it is even possible to hold that Veuillot comes out the better. Veuillot always fought in the open, while Dupanloup at least was not averse from subterranean methods. His hand was in many things in which it did not overtly appear. It is hard, too, to acquit Montalembert of personal animus against Veuillot. For all his noble qualities he seems to have been a rather difficult person to get on with unless you would " toe his line " in all respects : and his remorse for the support he had given to Louis Napoleon undoubtedly embittered his temper. But he should have reflected that Veuillot had only taken up his own position in 1849-50 ; and that it was he who was inconsistent with his past and not Veuillot, whose political attitude throughout his career appears (as Jules Lemaître said) to have been " completely of a piece." No doubt he made mistakes as to the means—especially in his

---

[16] E. and F. Veuillot, *op. cit.*, iv. 764.

whole-hearted backing of Napoleon III. until he found him out. But the end and principle were always the same—the triumph of religion as he conceived it.

All this may be admitted even by those who entirely disagree with Veuillot's views and detest the methods of controversy which he adopted. In regard to his views it is no part of the present writer's purpose to sit in judgment on Ultramontanism —to assess its truth or falsehood or what elements it may contain of either. It may suffice to say that it is a perfectly consistent and logical position if once its premises be accepted : and Veuillot, accepting the premises *ex animo,* was never afraid to press their consequences to the uttermost. His methods are rather a different matter. Controversy is inevitable, especially on matters of such fundamental importance as those with which Veuillot largely dealt. But it needs to be carried on in a moderate and charitable spirit—with a due desire to understand and give full weight to the position of the other side, to persuade by argument and not wantonly to exacerbate and wound. It was here that Veuillot failed. Nature had endowed him with superb gifts of expression. He is an acknowledged master of the French language, with special gifts of wit, irony, epigram and invective—all those gifts, in fact, that are most dangerous to their possessor. To Veuillot they were specially dangerous because of the ardour of his temperament and the intransigence of his views. The result was deplorable. The annals of religious journalism are not particularly edifying : but Veuillot enjoys an unenviable reputation even here. A story is told of a conversation between a Catholic and an unbeliever. "I never read the *Univers,*" said the former, "because I want to remain a Christian." "And I read it every day," replied the other, "because I don't want to become one."

Unfortunately, Veuillot's defects were no obstacle to his success—rather they were a cause of it. Extreme views, especially when expressed with such verve and brilliance as Veuillot's, will never fail to find and win hearers : and for some two generations the great Catholic journalist occupied the position of a sort of lay Pope in France. To a man of his stamp such a position was perilous indeed. He was considerably smitten with self-importance and vanity. He loved to be in the limelight, to receive praise and flattery—and he had far too much of both for his own good. He was intensely sensitive to criticism and could never endure it in silence, but must always give as good as and better than he got. With such a disposition nothing is more dangerous than to believe oneself identified with the cause of absolute and eternal truth : for self-assertion and prejudice, vanity and dogmatism so readily disguise themselves under the mask of a champion of God—especially if (as in Veuillot's case) God's Vicar is usually ready to back one up and compliment one at every turn. Yet even Pius IX. was sometimes of opinion that Veuillot's zeal outran his discretion.

Whatever the manner of their rendering, Veuillot's services to the Ultramontane cause are beyond dispute and almost beyond calculation. The priests and laity of France in ever increasing numbers looked to him as to an oracle, and rejoiced to help in the dissemination—and even the exaggeration—of his views. Nor were these views without echo and support within the episcopate itself. The French bishops, almost exclusively Gallican under Louis Philippe, found themselves under Napoleon III. divided into two opposing camps—Gallicans and Liberals [17] on the one side, Ultramontanes on the other. The latter were not always in sympathy with Veuillot's political attitude : but they shared (in varying degrees) his ecclesiastical views, even though at times they might desire a little more moderation in their expression. Among them were two former disciples of Lamennais : Salinis, Bishop of Amiens (who, like Veuillot, enthusiastically supported the revived Napoleonic dynasty) and Gerbet, Bishop of Perpignan. The principal champion of Ultramontanism in the episcopate under the July monarchy, Parisis of Langres, falls into the background after 1848. In his place the leadership

---

[17] The Gallicans and Liberals differed in many ways from one another : but their common aversion for Ultramontanism tended to draw them together in the sphere of ecclesiastical politics.

passed more and more to the youthful and vigorous Mgr. Pie, appointed Bishop of Poitiers in 1849. [18]

As regards secular politics Pie was far from sharing Veuillot's position : for he had been cradled in the Legitimist faith and was throughout his life a warm and uncompromising supporter of the claims of the elder Bourbon line. Napoleon III. he neither liked nor trusted, and he used plain speech even to his face. But in the sphere of ecclesiastical politics he was as fanatically Ultramontane as Veuillot himself. Between him and Dupanloup there was little love lost and a strong personal rivalry : and the duel between them was incessant as protagonists of the Ultramontane and the Liberal Catholic side respectively. A thorough-going reactionary in both political and religious matters, Pie hated liberty in all its forms—liberty of conscience most of all. He would accept freedom for the Church if he could get nothing better : but he had in him all the stuff of a highly conscientious persecutor. Had he lived in the Middle Ages he might have left behind him a somewhat execrable memory. But he was a strong, able and resolute man who united a fanatical devotion to the Church to an autocratic temper and an immense self-importance. His pompous harping on the phrase " *Ego episcopus sum,*" when, as a young man of thirty-four, he took possession of his see, [19] strikes the keynote of his career. He was deeply in the confidence of Pius IX., whose views he completely shared.

Another influence operating in favour of the Ultramontane cause—less prominent to the eye yet not less steady and effective—was that of the religious orders. These had been swept away in France by the Revolution : and the Concordat had made no provision for their restoration. But gradually— and especially after 1830—they had come back : and to the old historic orders was now added a considerable number of new congregations, large and small. Most of them made no attempt to secure the State authorization that was in theory required by the law : but they showed no signs of suffering

[18] For Pie's career see Baunard : *Histoire du Cardinal Pie,* 2 vols. 1883. The book exhibits in a marked degree the hagiographical tendency usual in French (and not only French) ecclesiastical biography.
[19] Baunard, *op. cit.,* i., 243f.

in consequence. The *militia Christi* (as the religious orders are often called) have been ever for the most part a *militia Papae* as well: and the Holy See has always been disposed to rely on them as a counterweight to the episcopate. The Jesuits in particular have been the unwearying champions of the papal claims. In 1846 their order had been suppressed in France by the government of Louis Philippe: but the suppression had been no more than nominal and the Revolution of 1848 soon restored to them full liberty of action. Other famous orders like the Dominicans shared their devotion to the Holy See: and among the new congregations the Assumptionists [20] were to achieve special note and effectiveness in this direction.

It was, however, an order that has not always perhaps been so completely the willing slave of Rome as some others—the Benedictine—that produced the foremost champion of Ultramontanism among the French religious of the nineteenth century. As such, the name of Dom Guéranger, Abbot of Solesmes, [21] stands beside that of Pie and Veuillot. It was by him that the Benedictines were restored to France in 1832, when at the head of a small group of monks he took possession of the deserted priory of Solesmes. A pontifical brief of 1836 assigned to them the special duty of " restoring the sound traditions of the pontifical jurisprudence and of the sacred liturgy." A devoted servant of Rome and a deeply learned liturgiologist, and at the same time a man of singularly forceful and militant character (Pius IX's playful nickname for him was " Dom Guerroyer " [22]), Guéranger was to prove fully worthy of his task. In political matters he was not always wise. Like Veuillot, he fell an easy victim to the professions of Louis Napoleon. His adulation of the " Saviour of Society " was almost nauseating; his contempt for freedom profound. Yet, like Veuillot again, if he supported the revived Empire, it was because he believed that it would serve the turn of the Church and its Head.

[20] Its founder, Père Emmanuel d'Alzon, had been a member of the Lamennais circle.
[21] On Guéranger's life and activity, see [Delatte]: *Dom Guéranger, abbé de Solesmes,* 2 vols. 1910.
[22] Weill, 122.

Guéranger's chief service to the Ultramontane cause, however, was the part played by him in bringing about the substitution of the Roman liturgy for the old diocesan liturgies of France. No triumph of ecclesiastical centralization was quite so striking as this. The change more particularly affected the breviaries, which at the end of the seventeenth and beginning of the eighteenth century had undergone drastic remodelling under Gallican and Jansenist influence with the object of making them "more conformable to the dignity of the Church and the doctrines of antiquity."[23] Rome had frowned on these new " Gallican " breviaries : but her censures had beaten in vain on the nationalist spirit of the Church of the old regime. Now, however, that Church was a thing of the past : and the increasing tendency of French Catholicism to turn to the Holy See for inspiration gave Rome her opportunity. The bishops were, for the most part, against the change : and one of them, Archbishop d'Astros of Toulouse, replied to Guéranger's strictures in 1843 in a pamphlet entitled *L'Église de France injustement flétrie*. The attachment of the French dioceses to their old usages, and the trouble and expense involved in changing them, were powerful practical arguments for their retention. On the other hand, it is obvious that their variety was a source of great inconvenience and confusion—a confusion increased by the rearrangement of diocesan boundaries under the Concordat, as a result of which a new diocese often comprised portions of several old ones, each with its own liturgy. Rome, of course, favoured the change. In 1842 Gregory XVI. deplored the "variety of Uses " and praised " those who adopted a universal Use," though he gave no actual injunctions in the matter. Under Pius IX. more definite pressure was brought to bear : and the combination of doctrinal and practical considerations won the victory for a liturgical revolution which swept away not the diocesan breviaries only but many time-honoured local usages

[23] On the Gallican breviaries see Guéranger: *Institutions liturgiques,* vol. 2 ; Batiffol: *Histoire du bréviaire romain,* 353ff. ; and the article by Dom Leclercq in *Dictionnaire de l'Archéologie chrétienne et de Liturgie, s.v.* Liturgies néo-Gallicanes, vol. IX., 1636ff. ; also an excellent note by R. E. Balfour in *Journal of Theological Studies,* July 1932.

as well, and enthroned the Roman rite in all the dioceses of France. The first of these to adopt it was Langres in 1839, the last Orléans in 1875.

Nor was it only in regard to the liturgy proper that the Italian inspiration displayed itself. The old-fashioned French piety—the piety of Saint Sulpice—with its grave, restrained flavour was compelled to give way to a more flamboyant type of devotion imported from beyond the Alps. The older generation of French Catholics, as of English, disliked the extravagances of the latter : but its appeal to popular sentiment (and, it may be added, to popular superstition as well) won the hearts of the younger, especially among the ignorant and uneducated. This attraction was diligently exploited by the more popular religious congregations, which sought thus to further their policy of acclimatizing the Ultramontane idea.

In all these ways the once proudly independent Church of France was led to seek for its main inspiration and guidance no longer within its own borders but from outside. The old Gallicanism of Bossuet had, of course, always acknowledged the spiritual supremacy of Rome : but its devotion had been very far on this side idolatry and had been restricted within carefully defined limits. Now those limits were rapidly swept away. The eyes of French Catholics turned more and more to the Vatican—and most of all when, between 1860 and 1870, the rage of the despoiler was launched against its august occupant and all faithful hearts were wrung by the contemplation of his woes. The Holy Father might weep tears of rage and grief over the piecemeal destruction of his Temporal Power. Yet it remains true that nothing did more to gather the love and devotion of Catholics round him, and to prepare their hearts for the mighty affirmation of his spiritual authority in 1870 and its acceptance throughout the Catholic world.

CHAPTER I

THE REVOLUTION OF 1848 AND THE RISE OF LOUIS NAPOLEON
1848—1851

REVOLUTIONS are seldom kind to the Church. The cause of institutional religion is normally too much bound up with the conservative principle for that. But to this general rule the French Revolution of 1848 forms a notable exception. Unlike its predecessor at the end of the eighteenth century and its successor of 1870-1, it was not merely friendly to the Church, but even sought its benediction and allowed itself to submit—in a measure and for a short while—to its influence and control.

The explanation of this phenomenon is worth examining. It may be largely summed up in a single name—Lamennais.[1] True, that strange wandering star had many years before cut himself off from the Church whose cause he had once so warmly, so intemperately espoused. But his influence and ideas lived on in his disciples. For nearly two decades they had inspired in France a notable revival of Catholic life and corporate action, and (as Pius IX. himself testified in a letter to Montalembert written in 1848[2]) had won from the nation a new respect for the Church. The old alliance between the Church and the cause of the *ancien régime* had been weakened, if by no means destroyed. The " principles of 1789 " had secured a lodging within its bosom : and in the curiously intoxicating air of those spring days of 1848 they

---

[1] It seems well-nigh impossible to exaggerate the influence of Lamennais. Weill says with truth that each of the systems he in turn evolved gave birth to an important school. The Lamennais of the *Essai sur l'indifférence* produced the Ultramontanes, the Lamennais of the *Avenir* the Liberal Catholics, the Lamennais of 1834 onwards the democrats and anti-clericals ; *op. cit.* 51.

[2] Dated March 26th. Lecanuet : *Montalembert* ii. 378.

were to lay hold not only on the minority of Catholics which already accepted them but also on hearts (even episcopal) that had been hitherto suspicious or hostile. There was indeed no particular reason why the Church should regret the fall of the government of Louis Philippe. That government had never been its friend, had sought to use it for its own purposes rather than really favoured or helped it. The victories of the Catholics had been won less by the aid of the civil authority than in its despite.

The influence of Lamennais, however, had been by no means confined to the Church. He had ceased to be a Catholic, had even ceased in any very definite sense to believe in God. But the Christian colour and inspiration of his ideas had never left them—rather, in a sense, had increased with the passage of years. He had once believed in Jesus Christ as the Divine Founder and Living Head of the Catholic Church. That belief he held no longer : but he still believed in Jesus as the supreme embodiment of humanity, the prophet of love and brotherhood, the spiritual genius whose ideals, at this late hour, were to fashion anew the sorry fabric of human society. It was these ideals that he had preached and fought for ever since he left the Church. It was the same ideals that actuated the Utopians and visionaries in whom the age so plentifully abounded—the Saint-Simonians, the Fourierists and the rest—and had been brought home to a far wider public in the novels of Georges Sand. And now they seemed on the point of coming into their own. The men who were to play the leading part in the Revolution had drunk deep of the inspiration of Nazareth. Some (like Buchez, the first President of the National Assembly) even combined a practising Catholicism with their devotion to the revolutionary idea ; though these were the exception. But all (and not least Lamartine, the presiding genius and idol of the Revolution in its first stage) believed that the morality, if not the Person, of Christ was divine and saw in the watchword of the Revolution—" Liberty, Fraternity, Equality "—the practical embodiment of the message for which He had lived and died. As Debidour says, " In 1848 the Gospel was the order of the

day." [3] If then the Church was willing—and, for the moment
at least, it seemed willing—to work with such men towards
the setting up of a better social order, they would not refuse,
but would gladly avail themselves of, its co-operation.

Even at the height of the revolutionary outbreaks which
raged in Paris through the " days of February," the Church
was treated with respect. No longer identified (as in 1830)
with the cause of monarchy, it remained unvisited by the
wrath of the destroyer. The working men who pillaged the
Tuileries bore the crucifix and sacred vessels from its chapel
with reverence to the Church of St. Roch. The National
Guards carried their colours to the palace of Archbishop Affre
of Paris to be blessed. Such gestures of goodwill were not left
without response. The Archbishop sang a solemn Te Deum
in honour of the new order. The Bishops, in a shower of
charges, hymned its coming in strains of lyrical enthusiasm.
" The principles " (wrote the Archbishop of Bourges) " the
triumph of which must begin a new era, are those which the
Church has always proclaimed and has just proclaimed afresh
by the mouth of its august head, the immortal Pius IX."
" Nothing can be more profoundly, nay, more exclusively
Christian than the words inscribed on the national flag," wrote
the Bishop of Langres, Mgr. Parisis. [4] The lower clergy followed
enthusiastically in the wake of their superiors. All over France
the pulpits rang with the praise and promise of the Revolution.
Many curés chanted mass in the public places to win the
benediction of heaven on the new era, or blessed the " trees of
liberty " that were everywhere planted as the symbol of its
inauguration. Veuillot himself declared in the *Univers* that

[3] Debidour: *Histoire des rapports de l'Église et de l'État en France,
1789—1870*. 1911. This is an accurate, comprehensive and well-written
book : but its tone is vehemently anti-clerical and the author's judgments
(though not his facts) should be accepted with caution. See also Weill,
Histoire du catholicisme libéral en France, ch. v., Lecanuet, *op. cit.*, ii.,
iii., Lagrange, *Vie de Dupanloup*, i., ii., Veuillot, *Louis Veuillot*, ii., and
other works cited below in the notes.

[4] These and similar episcopal effusions are quoted in Debidour, *op. cit.*
484 n. Parisis had already, in his *Cas de conscience* (1847), outlined the
future Liberal-Catholic position (Weill, 85ff). But under the Empire his
tone was to be very different (*v. infra* p. 54): and he regretted his
previous utterances.

the Revolution was a " notification of Providence " and that, if the Republic would grant liberty to the Church, " there will be no more sincere republicans than the French Catholics." [5]

Such sentiments, it is true, were not universal in Catholic hearts, nor, perhaps, even when expressed, wholly sincere. Those who still clung to the elder Bourbon line as offering the only permanent safeguard of the interests of religion could hardly regard with satisfaction an event which appeared to make the chances of its restoration more remote than ever. Even the Liberal Catholics were not wholly of one mind. If Lacordaire hailed the Revolution with joy, the aristocratic and Orléanist Montalembert was uncertain and mistrustful—inclined at best to tolerate it as a *fait accompli*. When Lacordaire [6] announced his intention of joining with Ozanam and the Abbé Maret in starting a new journal, the *Ère Nouvelle*, with the aim of "reconciling the Church and democracy," Montalembert warned him earnestly of the " dangers and disappointments " that might await him. The *Ère Nouvelle* appeared, all the same, for the first time on April 15th—with the warm approval of the Archbishop of Paris, but to the " great despair " of the Papal Nuncio. Declaring the Revolution "not only permitted but willed by God," it called all Catholics to rally to its aims without misgiving. For the moment it won considerable support, especially from the younger clergy. [7]

The Provisional Government having decreed the summoning of a Constituent Assembly based on the principle of universal suffrage, the election of its members became a matter of prime importance. For all his distrust of the Revolution, Montalembert was not the man to sulk in his tent and neglect his duty as a Catholic. His *Comité Central pour la Défense Religieuse*, which had done such yeoman work for the Church in the past, was still in existence. Without delay he called its members together (February 28th), and issued in

[5] Veuillot, *Louis Veuillot*, ii., 210, 212.
[6] The main authority for the life of Lacordaire is Foisset, *Vie du R. P. Lacordaire*, 2 vols., 1870. For an admirable sketch see D'Haussonville, *Lacordaire* (Eng. tr. 1913).
[7] Lecanuet, ii. 379f.

the columns of the *Univers* a stirring message to its provincial sub-committees. Without declaring himself for or against the Revolution, he based his appeal on the principle of freedom—religious freedom above all. " The Catholics," he wrote, " will descend into the arena with their fellow-citizens to claim all those political and social liberties which will be henceforward the imprescriptible patrimony of France." [8] The appeal was answered with enthusiasm; Montalembert himself of course taking the lead and Veuillot supporting the same policy of " *catholicisme avant tout*." Lists were drawn up of candidates whom Catholics might safely support. Pamphlets were showered upon the electors to guide their choice. The bishops were urged to come into line—and not in vain. Montalembert had a personal interview with Thiers at the latter's request; and won from that astute and aspiring politician the admission that " Catholicism is the great social rampart that must be defended at all costs." "And freedom of education?" queried Montalembert. " I admit it," replied Thiers: " I am changed." [9] So Thiers duly appeared on the Catholic list, and eventually secured a seat (though not till some months later)—with important results in the sequel.

As the consequence of these strenuous efforts, the Catholics to a large extent controlled the election. The Provisional Government put no obstacles in their way, recognising the need of guidance for the untutored masses in this their first exercise of the vote. Not all the candidates they put forward were elected : but hardly anywhere was a candidate successful whom they openly opposed.

The newly elected Assembly met for the first time on May 4th. The majority was composed of earnest, if inexperienced, liberals, who were no doubt sincere in their desire to found a Republic but whose republicanism was hardly stout or seasoned enough to withstand the shocks it was destined to receive. The minority included, on the Extreme Left a number of revolutionary extremists like Louis Blanc, on the Right the adherents of the fallen dynasties, whether of the Orléans

[8] Lecanuet, ii. 386.
[9] *Ibid.*, ii. 391.

family or of the representative of the elder Bourbon line, the Comte de Chambord, grandson of Charles X. Pledged neither to republicans nor to non-republicans, but ready to ally itself with either, was the small group of *catholiques avant tout,* with Montalembert (elected member for the Doubs) at their head. The representatives of the sovereign people included a considerable number of clerics—among them Lacordaire (who, to Montalembert's vexation, insisted on taking his seat on the extreme left, not far from his old master Lamennais) and three bishops—those of Langres (Parisis), Quimper (Graverand), and Orléans (Fayet)—nicknamed " Taedificat," " Aedificat," and " Laetificat " respectively, according to the nature of their oratory. Some 250 of the members of the Assembly stood pledged to support the cause of freedom of Catholic education.

If, however, the extreme revolutionary and anticlerical element was but feebly represented in the Assembly, it was otherwise outside. And as the weeks passed this element more and more assumed control of the course of events in Paris. The agitators stirred up the populace, which, owing to the dislocation of trade and consequent shortage of employment that the Revolution brought in its train, fell a ready prey to their inflammatory outpourings. At the opening session of the Assembly the Palais Bourbon was surrounded by a vast mob. These, when the deputies had acclaimed the Republic seventeen times, insisted on obtaining a sight of their representatives. The members of the Assembly ranged up under the portico and were welcomed with wild acclamations by the crowd that surged against the railings. Lacordaire descended the steps, to receive a positive ovation and to be carried in triumph round the Palais.

Eleven days later (May 15th) the people returned—in a very different mood. The extremists had persuaded them that the Assembly was the tool of reaction and must be dissolved. Amid the roar of 20,000 throats the hall was invaded, and a crowd of men in blouses occupied the benches of the deputies. This scene of wild confusion lasted for three hours, during which the deputies were repeatedly threatened with death.

Finally the Assembly was declared dissolved, and the deputies fled pursued by the mob. Next day Lacordaire gave in his resignation. He had had enough. " The Republic is lost," he groaned. A few weeks later he quitted the *Ère Nouvelle,* leaving its direction in the more extreme hands of Maret, who at once declared himself in favour of " an openly avowed alliance with democracy." [10]

Even this, however, was nothing to what was to happen a month later. By the creation of *ateliers nationaux* to provide work for the unemployed, the Provisional Government had forged a weapon that was now to be turned with terrible effect against itself. 20,000 workmen were inscribed on the list of these *ateliers.* Ill-conceived and incompetently run, they turned out a miserable failure from a practical point of view. As work could not be provided in sufficient quantities, the workmen received money—and arms. Meanwhile the idle and disillusioned mass was feverishly worked upon by the Socialist agitators and the extremist press. The unpractical idealists who composed the Government did not know how to cope with the situation, and lost their heads. Various schemes were propounded in the Assembly, but without résult. One of these schemes—for the confiscation of the great railways— was denounced by Montalembert in an eloquent speech— much to the fury of the Socialists who dubbed him " the pontiff of the golden calf " and " the Jeremiah of property."

Next day (June 23rd) the Revolution burst anew into flame —the immediate cause of its outbreak being a report by Falloux (made at the request of the Assembly) declaring for the dissolution of the *ateliers nationaux.* Barricades appeared everywhere in the approved Parisian manner, and the sound of gunfire filled the streets. The Government entrusted General Cavaignac with the task of crushing the revolt. The insurgents fought with fury, but were gradually compelled to submit. Almost the last blood shed in these terrible " days of June " was that of Archbishop Affre, who crowned a blameless if somewhat mediocre career by a truly heroic death (June 25th)—the first of three Archbishops of Paris who in less than

[10] Weill, 96. On Maret see Bazin, *Vie de Mgr. Maret,* 3 vols., 1891.

a generation were to meet with a violent end. Having mounted a barricade to exhort the insurgents to surrender and so save further bloodshed, he was (? accidentally) shot and fatally wounded. The manner of his death naturally lent enormous prestige to the Church : and his funeral was the occasion of an imposing demonstration.

This sudden yawning of the pit beneath their feet struck terror into the hearts of all who had a stake in the maintenance of the existing social order. The rosy visions of a few months back were rudely dissipated : and men began to wonder whether " the sovereignty of the people " was really such a blessing after all. The republicanism of the majority in the Assembly was shaken to its foundations. A violent reaction set in. The insurrection was crushed with merciless severity. 11,000 of the rebels were arrested, and an unknown number summarily shot. Even after the immediate danger was over, the Assembly continued the dictatorship of Cavaignac, maintained the state of siege and revived the stringent press law of 1822. A speech by Proudhon in the Assembly advocating the spoliation of the rich for the benefit of the poor was received with yells of rage.

The Catholics were not slow to take advantage of the new situation. The Assembly, never ill-disposed to religion, was now more ready than ever to view with a friendly eye the one social force that seemed able to bridle the inconvenient cupidity of the masses. This attitude was reflected in the Constitution that it now set itself to elaborate. [11] It was declared in the preamble that " there exist rights and duties anterior to positive laws," and that " the citizen must be protected in his religion." The union between Church and State was maintained. " The ministers of religious bodies recognized . . . by the law have the right to receive payment from the State." Attempts made in the *comité des cultes* to secure modification in the terms of the Concordat in a democratic direction—including a proposal to extend the privilege of *inamovibilité* among the lower clergy—failed to win support. [12]

[11] Debidour, 487.   Lecanuet, ii. 413.
[12] Debidour, 488f.

Above all, the Assembly accepted definitely the principle of freedom of education, if with important qualifications. Article 9 of the Constitution ran thus : " Education is free. The liberty of education is exercised according to conditions of capacity and morality determined by the laws and under the supervision of the State. This supervision extends to all educational and teaching establishments without any exception."

The Constitution having been framed and (Nov. 12th) solemnly promulgated with religious rites, the next step was to elect a President of the now definitely constituted Republic. The election was fixed for Dec. 10th. The choice lay between two candidates. One of these was Cavaignac, who had certainly deserved well of the party of order and, as being still *de facto* head of the executive, was (so to speak) the " man in possession." But lately a new and rather sinister star had risen on the political horizon. Louis Napoleon was the nephew of the great Emperor, the son of Louis Napoleon, King of Holland, by his wife Hortense, sister of the Empress Josephine. After a chequered and impecunious career (in the course of which he had twice made a grotesque attempt to overturn the July Monarchy in his own interest) he returned to Paris after the fall of Louis Philippe. The troubled waters of the inchoate Republican regime were for him a thoroughly congenial element. He lost no opportunity of pushing himself forward ; while his supporters diligently exploited the Napoleonic legend on his behalf. Elected deputy in June, he was refused admission by the Assembly : but having been elected again—in Paris—he was allowed to take his seat on the Left. At first he was viewed not only with dislike but with contempt. Soon, however, the conservatives (including Thiers, who saw in him a convenient " warming-pan " for himself) began to mark him out as a possible candidate for their suffrages in the coming presidential election. Cavaignac they disliked because of his sturdy republicanism. Louis Napoleon might be a more malleable instrument.

For Montalembert and the Catholics the main question was : " Which of these two candidates was likely to be the better friend to the Church? " In this connection two matters were of special urgency at the moment. The Pope was in exile at Gaeta and had issued an appeal to the Catholic governments for aid. The liberal experiments at the outset of his pontificate (which drew from Metternich the exclamation, " I had foreseen everything except a Liberal Pope ") had proved short-lived. His Prime Minister, Rossi, had been assassinated : and he himself had been compelled to flee from Rome, with a fixed determination in his heart to have done with " Liberalism " for good and all. Would France be ready to co-operate in restoring him to his States? The other matter was the old question of freedom of Catholic education. This (as we have seen) had been accepted by the new Constitution in principle. But the Catholics disliked the qualifications with which the concession was surrounded, and hoped to extract better terms.

Opinion in the Catholic camp was divided as to the merits of the rival candidates. Falloux, Sibour (now Archbishop of Paris) and the eloquent Jesuit, Père Ravignan, favoured Cavaignac. Dupanloup counselled reserve, while Parisis and others supported Louis Napoleon. Veuillot had not yet made up his mind. In consultation, therefore, with his committee, Montalembert decided that both candidates should be approached with a view to ascertaining their respective positions on the main points at issue. Cavaignac declined to give the required guarantees. He had offered the Pope (before he left Rome) an asylum in France, and had even proposed to send a small force to Civita Vecchia to ensure his personal safety. But he would not agree to use the French arms to strangle the infant Roman Republic. As to freedom of education, he refused to commit himself. Montalembert himself undertook to sound Louis Napoleon in a personal interview. The latter's answers were not wholly satisfactory : but soon all doubts were set at rest by a passage in his electoral manifesto declaring that " the freedom of religion involves as a corollary freedom of education." [13] Further, in a letter to the Nuncio he asserted that " the temporal sovereignty of the Pope is intimately bound up with the state of religion, as with

[13] Lecanuet, ii. 418f.

the freedom and independence of the Church." This clinched
the matter. The *Comité Catholique* was still unwilling to make
him its official candidate. But Montalembert used all his
influence on his behalf; Thiers and the *bourgeois* Liberal-
Conservatives gave him their warm support; and he was
chosen by an enormous majority (December 1848).

Elected by the conservatives, Louis Napoleon naturally
turned in their direction in forming the new Cabinet. The
Republicans were excluded: and the Orléanist Odilon-
Barrot became Prime Minister. The post of Minister of
Public Instruction and Religion was offered to Falloux.[14] A
Legitimist by conviction, but of the more progressive sort, and
a man of marked ability, he was closely allied with the *parti
catholique,* which saw in him (and with good reason) the man
for realising its designs. At first he was most unwilling to take
the post. He had not voted for Louis Napoleon and profoundly distrusted his policy. Montalembert and Ravignan,
in a three hours' interview, passionately urged him to accept,
without overcoming his resistance. In reply, however, to
further entreaties from Dupanloup (who informed him that
the President had hinted that " he would see M. Jules Favre ")
he consented to go and see Thiers. " I accept the ministry,"
said Falloux to Thiers, " if you promise to prepare, support
and vote with me a law of freedom of education." " I
promise, I promise," replied Thiers. So Falloux became
Minister—and during the next few months the chief influence
in the government. His aim was threefold—to suppress
anarchy, to re-establish the Pope in Rome and to secure
freedom of education for the Catholics.

Of these, the second was for the moment the most pressing.
Cavaignac had countermanded the expeditionary force to
Civita Vecchia, as soon as the Pope was safe in Gaeta. What
was the new President going to do in the matter? His Carbonarist past and personal inclinations might have inclined
him to accept the new republican regime in Rome. But he

---

[14] See Falloux' own very important *Mémoires d'un Royaliste,* 2 vols.,
1888. His account of his ministry is in vol. i., ch. 11-14. See also
Lecanuet, ii. 421ff.

needed the support of the *parti catholique* and had definitely committed himself to a policy of intervention, if necessary. Also, he was keenly alive to the risk that Austria would intervene if France did not, and so involve him in a loss of prestige. At first he seems to have cheated himself with the hope that neither France nor Austria, but Sardinia, would essay the task. Sardinia, however, was not thinking about the Pope. Her aim was to avenge the defeat inflicted on her by Austria in 1848 at Custozza. But at Novara (March 23rd, 1849) it was not Sardinia but Austria that was victorious. The President had now more reason than ever for seeking to snatch the laurel from Austria. At the same time the approach of the elections for the Legislative Assembly that was to succeed the expiring *Constituante* made it even more necessary to retain the support of the *parti catholique*.

Meanwhile, however, the republican *Constituante* was still in existence. On April 16th the President asked it to vote a subsidy for a military force which, under General Oudinot, was on the point of starting for Civita Vecchia. The Assembly granted this, but with the understanding that the troops should not be used to suppress the Roman Republic. Soon afterwards the news arrived that Oudinot had marched on Rome and made an unsuccessful assault on the city. The Assembly indignantly requested the Government " to take the necessary measures that the Italian expedition should no longer be diverted from the purpose which had been assigned to it " (May 7th).

The President was in a quandary : for no one could yet say what the character of the new Assembly was going to be. For the time being he decided to try to run with the hare and hunt with the hounds. Ferdinand de Lesseps was despatched to Rome to negotiate with the triumvirate (headed by Mazzini) in control of the Republic. The negotiations lasted from May 17th to 31st, during which time Oudinot completed his preparations for attack and the Papal States were invaded by Austrian and Neapolitan troops from the north and the south respectively. Lesseps finally concluded an agreement placing the Republic under the protection of the French arms.

By this time the result of the elections was known. The conservatives were a strong majority : and this meant the triumph of the Catholics as well. As Tocqueville was to write not long after : " The fear of Socialism has produced for the moment on the middle classes an effect similar to that produced by the French Revolution on the upper." [15] The President was now able to throw off the mask. Lesseps was disavowed on his return : and on June 1st Oudinot began the siege of Rome. A successful attack on one of the city gates (June 29th) forced the triumvirate to flee : and on July 3rd Oudinot entered Rome, to inaugurate that French occupation which was to be a continual thorn in the side of Napoleon III. until the hour of Nemesis sounded more than twenty years later.

The pontifical government was re-established immediately : but Pius IX. was in no hurry to put himself again at the mercy of his rebellious children. From the security of Gaeta he carried on the government of his States through his minister Antonelli, in complete disregard of a request of the French Government that he would grant to his people " serious liberal institutions." In truth, he cared much more for Austria than for France. In the hope of bringing him to his senses, Louis Napoleon addressed his famous letter to Colonel Edgar Ney, [16] complaining of the papal ingratitude and instructing his correspondent to ask Pius to grant an amnesty, secularize his administration and set up a liberal government (August 18th). The Pope was quite unperturbed and merely issued (Sept. 12th) a *motu proprio* embodying vague promises of reform. The Legislative Assembly approved the *motu proprio*: and, carried away by a magnificent speech of Montalembert [17] (culminating in the famous exclamation *"L'Église . . . c'est une mère!"*), declared that " the pontifical freedom and dignity " must be safeguarded (Oct. 20th). Louis Napoleon, on the other hand, showed his vexation by dismissing first Falloux and then the rest of the ministers. Pius IX., however, paid no attention :

---

[15] Weill, 99.
[16] Printed *in extenso* in Falloux, *op. cit.*, i. 528—9.
[17] A full account of this speech is given in Lecanuet, ii. 447.

and on his return to Rome took care to see that the old reactionary clerical government, with all its abuses, was as far as possible brought back.

The Temporal Power restored, it still remained to secure the other prime demand of the *parti catholique*—freedom of education. Ever since his appointment as minister, Falloux had been working towards a settlement. Essentially a realist and a practical man, he saw clearly that if anything was to be gained for the Catholics it could only be by means of a " transaction " with the Université—the stronghold of the State monopoly of education. This in itself was quite enough to antagonize the Catholic extremists, who regarded the Université as the accursed thing and demanded nothing less than its complete destruction. Veuillot (between whom and Falloux there was never any love lost) opposed the minister's plans from the start and bitterly attacked him in the *Univers,* nicknaming him " *Falloux Fallax.*" [18]   Placed thus between two fires—the Catholic extremists on the one hand and the fanatics of the Université on the other—Falloux had a difficult game to play. But he went on with his projects, and was at last able to bring them to a successful issue.

His first step was to bring about a conference of the main interests concerned, with a view to a settlement by agreement. A commission of twenty-four was appointed, consisting of representatives of the Université and of the Catholics (of the more moderate type in each case) together with a number of politicians of different shades of opinion (including Thiers) to hold the balance. [19]   The Catholics included Montalembert and Dupanloup, whose reputation as an educationist gave him great authority. Neither Parisis nor Veuillot was included, as both had pronounced against any " transaction " at all.

The question of primary education was first dealt with. Thiers expatiated at great length on the " social peril," and declared that in order to conjure it it was necessary to place the education of the masses on a religious basis. When, however,

[18] Weill, 102.
[19] The proceedings of this commission have been published by H. de Lacombe, *Débats de la Commission de 1849.*

it came to secondary education he took a very different line. He had no objection to calling in the Church to keep the masses in order. But the Université was still to control the education of the upper classes and " stamp the effigy of the State " upon them. In particular he showed a strong prejudice against the educational work of the religious orders, especially the Jesuits. Dupanloup, in reply, indicated the Catholic position : and gradually the outlines of an arrangement began to emerge. Thiers professed himself convinced by Dupanloup's defence of the religious orders. Turning to Victor Cousin he said : " Cousin, Cousin, have you noticed what a lesson we have received ? The Abbé is right. We have been fighting against justice and reason : and we owe them reparation." [20] Cousin was not to be so easily convinced, and adhered to his hostile attitude. But Thiers' surrender won the day for the Catholics : and the *projet Falloux* was the result.

The measure, having been approved by the government, was brought before the Legislative Assembly, which in accordance with the usual procedure submitted it to a committee for examination. As eight out of fifteen members of this committee were its declared supporters and as these included both Thiers (the Chairman) and Montalembert, its report could not fail to be favourable. But, soon after, the retirement of Falloux from Paris owing to ill-health, closely followed by his dismissal from office, seemed to jeopardize the measure's chances of success : and the Left in the Assembly seized the opportunity to get it referred (Nov. 7th) to the Council of State, which attempted to introduce certain important modifications unfavourable to the Church. These, however, were rejected by the parliamentary committee : and the *projet* at length came up for consideration by the Assembly in January 1850.

In the course of the debate it was violently attacked from both sides. Victor Hugo denounced it as " a law under a mask, . . . a monopoly in the hands of those who wished to make education proceed from the sacristy and government

[20] Falloux, *op. cit.*, i. 431. .

from the confessional." [21]　The Catholic extremists declared the concessions to the Church insufficient : and their attacks were echoed outside by the furious diatribes of the *Univers,* which pronounced the measure " detestable."　Parisis, while supporting it as a *pis-aller,* denounced the Université as " a focus of immorality, atheism, unbelief and the spirit of anarchy and revolution." [22] On the other hand, Montalembert assumed the defence of the bill, urging the need of an *union des conservateurs* to avert the " social peril." [23] Thiers, faithful to his bargain, was no less eloquent on its behalf, and the law was carried on March 16th, 1850—" *le plus beau triomphe,"* as Weill says, " *du catholicisme libéral."* [24]

The details of the *Loi Falloux* are too intricate and elaborate to be set forth at length.　It must suffice to indicate its main provisions. [25]

The monopoly of the Université was swept away.　In place of the old *Conseil Royal de l'Université* was set up a new *Conseil Supérieur de l'Instruction Publique,* in which the eight representatives of the Université formed a minority in face of the other nineteen members.　These comprised four bishops, two ministers of Protestant denominations and a Jewish rabbi, together with three representatives each of the Council of State, the Cour de Cassation and the Institut de France—all elected by their colleagues—and finally three representatives of the non-State schools nominated by the Government. In the same way the existing twenty *Académies* for the local control of education gave way to eighty-six *Conseils Académiques* (one for each department), in which the Université was still more disadvantageously represented.　Schools were to be of two kinds : (1) " public," i.e. supported by the State, department or commune; (2) " voluntary " *(libres)* i.e. conducted by individuals or associations.　There was no mention of the religious congregations : but it was understood that members of these shared in the permission accorded to every French

[21] Debidour, 511n.
[22] *Ibid.*
[23] For an account of Montalembert's speech see Lecanuet, ii. 484ff.
[24] *Op. cit.,* 102.
[25] The law is printed *in extenso* in Debidour, 701ff.

qualified teacher to open a school, on condition of making his intention known to the *maire* of the commune and incurring no objection on moral grounds from the local *Recteur d'Académie*.

The tests of professional capacity for teachers were not exacting. The normal qualification was the *brevet de capacité* granted after examination by the *Conseil Académique*. But if this was not forthcoming, it was sufficient in the case of primary schools that the teacher should be a "minister of a recognised religious body," or have served three years as pupil teacher in a public or voluntary school. For teachers belonging to recognized female teaching congregations the requirement was less exacting still. All that was needed in their case was to produce the "letters of obedience" granted by the congregations to which they belonged.

The inspection of secondary schools was entrusted to *inspecteurs d'académies*; that of primary schools to *inspecteurs primaires* in collaboration with local representatives, including the *maire* and curé. In the case of *écoles libres* the functions of inspectors were to relate only to "morality, hygiene and health," and were to have nothing to do with the teaching given except to certify that it was not contrary to "the constitution or the laws." The teaching given in all primary schools was to include "moral and religious instruction."

As the *Univers* continued its protests even after the measure had passed into law, Montalembert wrote to the Pope to ask him to make a pronouncement in regard to it. The Pope replied by a circular letter to the bishops, declaring that, if the law did not entirely meet the wishes of Catholics, yet it should be accepted until better terms could be had, and instructing the bishops to co-operate in its arrangements. [26] After this the *Univers* held its peace.

The attitude of the President throughout the proceedings incidental to the passing of the *Loi Falloux* had been somewhat lukewarm. But his word was pledged and he dared not draw back. Moreover, he still needed the support of the *parti catholique* in his schemes of further self-aggrandisement. The

[26] The letter is summarized in Lecanuet, ii. 494.

Catholics used their opportunity to the uttermost; and in addition to their victory in the sphere of education were able to secure for themselves a preponderant influence in the new provisions for the administration of poor-relief that were decreed by the Assembly in the course of 1850-1. [27]

For such triumphs the price had, of course, to be paid. The Catholics were ready to pay it. Montalembert, blinded by his zeal for religion, had not yet found Louis Napoleon out: moreover, he was honestly afraid of the return of the Revolution, which seemed the only alternative to the existing regime. This attitude was clearly shown in his reply to the famous speech in which Thiers (from whose eyes the scales had already fallen) exposed the designs of the future Emperor, exclaiming, " *L'Empire est fait!* " (February 1851). Montalembert warmly defended the President, expressing his satisfaction at being able to " render him this public tribute," and declaring that he had " in no wise proved himself unworthy of the great cause of order." [28] In the following July he supported the attempt to secure a revision of the constitution which would not only permit the re-election of Louis Napoleon as President in 1852 but secure the prolongation of his powers for ten years. The Assembly rejected the proposal : but in the following November Montalembert and his friends collaborated in a scheme for renewing the attempt, with an appeal to the people if it were rejected again.

Meanwhile, however, the President was meditating a more drastic solution of the problem. A few days later Montalembert was staggered by the news of the *Coup d'État* of December 2nd, 1851. The Assembly was dissolved, the Constitution suspended and 200 deputies who dared to protest were sent to prison. Having gagged every organ of opinion that might express opposition to his schemes, the President now decreed that France, by the exercise of universal suffrage, should decide whether it was willing to renew his powers and entrust him with the task of personally setting up a constitution. The plebiscite was fixed for December 21st.

[27] For details see Debidour, 513.
[28] Lecanuet, iii. 18f. Debidour, 516.

Once again, as on the occasion of Louis Napoleon's first election in 1848, Catholic opinion was divided, though very unequally.   Lacordaire, Dupanloup (since 1849 Bishop of Orléans) and Ravignan condemned the *Coup d'État*.   But Montalembert was still the dupe of his illusions. Committing what he was to describe later [29] as " the capital error of my life, my regret for which will last as long as life lasts," he urged the Catholics to vote for the President.   " To vote against Louis Napoleon," he wrote on December 12th, " is to support the Socialist revolution. . . . To vote for him is not to approve all that he has done : it is to choose between him and the total ruin of France." [30]   Veuillot, who in the previous year had supported a scheme for the fusion of the claims of the rival Bourbon houses with a view to a restoration, now intoned the praises of Louis Napoleon without reserve. " Since December 2nd," he wrote, " there is in France a Government and an army, a head and an arm." [31]   The *mot d'ordre* was given.   On December 21st France, by an enormous majority, flung itself at the feet of its new master.

[29] In a letter to M. Daru (1867)—quoted Lecanuet iii. 39.
[30] *Ibid.*, 38.
[31] Quoted by Debidour, 519.

CHAPTER II

CHURCH AND STATE IN THE FIRST YEARS OF THE SECOND EMPIRE, 1851—1856 [1]

THE alliance between the *parti catholique* and the new Prince-President of the French Republic was on both sides a *mariage d'interêt,* not a match of genuine affection. Each of the two parties had an eye to the main chance : and each was, in the long run, to find the price of its partner's favours too heavy for its pocket. For Louis Napoleon, in particular, being as he was far more dependent on the Church than the Church was on him, the alliance was to prove a dragging chain that became more and more intolerable as the years wore on : a chain endowed with the live quality of some great tropical creeper—broken continually yet never broken completely, and always liable to knit itself up again.

Louis Napoleon's individual attitude towards religion partook of the enigmatic quality of his whole personality. Actually, he would appear to have taken little interest in the subject apart from its bearing on his own designs. Such an attitude was indeed only the natural one for a man who was at once a dreamer and a cynic. Neither his heredity nor his Carbonarist past held the promise of any particular devotion to Holy Church. He was not indeed an enemy of religion, and perceived clearly enough its value as a cement for the social

[1] For the relations between Church and State throughout the period of the Second Empire, the capital work is Maurain, *La politique ecclési-astique du second Empire de 1852 à 1869.* 1930. This is a book of the first order,—written on an ample scale, richly documented, and strictly " objective " in its handling of the issues involved—the work of a really scientific historian. [See review by the present writer in *English Historical Review,* October 1932.] It is largely based on an exhaustive study of hitherto unpublished documents in the archives of the French Foreign Office and of the Ministries of the Interior, Education and Religions. M. Maurain has also edited a collection of such documents relating to the part played by Rome in the establishment of the imperial regime and the triumph of Ultramontane principles in France, under the title *Le Saint-Siège et la France de décembre 1851 à avril 1853: Documents inédits.* 1930.

edifice. But his views on the subject were vague and bore little sign of having been really thought out. In a newspaper article on " The Clergy and the State," written in 1843 during his captivity at Ham,[2] he had recommended the clergy to conceive of their function as a duty to teach " the morality of Christ " in such a way that " the priests might become citizens and the citizens might become more religious." This was all very well : but it accorded little with the theocratic ideas that held sway in the Vatican under Pius IX. and were proclaimed with such ecstatic fervour by the neo-Ultramontanes who, for the moment, supported the Napoleonic cause in France.

The entourage of Louis Napoleon shared the point of view of their master. For nearly all of them, religion was not a matter of conviction or principle, but simply of gaining support for the new regime. The Church was to be used as an instrument for conciliating the favour of the Legitimists and (above all) for holding the forces of the Revolution in check. Further, it was impossible for any government of France to escape from the " Gallican " attitude towards the Church that seemed bred in the bones of her official class. The Organic Articles[3] had only crystallized into a series of propositions the traditional jealousy of the civil power in France towards outside interference in ecclesiastical affairs. Even Charles X., for all his bigoted Catholicism, had had neither the power nor even the will to sweep them away. The Pope indeed had never ceased to protest against them : and the Catholics were in high hopes that with the advent of Louis Napoleon the time had now at last come for their abrogation. But the Prince-President had no idea of gratifying their wishes. He was willing to show the Church all the favour he could : but he would never surrender the grip upon it inherited from his predecessors. Besides, the new regime rested on a frank acceptance of the " principles of 1789," with their explicit assertion of the exclusively " lay " character of the State, its freedom alike from religious discriminations and ecclesiastical influences.

[2] Quoted Maurain, *op. cit.*, 14f.
[3] *V. ante*, p. 5n.

For the moment, however, there was no disposition to push these " principles " to their logical issue. Indeed they had never been rigorously applied—at least not since 1801. The very existence of the Concordat was a proof that the State was unable to maintain its theoretical aloofness from all concern with religion. Not only the Catholic bishops and priests, but Protestant ministers and Jewish rabbis as well, received payment from the State. To attack religion was an offence punishable by law : the observance of Sunday was obligatory in theory if not in fact. Divorce, recognized by Napoleon, had been abolished since 1817 ; while the *Loi Falloux* had made religious instruction compulsory in all primary schools. There was no reason, therefore, why the new regime should not, if it chose, push its deference for the interests of religion to still greater lengths.

If, then, the bulk of the Catholics hailed the government of the Prince-President with rapture, it was not without its giving them reasons to do so. Already the restoration of the Pope to his States was of Louis Napoleon's doing : and if he had not greatly helped the passage of the *Loi Falloux,* neither had he put any serious obstacles in its way. The bishops were allowed to go to Rome as they chose and to receive the Pope's bulls, etc., without any cognizance of these being taken by the Government. All over France synods and provincial councils were permitted to meet and to pass resolutions at which previous governments would almost certainly have taken alarm. At the Council of Bordeaux, in 1850, under the influence of Pie of Poitiers, a series of resolutions had been passed which breathed the purest spirit of Ultramontanism.

Further marks of favour were to follow. The Constitution of 1852, while entrusting the Senate with the duty of safeguarding freedom of worship, also bade it maintain the interests of " religion." By the same Constitution the French Cardinals were given the right to sit in the Senate. Their emoluments, as well as those of the bishops, were largely increased. Religious processions displayed the pomp of the Church openly in the streets, without let or hindrance : and at these and other important ecclesiastical functions the prefects and similar high officials would be present in full uniform together with the troops of the local garrison. A censorship was imposed upon books, pamphlets and newspaper articles that betrayed hostility to religion. The works of Voltaire and Diderot were again proscribed. The Prince-President himself on his frequent progresses in the provinces was careful to show the utmost deference to the bishops and made many generous gifts to churches and convents. His marriage (January 1853) to the beautiful Spanish countess, Eugénie de Montijo, set at his side a consort who was a fervent Catholic and always susceptible to Clerical influences.

The religious orders multiplied their numbers with striking rapidity. A decree of January 31st, 1852 [4] enabled communities of women to be authorized (under certain conditions) by a presidential decree instead of by legal enactment, as required by the law of 1825. Between 1852 and 1860 982 new communities were thus authorized—a larger number than during the whole of the Restoration period. The orders that were unrecognized by the State—such as, e.g. the Jesuits—underwent a similar expansion. This increase in numbers was accompanied by a corresponding increase in wealth. The State supervision of authorized congregations enjoined by the law was allowed virtually to lapse; while in the case of unauthorized congregations the question of supervision did not arise at all.

It was in the sphere of education that the increased influence of the religious orders specially manifested itself. The *Loi Falloux* had resulted in the transfer of thousands of communal schools all over the country to the care of the teaching congregations. A similar progress was discernible in regard to secondary education. In 1854 the number of pupils educated by the Church equalled the number of those educated by the State. [5] The schools of the Jesuits, in particular, held out strong attractions for the rich *bourgeoisie* in view of the social *cachet* and professional opportunities they were supposed to confer : and many of its sons were enrolled among their pupils.

---

[4] Text printed in Debidour, 718f. See also 526.
[5] Debidour, 528.

The tone of the *écoles libres* in general was hostile to modern ideas and liberties. Falloux had hoped by means of his law to facilitate co-operation between the Université and the Catholic schools : but the latter preferred to adopt a policy of " splendid isolation." As Weill says, " The Law of 1850 was voted in accordance with the wishes of Falloux : it was to be applied in the spirit of Veuillot." [6]

It would even appear that early in 1852 the Prince-President suggested to Montalembert a reconstitution of the Université under clerical direction. But Montalembert had sense and fairness enough to reject the idea, which in any case can hardly have been meant seriously. [7] It was clear, however, that for the time being the Université had fallen sadly from its former proud monopoly. It was indeed too closely identified with subversive ideas in both politics and religion to expect much favour from the " Saviour of society." Some of its most eminent professors (including Michelet) were deprived of their posts for refusing to swear allegiance to the new regime.

The importance of the Church was seen not only in the domain of education but also in the hardly less covetable sphere of charitable relief—always so fertile a field for bringing Catholic influences to bear upon the poorer classes. In the measures passed by the Legislative Assembly for dealing with the problems of poverty a preponderant influence had been assigned to the clergy and the organizations they controlled—both religious communities and voluntary associations of the laity. The opportunity was eagerly turned to account. The Sisters of Charity and the Little Sisters of the Poor (the latter founded in 1840) rapidly increased both in numbers and in resources : and the former were systematically introduced into the hospitals. New charitable organizations were created in all directions; while those already existing underwent a notable development. The Society of St. Vincent de Paul, in particular, which had been founded by Frédéric Ozanam (with six members) in 1833 and had been steadily growing ever

[6] Weill : *Histoire du libéralisme catholique en France,* 105.
[7] Lecanuet, iii. 45.

since, now took a great leap forward and, with its widespread
network of conferences and the many charitable activities
carried on by these, rapidly assumed an importance that
excited deep misgivings and suspicion in the enemies of the
Church. Among the Catholic laity the Vicomte Armand de
Melun was specially distinguished for his zeal on behalf of the
poor. On his election to the Legislative Assembly he had
declared, " I will be the representative of the poor and
humble " : and his whole life, so fertile in good works,
especially on behalf of working-class youth, was to prove that
this was no idle boast.

So far the situation of the Church gave ground for satisfaction, and could hardly fail to inspire in Catholics a feeling of
confidence and gratitude towards the new regime. Yet after
all their main grievances remained. Their position was still
too entirely dependent on the favour of the Government : it
had no permanent foundation in the *droit civil*. In three
directions in particular they desired a change : and in the
course of December 1851 Montalembert had acted as their
spokesman in a series of private interviews with the Prince-
President. [8]

The first and chief of the concessions sought was the
abolition of the Organic Articles. We have already seen what
was the attitude of Louis Napoleon on this question. The
Organic Articles were the work of the founder of his dynasty :
and he had not the slightest intention of letting them go. The
Government might not always choose to insist on their strict
observance : but the weapon would be there if required. In
consequence, when Montalembert presented to him for inclusion in the new Constitution a *projet* abrogating the
Articles most offensive to Catholics, he formally handed it to
the President of the Council, Troplong—and no more was
heard of it.

A similar fate befell Montalembert's attempt to secure a
second concession—the further extension of the educational
freedom and privileges accorded to the Church by the *Loi
Falloux*. The Catholics desired two things in particular :

[5] Lecanuet, iii. 42ff.

(1) the liberation of the Catholic secondary schools (and especially the diocesan *petits séminaires*) from inspection by the Université, and their eligibility to receive assistance from the public funds; (2) permission for the Church to found Universities of its own, with the right of conferring degrees that should be regarded as equivalent with those granted by the State Faculties. Montalembert presented to Louis Napoleon a second *projet* embodying these demands. " I will consult Fortoul " (the Minister of Education) " about that," remarked the Prince-President. But Montalembert knew that nothing would be done. Indeed the Government, so far from extending the concessions of the *Loi Falloux,* actually contracted them. A decree of March 9th, 1852, gave to the State the nomination of all the members both of the *Conseil Supérieur de l'Instruction Publique* and of the departmental *Conseils Académiques,* thus depriving the Church of its right to choose its own representatives on the bodies concerned. [9]

The third direction in which the Catholics desired an extension of the Church's legal privileges was that of charitable assistance. As we have seen, the Legislative Assembly had done not a little to extend the influence of the Church in this sphere. But the Catholics were not satisfied. It was the Vicomte de Melun who in this case drew up a *projet* for submission to the Government, while Montalembert seconded his views privately with the Prince-President. His scheme demanded for the Church a " *liberté de la charité* " similar to the educational freedom secured for her by the *Loi Falloux.* Diocesan and parochial committees were to be set up that should be recognized by the State and be subsidized from public funds. To these committees the communes might, if they chose, hand over the administration of their poor relief. The *projet* was referred to the Ministry of the Interior, which received it with scant sympathy. " It is not," was the comment, " freedom to give relief that M. de Melun demands for the clergy : that already belongs to everyone. He demands that in future there shall be two administrations for public relief, the one clerical, the other lay." Nay, more, the clergy will

[9] Maurain, 131.

not be satisfied " until they have got the entire control of public relief." The scheme was therefore rejected. [10]

It was clear that the Catholics had over-estimated their credit with the new Government. Their support of Louis Napoleon in the critical events of December 1851 had been invaluable, and he still needed their services. But those services were not to be rewarded with the gift of a blank cheque.

Montalembert was profoundly disappointed. After December 26th he visited the Elysée no more. Three weeks later the offer of a seat in the Senate was refused. The developments of the early months of 1852 completed his disillusionment. Montalembert was rather a Whig than a Liberal : he was not an aristocrat for nothing and never pretended to believe in democracy. But he had no love for tyranny either. The exile of Thiers and many other eminent citizens of France greatly distressed him. The new Constitution displeased him by its autocratic character and its frank disdain of parliamentary institutions : and the complete stifling of the liberty of the press that quickly followed was as little to his taste. But the bitterest blow of all was a decree published on January 23rd confiscating the property of the exiled House of Orléans, to which he was bound by close ties of personal friendship and political loyalty. The gift of five million francs from the proceeds to the Church only added insult to injury. On reading it he at once sat down and penned a letter resigning his seat on the *Commission Consultative,* to which he had been nominated after December 2nd. [11] " Although," he wrote, " the Committee has been consulted on none of the acts of the Government, there none the less results for its members in the eyes of the public a sort of solidarity with the governmental policy that I can no longer accept." The letter was not allowed to be published : and on hearing of the resignation, the Prince-President merely shrugged his shoulders and said, " I am delighted to be rid of M. de Montalembert. He would only have embarrassed me."

[10] Maurain, 19.
[11] The text of this letter is printed in Lecanuet, iii. 50.

In the hope, however, of still being able to exercise some influence on affairs Montalembert consented to stand for the Corps Législatif, and he was chosen as member for Besançon by a large majority. But he was to find that the assembly to which he had been elected was a thing of straw. His career as an active political force was at an end.

Louis Napoleon could the better afford to be indifferent to Montalembert's defection inasmuch as the latter's following was comparatively negligible. The group of " Liberal Catholics " was certainly distinguished enough : but it was small and enjoyed little support from the Catholic rank and file. *Their* prophet was Veuillot : and he had as yet no misgivings regarding his hero, whom he took every opportunity of lauding to the skies. The autocratic character of the new Constitution, so far from disgusting him, filled him with delight. Its first article, recognizing and guaranteeing " the great principles proclaimed in 1789," he refused to take seriously. " We persist," he wrote, " in regarding the 2nd of December as the most anti-revolutionary date of our time." His scorn for representative institutions was unbounded. " France will reject parliamentarianism as she has rejected Protestantism, or she will perish in trying to vomit it up. . . . . She has said [to Louis Napoleon], ' My orators fatigue me : rid me of them. Govern me.' The real mandatory of the country is the Government." [12] Meanwhile (as we shall see in the next chapter) the political cleavage between Veuillot and the Liberal Catholics was being reinforced by a discord on religious questions that became more and more exacerbated as time went on.

It was not only the *Univers* and its followers that supported the new Government. It also enjoyed the favour of the Sovereign Pontiff himself. It was not unnatural indeed that Pius IX. should feel goodwill and gratitude towards the man who had restored him to his States and was maintaining him in possession of them by the arms of France. Nor did he entertain any abstract love of liberty that would lead him to shrink from arbitrary acts and autocratic methods of govern-

[12] *Univers*, Dec. 26th, 1851 ; Jan. 4th, 1852.

ment. He himself had been a victim of the Revolution and could not but rejoice to see the monster trodden underfoot. Less than a fortnight after the *Coup d'État* he expressed privately to the Government his warm approval of that event: and on January 1st, 1852, addressing the officers of the French army of occupation, he delivered a panegyric on the troops " that have saved France and Europe from the deadly and sanguinary excesses plotted by the men of anarchy." The *Univers* quoted a remark of his declaring that " Heaven has just acquitted the debt of the Church towards France." [13]

This friendly attitude on the part of the Pope was not only gratifying in itself. It might also be turned to very definite account. For Louis Napoleon the *Coup d'État* and the new Constitution were only a preliminary to a further step—the reestablishment of the Empire. In all things he desired to follow in his illustrious uncle's footsteps. If, then, he was to become Emperor, why should he not be crowned, like Napoleon I., by the Pope himself? Pius VII. had journeyed to Paris to set the seal of his august approval on the inception of the Napoleonic dynasty. Why should not Pius IX. similarly bless its revival? In the latter part of 1852, therefore, Bonnechose,[14] Bishop of Carcassonne, was sent to Rome to conduct a secret negotiation with this object. His efforts were seconded by Mgr. de Ségur, the new Auditor of the Rota for France at Rome. The Pope's attitude was kind but very reserved. He himself was not unwilling to do what was asked: but his entourage was strongly against it.

Meanwhile, in France, the steps preliminary to setting up the Empire proceeded apace. In the autumn of 1852 the Prince-President made a tour of the south of France with a view to testing public opinion. Everywhere he was ceremoniously received by the bishops and made loud profession of his respect for religion. At Marseilles he was even greeted by a Legate of the Pope. Speaking at Bordeaux he delivered himself as follows: " I desire to win for religion, for morality

---

[13] Maurain, *Le Saint Siège et la France*, 18, 23 n.: *Univers*, Jan. 7th, 1852.
[14] On Bonnechose see Besson, *Vie du Cardinal de Bonnechose*, 1887.

and for a decent standard of living *(l'aisance)* that still so numerous part of the population which in the midst of a country of faith and belief hardly knows the precepts of Christ." [15] Here, in fact, was the official theory of the relations between the Second Empire and the Church—a theory that was to take the place of the old Bourbon alliance between the Altar and the Throne. The Government was to show favour to the Church, which in return was to help it to curb the forces of the Revolution.

On November 6th, 1852, the Senate decreed the re-establishment of the Empire: and on November 20-21st a second plebiscite confirmed this decision by an overwhelming majority. The negotiations for the Pope's presence at the imperial coronation were pushed forward with energy. The proclamation of the Empire had been received at Rome with less of overt enthusiasm than the *Coup d'État*. This was due not to any lack of satisfaction on the Pope's part but to a fear of wounding the susceptibilities of the other Catholic powers —Austria in particular. The same fear was also alleged as a reason for not granting the new Emperor's request. If the Pope came to Paris to crown the Emperor of the French, other Catholic sovereigns would expect a similar favour at his hands. It was indicated, however, that even this difficulty might be overcome if Napoleon would make it worth the Pope's while—by abrogating the Organic Articles and abolishing civil marriage. " If the Emperor," said Pius IX. one day, " wants me to go to Paris, he must open the door to me. Let him abolish any decree that is contrary to the Concordat. I will allow three months to elapse so as to avoid the appearance of a bargain, and then—*en voiture!* " [16]

The price, however, was too much for Napoleon to pay. Public opinion was strongly against it. The old Gallican mistrust of Rome was aroused, and was not diminished by the Pope's open support of the Ultramontane cause in France. On May 8th, 1853, the Emperor went so far as to solicit the Pope by an autograph letter [17] couched in the most edifying

[15] Maurain, 41.
[16] Debidour, 535.

[17] Printed in Maurain, *Le Saint Siège et la France: documents inédits,* 216.

terms. "*Ecco una magnifica lettera!* " exclaimed the Pope. But Napoleon had by this time little hope of success : and the negotiation, though not completely abandoned, was generally and rightly held to have failed.

This failure may be regarded as the beginning of the rift between the Emperor and the Church that was to assume such serious proportions as time went on. For the time being, however, the outward appearances of union continued. The Organic Articles may have remained theoretically in force : but the Government was not assiduous in applying them. The bishops continued to hold their synods and provincial councils and to pay their visits to Rome unhindered : and under these favourable conditions Ultramontanism made rapid strides. The *budget des cultes* steadily rose in amount. [18] The Government did what it could to encourage the observance of Sunday as a day of rest, while refusing to render it compulsory (as the clergy would have wished). The attendance of civil dignitaries at religious functions was also encouraged. Attacks on religion were punished, but scandals in the clerical body were carefully hushed up with the connivance of the law. [19]

The clergy on their side were still loud in praise of the Government. The fulsome eulogies of Veuillot had led Montalembert, more and more disillusioned by the progress of events, to publish in October 1852 his celebrated pamphlet entitled *Les Interêts catholiques au XIXme siècle*. [20] In this he examined the causes of the revival of religion in France since the Revolution and found them in " liberty and the struggle made possible by liberty." He further maintained that, in the existing circumstances of Europe, representative government is the only possible form of political freedom. It follows that this kind of government is also the kind most favourable to the Church. But now in France it has disappeared and given place to despotism. What, then, shall the Catholics do? Certainly not initiate a policy of hostility to the new regime, which would at once be dangerous and futile.

---

[18] From 39½ million fr. in 1852 to 46 million in 1859. Maurain, 55.
[19] *Ibid.*, 77ff.
[20] Analysed in Lecanuet, *Montalembert,* iii. 69ff.

But let them be careful not to identify the cause of the Church with that of absolutism. The proper course is " to maintain a reserved and independent attitude between a systematic opposition and an undignified submission."

The pamphlet was widely read : and the Liberal opponents of the new regime were delighted. But the bishops (to each of whom Montalembert sent a copy) were very guarded ; and while congratulating the author were careful not to commit themselves on the point at issue. Dom Guéranger went much further. " I regard this pamphlet as a mistake," he wrote,[21] " and I tell you so flatly." He absolutely denied the alleged connection between liberty and the revival of Catholicism, and declared that the only possible government for France was a despotism. On the other hand, Lacordaire, whose Liberalism had never faltered and whose hope it was that he might die " as a penitent Catholic and an impenitent Liberal," was over-joyed at the return of his old comrade-at-arms to his former faith. " It was an unspeakable joy to me," he wrote, " to find you again the friend whom I clasped to my arms two-and-twenty years ago."[22]

It was from the *Univers,* however, that the most furious onslaught on Montalembert's pamphlet proceeded. It called it *"une Marseillaise parlementaire"* and attributed its compo-sition to a fit of sulks. " *M. de Montalembert s'ennuie.* He gives way to his disgust at being no longer anything."[23] It sang the praises of autocracy and (rather oddly, one feels) exalted the Government of Louis XIV. as " the ideal of a truly liberal and Catholic Government."[24] This was on the eve of the revival of the Empire. That revival accomplished, it pursued the same strain with even greater enthusiasm. It denied that it was absolutist : yet no words were too strong to express its detestation of liberty in every form. For the *Univers* only one kind of liberty existed—the liberty of the Church (by which, of course, was meant its exclusive domina-tion). As for parliamentary government, it was " *un bourbier*

[21] In a letter dated Nov. 22nd, 1852, printed in Lecanuet, 79f.
[22] *Ibid.,* 81.
[23] *Univers,* Nov. 1st, 1852.
[24] *Univers.,* Nov. 17—18th, 1852 (quoted Lecanuet, 82).

de servilisme et de corruption." [25] The Emperor was praised in
the most fulsome terms. In a note addressed to him in 1854
Veuillot described him as " a mind truly great, truly liberal,
truly royal," and his government as " a gift of Providence." [26]

The ecstasies of the *Univers* found an echo on episcopal
lips. Mgr. de Salinis, who had exalted in 1848 " the divine
perception of the people of February," now professed on
behalf of the Church " the most profound gratitude to the
Emperor " and exhorted it to give him " its most active
support." Mgr. Parisis even went so far as to apply to him
the words of Holy Writ concerning the Divine Wisdom—
" reaching from one end to another and sweetly ordering all
things " ! [27] After this there was not much more to be said.

None the less, the rift was there. The secret irritation of
the Government at the non-compliance of the Pope with the
Emperor's wishes respecting his coronation betrayed itself in
a serious modification made in the *Loi Falloux.* By a law of
June 14th, 1854, the number of *Académies* and consequently
of *Conseils Académiques* was reduced from 86 to 16. In these
the representatives of the Université were to be no longer a
minority, but a majority : and the Rectors once more became
persons of importance. Further, the teachers were henceforth
to be appointed and displaced by the prefects, who were also
to preside over the former *Conseils Académiques,* now turned
into *Conseils Départmentaux,* with the control of primary and
of voluntary secondary schools. [28] The authority of the Université, and still more of the Government, in the sphere of
education, was thus greatly increased : and that of the Church
was correspondingly diminished.

The bishops were strongly opposed to the new law and even
more to a decree of Dec. 31st, 1853, providing for the inspection of the *pensionnats congréganistes*—boarding-schools
for upper class girls conducted by religious communities [29]—
which had hitherto been exclusively under their control. But

[25] *Univers.,* April 10th, 1853.
[26] Debidour, 530.
[27] Lecanuet, 87f.
[28] Maurain, 147.
[29] *Ibid.,* 147.

in both cases their opposition was unavailing, though no action was taken against those bishops who refused to apply the decree.

Early in 1855 further tension arose in connection with the Bull issued by Pius IX. on December 8th, 1854, declaring *de fide* the dogma of the Immaculate Conception of the Blessed Virgin. The Bull was issued by the Pope on his own authority. No General Council had been summoned : the bishops had been merely consulted individually by letter. It was, in fact, a direct and deliberate exercise of that " infallibility " which was to be formally sanctioned by the Vatican Council of 1870. The French bishops made no difficulty about accepting the Bull, and many of them promulgated it at once. But the Gallican lawyers in the Council of State objected strongly—to the manner of its setting forth even more than to the dogma itself—and proposed to apply to it the first of the Organic Articles, forbidding " any bull, brief or rescript " emanating from the Pope to be " received, published or executed " in France without the authorization of the Government. The Bull was therefore submitted to the Council, where it was severely criticized. Eventually it was declared received, but with the traditional reservation of the rights of the civil power and the liberties of the Gallican Church. It was well understood that the Government disapproved of it.

Meanwhile, a negotiation had been dragging its slow length along which, though ultimately settled in accordance with the wishes of the Government, did nothing to improve the relations between it and the Holy See. [30] In the days following the *Coup d'État*, Baillés, Bishop of Luçon in La Vendée and a bigoted Legitimist, specially signalized himself by his open opposition to the new regime. He requested his clergy not to take part in the plebiscite of 1851, and after the election of Louis Napoleon refused to allow public prayers to be offered for him in the churches. The Government appealed first to his metropolitan, then to the Pope : but the pugnacious and obstinate old man refused to be guided by either. He embarked on a feud with the civil authorities of his region and

[30] Maurain, 86ff.

gave them all the trouble he could. The exasperated government decided (August 1853) to request the Pope to suspend Baillés and entrust his diocese to a vicar apostolic. The Pope, however, replied that he could not take such a step without a regular canonical trial of the offender. He could only ask Baillés to choose between abandoning his opposition and resigning his see. But Baillés (though an Ultramontane) would do neither. Further pressure from the new Nuncio at Paris, Sacconi, produced as little effect. The bishop continued to fight the Government, which made repeated applications to Rome. Meanwhile, Baillés's clergy were becoming more and more alienated from him.

At last, early in 1856, the Pope summoned Baillés to Rome in the hope of inducing him to resign. The bishop refused to go. The question then arose of appointing an administrator for his diocese. The Pope was now willing to do this, but demanded a *quid pro quo*. The Bishop of Pamiers, Alouvry, a strong Gallican, was accused of financial and other malpractices. The Pope desired that he should be deprived of his functions at the same time as Baillés. The Government would have liked to refuse : but, having abandoned the principle of the *inamovibilité* of bishops laid down by the Concordat in the case of Baillés, it could not plead it in that of Alouvry. The Pope then asked both bishops to send in their resignation. He informed Baillés that he must resign or go to Rome in twenty days, or an administrator would be appointed. Baillés saw that the game was up and resigned. Alouvry held out a little longer : but the Pope appointed an administrator and he resigned.

The subsequent fate of the two bishops was very different. Baillés the Ultramontane went to live in Rome, where the Pope showed him much favour and gave him a post in the Curia. Alouvry the Gallican simply faded out.

The changes in the educational system and the attitude of the Government in regard to the Bull of 1854 were not the only blows sustained by the Catholics in the years 1854-6. On March 27th, 1854, the Senate rejected almost unanimously a Catholic petition to make religious marriage obligatory : and

on the following July 6th a note in the *Moniteur* (the official
journal) intimated a similar refusal in regard to compulsory
Sunday observance. The upshot of the so-called *affaire de
la Salette* was not less disappointing—at least to the Ultramontanes. La Salette was a remote village in Dauphiné which
had become a celebrated (and also lucrative) place of pilgrimage in consequence of an " appearance " of the Blessed Virgin
to two children in 1846. The majority of the local clergy
were, however, suspicious of the alleged "miracles" : and two
of their number published attacks on their genuineness. [31]   A
woman whom they had accused of fraud in the matter brought
an action for defamation against one of them, the Abbé
Deléon, but was non-suited by the tribunal of Grenoble (May
2nd, 1855). The incident was eagerly exploited by the anticlerical journals of Paris : but the authorities took no steps
to silence them.

The Government, in fact, was beginning to need the help of
the Liberal and anticlerical press. Already the course of
events had begun which was to lead to Napoleon III's overt
espousal of the cause of Italian freedom in 1859. In the
pursuit of the new policy the attacks of such papers as the
Siècle on the corruption and mis-government of the reactionary governments of the Papal States and of Naples were
welcome aids. A latitude of comment was therefore permitted that had been hitherto denied : and their circulation
rose rapidly. Outwardly, indeed, the alliance between the
Empire and the Church still subsisted : and the baptism of
the Prince Imperial (for whom Pius IX. stood godfather) on
June 14th, 1856, seemed to give it an imposing consecration.
But beneath the surface the current was running hard against
the Church. The appointment of the rigidly Gallican
Rouland as Minister of Religions and Public Instruction
(August 13th, 1856) in place of the deceased Fortoul, whose
administration had been on the whole not unfriendly to the
Ultramontanes, was a sign that a new chapter of events had
begun.

---

[31] Maurain, 164f. One of the children confessed to the saintly Curé
d'Ars that he had lied, but retracted later.

CHAPTER III

ULTRAMONTANES AND LIBERAL CATHOLICS, 1851—1857

IT is when a cause feels itself strong that its adherents are most tempted to indulge in the luxury of quarrelling among themselves : just as opposition or persecution acts as a signal to close ranks and present a united front to the enemy. The history of the Church in France in the middle decades of the nineteenth century illustrates the truth of this statement on both its sides. Between 1830 and 1850 the Church was on the defensive : and its more active and aggressive elements were thus led to concentrate on the points where they agreed, not on those where they differed. In consequence, they were not only able to keep the peace among themselves but also to carry the mass of Catholics with them, at least to a considerable extent. With the passing of the *Loi Falloux,* the situation changed. It was the cause of educational freedom that had called the *parti catholique* into existence : and with the triumph of that cause, its *raison d'être* had largely ceased. The advent of Louis Napoleon confirmed the favourable situation of the Church. It is not surprising, therefore, that in the years following 1850 the Catholic body in France should have been torn by internal dissensions. Such dissensions were more or less inevitable : for the new Ultramontanism could not but be distasteful to those brought up in the old Gallican tradition respecting the relations between Church and State. But, in addition, a cleavage now appeared in the ranks of those who had hitherto marched together under the Ultramontane banner. It is in these years that the struggle began between the neo-Ultramontanes and the so-called " Liberal Catholics." [1]

[1] Of this much the best account is in Weill, *Histoire du catholicisme libéral en France,* 1907, ch. vi. and vii. This is an admirable book and carefully " objective " in method. It has been of the greatest value to the present writer for the whole period with which his book deals. Its scale prohibits great elaboration of detail : but it is based on wide know-

This struggle, as we have seen, had its origin partly in the political circumstances of the time. Veuillot and his friends passionately supported the Second Empire: Montalembert and his no less passionately opposed it. But there was also a disagreement in the sphere of religious ideas, the manifestations of which form the subject of the present chapter.

In assessing the position of the Liberal Catholics, it is necessary to understand wherein precisely their " Liberalism " consisted. In the current sense of the term a " Liberal Catholic " is one who seeks to effect a synthesis between the historic faith of the Church and the achievements of modern thought and research. It is only in a very partial degree that this sense holds good of the French Liberal Catholics of the mid-nineteenth century. It is true that they were not prepared, like Pius IX. and his Ultramontane stalwarts, to declare war on all the chief ideas on which modern civilization rests. Their belief in political liberty was sincere—even if some of them were willing to go much further than others in this respect. They accepted the " principles of 1789," and believed that the Church could and should recognize them as just and true. In the ecclesiastical sphere, too, they were opposed (like the Gallicans) to the claim of the Papacy to an exclusive domination of the Church. But in other and deeper aspects of men's right to think for themselves—and especially in the processes and achievements of historical criticism and scientific enquiry—they took little interest. They were Liberals —more or less—in politics : they were in no sense Liberals in theology.

Here lay the difference between them and their fellow " Liberal Catholics " of the Münich school in Germany. Such leaders as Döllinger and Hefele were deeply learned men who sought (if in a very cautious and conservative way) to apply modern critical methods to the history and traditional theology of the Church. But their French counterparts were neither

ledge and provides a first-rate conspectus of its subject. See also Maurain, *op. cit.* and (on the Ultramontane side) Veuillot, *Louis Veuillot,* and Baunard, *Histoire du Cardinal Pie;* (on the Liberal Catholic) Lecanuet, *Montalembert,* and Lagrange, *Dupanloup,* as above. Other books referred to are cited in the notes.

learned nor critically minded. Not one of them in any serious
sense can be described as a scholar. The true scientific spirit
—the spirit that is willing to follow the evidence wherever it
may lead—was always alien to them. They were all, first and
foremost, orators, swayed by emotion rather than by reason,
readily " inebriated with the exuberance of their own
verbosity." Of Lacordaire, a fellow-Immortal said that he was
the most ignorant man in the Academy.[2] His *Life of
St. Dominic* is a charming book, but entirely uncritical. In
the same way Montalembert's famous *Monks of the West,* for
all its eloquence and enthusiasm, has little value for the
scientific historian. Dupanloup was an inspiring educator of
youth : but he was neither learned in the least nor a profound
thinker. When Lord Acton met him in Germany in 1869 he
was "appalled at his ignorance," and said to Döllinger,
" What is to be expected if this is one of the best specimens ?"[3]
In him and his group Renan—an acute if prejudiced critic—
discerned " a complete absence of theology " : " they were
content to revere it from a distance."[4] His attitude to historical criticism is sufficiently summed up in the remark :
" *Surtout méfiez-vous des sources!* "[5] So far from reverenc-
ing scientific achievement, he fought the election of Littré to
the Academy tooth and nail : and when Littré was elected
despite his efforts he resigned his own seat rather than be
associated with a Positivist. The French Liberal Catholics in
fact never really faced the essential problem—to effect a
synthesis between truth revealed and truth discovered.
"Quirinus," the caustic critic of the Vatican Council, comment-
ing on the attitude of Dupanloup and other French bishops,
has some words in this connection that are severe but not untrue : " The same cleavage which divides Catholics divides
also the minority : the term ' Liberal Catholic ' rather obscures
than expresses the principle of the division. . . . It is not merely
freedom but truth that is at stake. . . . The spirit which falsifies

[2] Acton : *History of Freedom,* 399. The speaker was Circourt.
[3] Acton : *Correspondence,* i. 53.
[4] Renan : *Souvenirs d'enfance et de jeunesse,* Ch. iii. p. 130. (Nelson
edition.)
[5] Acton : *History of Freedom,* 400.

history and corrupts morals is the crying sin of modern Catholicism " : and the leading French Catholics largely share it. [6]

Yet, however superficial their treatment of it may have been, the Liberal Catholics were at least aware that a problem existed. Their aim was a noble one—to solve the eternal antinomy between authority and freedom. They saw that both are good : they saw, too, that God uses many means to achieve His purposes, and that humanity may progress and truth be achieved through agencies that have received no *imprimatur* from the Church and are even bitterly hostile to it. In this, of course, they had history on their side; whereas Veuillot's reading of history is completely fantastic and the facts give it the lie at every turn. But, unfortunately for them and the Church they loved so well, Veuillot had the supreme authority in the Church behind him. For Pius IX. there was no problem at all. If ecclesiastical tradition and modern civilization came into conflict, modern civilization was bound to be wrong : nor did he ever hesitate to say so. This being the case, the Liberal Catholic attempt to reconcile the two was certain to fail : and its failure left the Roman Church committed to a position that dooms it to be always the bulwark of political and intellectual reaction—however venerable it may often be in the sphere of moral witness and spiritual effort.

I

Signs of internal tension had appeared within the *parti catholique* as early as 1846. They were more or less connected with the appearance of Dupanloup [7] by the side of

---

[6] " Quirinus " (Döllinger): *Letters from Rome on the Council,* 1870, 441ff.

[7] The chief authority for Dupanloup's career is the official biography by one of his Vicars-General (later Bishop of Chartres), Lagrange, *Vie de Mgr. Dupanloup,* 3 vols., 1883. It is interesting and full of information, but (as Maurain justly says) *très tendancieuse, surtout par ce qu'elle tait.* Dupanloup fought Pius IX. and lost: and his biographer is correspondingly embarrassed—especially as he writes in a decided spirit of hero-worship and had shared his hero's views. The book provoked a severe criticism from the neo-Ultramontane side in Maynard, *Mgr. Dupanloup et M. Lagrange son historien,* 1884. There are character studies of Dupanloup from a non-partisan standpoint in Ollivier, *Concile du Vatican,* i. 442f, and Hanotaux, *Histoire de la France contemporaine,* i. 226.

Montalembert as a protagonist in the struggle for educational freedom. Dupanloup was at this time still Rector of the College of S. Nicolas du Chardonnet in Paris, which his brilliant gifts as an educationist had raised from a humble diocesan *petit séminaire* to be the most fashionable and aristocratic school in France. Essentially a man of affairs, he maintained in two successive pamphlets (1845 and 1847) that the *parti catholique* was more likely to achieve its object by effecting a transaction with the Government than by fighting it. Veuillot, on the other hand, was strongly opposed to a transaction : he would have all or nothing. Montalembert was really of the same opinion, but allowed himself to be identified with Dupanloup's policy. That policy, however, failed for the moment. The Government scheme of 1847 was a bitter disappointment to the Catholics. Even Dupanloup was unable to accept it.

The same divergence of opinion betrayed itself again, as we have seen, in connection with the *Loi Falloux*. Falloux himself was a transactionist : and he was supported both by Montalembert and by Dupanloup, who was largely responsible for the scheme. Veuillot retained his attitude of determined opposition to a compromise of any sort. He fought Falloux's bill with all his might; and when it became law only ceased to criticize it in deference to the Pope's wishes. The breach between him and Montalembert was temporarily healed by their common action in support of Louis Napoleon at the end of 1851 : but when Montalembert went over to the opposition it yawned wider than ever.

Between Veuillot and Dupanloup there was never any pretence of reconciliation. Dupanloup, since 1849 Bishop of Orléans, [8] had opposed the identification of the *parti catholique* with the fortunes of Louis Napoleon. He was even more opposed to the new Ultramontanism preached by the *Univers*. The *Ami de la Religion,* a newspaper of which Dupanloup assumed control in 1848, had many a brush with Veuillot's

[8] Dupanloup and his great rival Pie were both nominated to the episcopate by Falloux—as were also Salinis and the stormy-petrel Dreux-Brézé.

organ on the educational and other questions. In a letter to
a correspondent, Dupanloup described the *Univers* as "*une
plaie vive dans l'Église.*"[9]   Visiting Rome in the winter of
1850-1 the Bishop of Orléans even ventured to speak to the
Holy Father "*avec grande franchise*" concerning the "*impru-
dentes témerités*" which troubled the peace of the Church of
France. The experiment would not appear to have been very
successful : for, writing in his journal next day, Dupanloup
ruminated as follows : " There are people who seem able only
to receive congenial information and do not care for any
other."[10]   That Montalembert should quit the side of an old
comrade-at-arms to associate himself more and more with a
personality so antipathetic must have been a bitter blow to
Veuillot.

Dupanloup's place among the great figures of the French
Church is secure for all time. His remarkable gifts of utterance, his personal charm, his devouring activity combine to
make him stand out not only as a great Churchman but as
one of the most striking figures of his age. Yet if many loved
him much, many loved him little or not at all. He was the
sort of person who lays himself open very easily to criticism :
nor (to do him justice) was he altogether blind to his own
faults. The venomous hatred of Veuillot and his crew is
easily comprehensible when we remember that Dupanloup
was always the most formidable spoke in their wheel. Yet
even here we cannot hold him entirely beyond reproach. He
was the declared enemy of " disunion," his policy was one of
" pacification "—or so he is never tired of telling us. But his
olive branches were often " shot from a catapult." Not only
did he give as good as he got, but he seems to have delighted
in getting his blow in—nor did he always mind if it was a bit
" below the belt." To quote Emile Ollivier's brilliant contemporary character-study : " He is of a candid honesty and
in debate he has no scruples : he is so convinced of being right
that, to prove it, he now and then ceases to be truthful ! "[11]

[9] Lagrange, *op. cit.*, i. 511.
[10] *Ibid.*, ii. 29.
[11] Ollivier : *Concile du Vatican*, i. 443.

In any case it is clear that the scent of battle was far from distasteful to the bishop : he was always a *lutteur*. It is no less clear that he loved to be " in the limelight." Wherever there is an opportunity to say anything, he always likes to say it before anyone else and to say it as vociferously as possible— to *pousser son cri* (to use his unctuous biographer's constant expression).

In many ways Dupanloup reminds one of our own Bishop Samuel Wilberforce. There is the same ready eloquence, the same social charm, the same delight in the society of the great, the same easy and rather superficial handling of big issues, the same inability to make others entirely believe in their sincerity and straightforwardness. There is also the same pastoral zeal and energy. It has been said that Wilberforce revolutionized the English idea of a bishop and his office : and much the same may be said of Dupanloup and the French idea. One wonders indeed whether his clergy did not find him rather a trial at times. Renan tells us that he understood that he was always better loved by his laity than by his priests. [12] The Bishop was nothing if not an autocrat : and it is not surprising that the cause of the *inamovibilité* of the parish priest left him rather cold. [13] Yet in all this the organizing power, the ability to plan out big comprehensive schemes, combined with an immense grasp of detail, are not less patent than the restless energy and love of domination. Nor would it appear that the prelate's multifarious outside preoccupations were allowed to interfere seriously with his diocesan duties—in spite of the well known sneer that he was *"aussi peu évêque d'Orléans que possible."* He clearly liked to be an important figure in the world : there was nothing of the modest violet about him. In every way he was the obvious target for Veuillot's attack : and for the next thirty years the mutual antipathy of the two men was to find resounding opportunity of expression.

[12] Renan : *Souvenirs d'enfance et de jeunesse,* 137. (Nelson edition.)
[13] Lagrange, ii. 43.

II

It was not, however, between Veuillot and Dupanloup that the first serious encounter took place. Mgr. Sibour, Bishop of Digne, had been appointed Archbishop of Paris in 1849 in succession to the murdered Archbishop Affre. The correspondence between him and Montalembert quoted at the beginning of this work [14] shows that he had regarded himself as an " Ultramontane " in the earlier sense of that word. But with the Ultramontane doctrine as preached by the *Univers* he had no sympathy whatever. Veuillot's intolerance and obscurantism, his contempt for the bishops and exaggeration of the claims of the Holy See, filled him with alarm for the future of the Church. He was essentially a devotee of the *via media*. For him (to quote another sentence from the same correspondence) " wisdom as well as truth consists in taking a course between opposite extremes and the abysses that yawn on both sides." [15] Nor was he at all in agreement with Veuillot's reckless praise of absolutism. He had disapproved of the *Coup d'État*; and would have preferred the Catholics to abstain from voting in the plebiscite.

The Archbishop's uneasiness in regard to the excesses of the *Univers* was increased by the fact that the paper was published within his own diocese. At the outset of his episcopate he had suggested to Veuillot an arrangement that would give him a measure of control over its policy. The offer was not well received: and Sibour then started a rival journal, the *Moniteur Catholique*. This proved a failure. Undaunted, the Archbishop issued (August 31st, 1850) an *avertissement* condemning the *Univers* as " compromising the Church." [16] The *Univers* promptly appealed to the Pope, to whom Sibour also wrote defending his action. Rome was anxious for a settlement, and obtained it. On October 3rd the *Univers* withdrew its appeal. But it was understood that the Pope was not pleased with the Archbishop, whom indeed he had distrusted from the start.

[14] p. 1f.
[15] Lecanuet, ii. 105.
[16] Veuillot: *Louis Veuillot*, ii. 400f.

A second encounter followed almost at once. The old Bishop of Chartres, Clausel de Montals, a militant Legitimist and Clerical with a habit of getting into hot water, denounced in a pastoral letter the " democratic " tendencies evinced by Sibour in his episcopal charges.[17] At his request Veuillot published the letter. Sibour summoned the bishop to appear before the provincial council of Paris. He also severely reprimanded Veuillot and forbade him to publish any further comments on the matter on pain of excommunication—an undertaking that Veuillot declined to give. The effect of the incident was to reopen the question : " Does a journal with the circulation of the *Univers* depend on the Archbishop of Paris or on the whole episcopate? " The question was considered at Rome : and Veuillot was soon given to understand that he need fear no unpleasant results in that quarter. A " reconciliation " between Sibour and the Bishop of Chartres followed.

Shortly after this a further incident gave Dupanloup an opportunity of ranging himself on Sibour's side in no uncertain fashion. An eccentric and fanatically Ultramontane priest of Paris, the Abbé Combalot, ventured to attack a charge of Sibour's. Combalot and Dupanloup were old enemies : for the Abbé, during the controversy on the *Loi Falloux,* had distinguished himself by his venomous attacks on one who was rightly regarded as largely responsible for the measure. Notwithstanding this, he rashly sent to the Bishop of Orléans a copy of his pamphlet. Dupanloup returned a withering reply in which he compared the Abbé to Lamennais and animadverted in the severest terms on the " fraternal correction " he had presumed to offer to his diocesan. *" C'est le drapeau du présbyterianisme que vous levez,"* he informed him.[18] This letter he formally communicated to his clergy. Eventually Combalot was compelled to apologize to the Archbishop.

By this time a controversy had begun which was to bring Dupanloup into much prominence and set him in the vanguard of the opposition to the *Univers*. Early in 1852 the

[17] Veuillot: *Louis Veuillot,* ii. 439f.
[18] Lagrange, ii. 125f.

Abbé Gaume published a book called *Le Ver rongeur des sociétés modernes*. In this he denounced the use of the pagan classics of Greece and Rome in education, finding in this a chief cause of the irreligion of the modern educated world. In their place he proposed to substitute the " Christian classics," the Fathers of the Church. Dupanloup at once took fire. No doubt—and with good reason—he felt himself personally attacked : for had not the classics played a principal part in the education of his own pupils at St. Nicolas du Chardonnet? In a letter to the professors of the *petits séminaires* of his diocese he strongly dissociated himself from the views of the Abbé Gaume. [19] The letter gave the signal for the entry of the *Univers* into the fray. In a series of articles it upheld the Abbé and violently attacked the Bishop by name, accusing him of instituting in his seminaries " a system of education of which paganism formed the basis."[20] These charges stung Dupanloup to fury. Not only did he feel himself attacked, but the episcopal office as well : for what he had written he had written not as a private individual but as bishop of his diocese. And it was a mere layman who had presumed to act as his judge ! At this rate, what became of the sacred principle of hierarchy ?

The bishop's indignation found vent in a charge. In this he dealt with both aspects of the question. He defended the use of the classics : but above all he expressed his horror at the presumptuous interference of lay journalism within the hallowed sphere of episcopal jurisdiction. " The real issue," he wrote, " is to know whether the staff of the *Univers* are to have the right, in the place of the Pope and the Council of the province, to exercise control over our pastoral instructions and to establish themselves, in the teeth of ourselves, of our venerable colleagues and of the Holy See as the defenders of *la foi compromise* and the censors of the episcopate." " Nor," he continued, " is this an isolated fact. It is a custom with these men to settle precipitately, rashly, violently, all the most grave and difficult questions and, when once they have settled

[19] Lagrange, ii. 115.
[20] *Ibid.*, 129.

them, to refuse to tolerate any disagreement, from whatever quarter, however exalted, it may come." He censured the " mocking levity," the " tone of haughty raillery " adopted by his critics. In conclusion, he forbade any who held office in the seminaries of his diocese to become subscribers to the *Univers*.[21]

Even so, the bishop's rage remained unslaked. A condemnation of the *Univers* by a bishop here and there was not enough: the whole episcopal body must be brought into action. With this object he, with the Archbishops of Paris and of Besançon, drew up a Declaration which they (rather optimistically) hoped might secure the adherence of all the bishops of France. The Declaration[22] set forth the following four points:

(1) " That the acts of bishops are in no wise to be judged by newspapers but only by the Holy See and the bishops."

(2) " That the use in secondary schools of the pagan classics, suitably chosen, carefully expurgated and explained in Christian fashion, is neither evil nor dangerous, and that to pretend the contrary would be to condemn the practice of all Catholic bishops and of the most saintly religious congregations . . ."

(3) " That the use of the pagan classics ought not to be exclusive, but that it is advantageous to add to it the study and explanation of Christian authors."

(4) " That to the bishops alone belongs, each in his own diocese and without any control from writers or journalists, to determine in what measure these authors, Christian or pagan, are to be employed."

The Declaration obtained the adhesion of forty-six bishops. But others opposed it, if only on the ground of the method of procedure. Parisis even wrote to Veuillot a letter of sympathy. Pie referred the matter to Rome: and a letter from Cardinal Antonelli condemned the Declaration. No further step therefore was taken in regard to it. Veuillot, at the request of the bishops, ceased his polemic on the pagan classics. But the

[21] Lagrange, ii. 131ff.
[22] Text printed, *ibid.*, 137f.

cleavage in the ranks of the episcopate stood revealed : nor was there any doubt on which side the sympathies of Rome lay.

Thus encouraged, the Ultramontane section of the episcopate was not long in making a counter-demonstration. In January 1853 a Council of the province of Reims was held at Amiens. The majority of the assembled bishops were Ultramontanes, including the Cardinal Archbishop of Reims, Gousset,[23] and the Bishop of Amiens, Salinis. The Council condemned an anonymous memorandum—recently circulated to all the French episcopate and believed to have emanated from the leading anti-Ultramontane bishops—defending the *droit coutumier* of the Church of France and criticizing the Ultramontane attempt to substitute for it the *droit commun* of the Church. It also gave a partial support to the ideas of the Abbé Gaume on the classics and championed the rights of Catholic journalists.[24] After the Council Salinis betook himself to Rome to submit its acts to the Holy See. He was accompanied by Gaume and Veuillot.

No sooner had they arrived than tidings came of a new blow at the *Univers*—this time from Sibour. The original *casus belli* in the present instance had come from Orléans. One of Dupanloup's vicars-general, the Abbé Gaduel, writing in the *Ami de la Religion* had criticized severely a book by the Spanish Ultramontane, Donoso Cortés, that had appeared in a series edited by Veuillot called *Bibliothèque Nouvelle*. Veuillot took up the cudgels in his friend's defence and in a series of articles held up to ridicule not only the views but also the person of his critic. The Abbé made a formal complaint to the Archbishop of Paris, describing Veuillot's articles as "insulting, defamatory and scandalous."[25] Sibour thereupon issued an ordinance (February 17th) in which he not only expatiated at length on the misdoings of the *Univers* but forbade all his clergy to read it, still more to contribute to it. The

---

[23] Gousset was an Ultramontane *de la première heure*. It was he who first introduced "Liguorism" into France as a rival to the old quasi-Jansenist moral theology. Weill, 60.
[24] Maurain, 47.
[25] Lagrange, ii. 141.

Univers once more appealed to the Pope. Immediately afterwards Sibour also appealed—against a letter in which the Ultramontane bishop of Moulins, Dreux-Brézé, had called in question his claim to control the proceedings of the *Univers*. [26]

Veuillot, being in Rome, requested an interview with the Pope. Pius received him graciously, and later sent him a letter commending his work and at the same time exhorting him to " moderation and mildness." [27]

Something more public than this, however, was needed. The Pope had before him two specific appeals to his authority —the acts of the Council of Amiens and the issue respecting the *Univers*. On March 21st, 1853, therefore, he issued an Encyclical, *Inter multiplices,* addressed to the bishops of France and giving his decision on both questions. The decision was in all essentials a verdict for the Ultramontanes. The Council's acts were approved, and the bishops were exhorted to introduce the Roman liturgy into their dioceses and to use in their seminaries none but books approved by the Holy See. Sibour's ordinance was not mentioned : but the work of the Catholic journals was eulogized and the bishops were invited to treat them with kindness. Only in regard to the pagan classics did the Ultramontanes lose their case ; the use of them being allowed under certain reserves. [28]

The anti-Ultramontane offensive had thus failed. Sibour withdrew his ordinance : and the *Univers* went on its way rejoicing.

It was now the turn of Montalembert to come into the field. Whatever hope there might ever have been of a reconciliation between him and Veuillot had been ended for good and all by the latter's virulent attack on his pamphlet, *Les Interêts catholiques au XIXme siècle.* His own position was increasingly isolated. Only in the Academy (at this time the chief and almost the sole focus of opposition to the Empire) was he genuinely at home. He himself had been elected to it in 1851, Dupanloup in 1854 : Falloux and Lacordaire were

---

[26] Maurain, 48.
[27] Veuillot : *L. Veuillot,* ii. 555.
[28] Maurain, 49.

to be elected in 1857 and 1860 respectively. With the majority of the anti-Ultramontane bishops he had little in common : for they were devoted to the Government. More and more, therefore, he felt that some organ was needed that might express the specific Liberal Catholic point of view.

A newspaper was out of the question in view of the stringent press censorship. But a monthly review might serve *faute de mieux*. With this object Montalembert busied himself with reviving the *Correspondant*. Founded in 1828, this review had done good service to the Catholic cause in the past, but had fallen latterly on evil days. To assist in its revival Montalembert gathered round him a notable band of collaborators —the Prince Albert de Broglie (before 1848 a strong Gallican, but now come round to the Liberal Catholic standpoint [29]), Falloux, Dupanloup, Foisset (Lacordaire's friend and biographer), and the brilliant young Auguste Cochin. Lacordaire also was approached. Since 1853, when, in a transparent allusion, he had denounced Louis Napoléon from the pulpit as *"un grand homme par l'esprit et un misérable par le cœur,"* [30] he had ceased to preach in the churches of Paris and was now living in comparative retirement as head of the Dominican college of Sorrèze. After some preliminary misgivings he agreed to lend his aid.

A committee of six was appointed to control the policy of the new *Correspondant,* with Montalembert as its president. A striking article from Broglie's pen outlined its programme. The article asserted that the sympathy accorded to the Church in the years 1848-50 had recently undergone a serious setback, and attributed this to the deplorable way in which its cause had been defended since 1852. Reason and faith had been wilfully set in opposition : and the " principles

---

[29] Broglie's *magnum opus, L'Église et l'empire romain au IVme siècle,* 1856-69, was inspired—so its preface (1856, p. vf) informs us—by the desire of helping Catholics to treat the new social order created by the Revolution with the *douceur toute maternelle* shown by the Constantinian Church to the pagan world. For this reason it was fiercely attacked by Guéranger in a series of articles in the *Univers,* subsequently collected in a volume : *Essai sur le naturalisme contemporain,* 1858. Weill, 139f.

[30] February 10th, at St. Roch. Debidour, 532 n. See also D'Haussonville, *Lacordaire* (Eng. tr.), 180 f.

of 1789," on which modern civilization largely rested, had been held up to execration. As against this the promoters of the *Correspondant* stood for the following principles :

(1) They do not admit any antagonism between faith and reason; (2) they are not the enemies of modern society; (3) they admit religious freedom, if not as an absolute principle and for every age, yet as necessary to-day; (4) they maintain that political liberties have nothing in them incompatible with the Catholic faith. The Church may consist with any form of government : but freedom is that most to be preferred. [31]

The *Univers* was not slow to pick up the gauntlet. It began by sarcastically inviting the *Correspondant* to direct its fire on the enemy, not on its fellow-Catholics : and went on to ridicule " these temporizing journalists who shuffle with the Catholic creed and blush at Christ, His saints and the laws of His Church." [32]   The *Correspondant* did not endure these attacks meekly, but returned blow for blow, if with a somewhat more dignified air. What most of all irritated Montalembert was the claim of the *Univers* to speak in the name of the Holy See. In the hope of exploding this pretension he and Falloux addressed a letter to Pius IX., expounding their methods and aims and by implication denouncing their rivals. But they failed to get much satisfaction. The Pope deplored the exaggerations of the *Univers:* but he praised its services to religion all the same. In his reply to Montalembert (March 17th, 1856), while denying that the *Univers* was in any sense his organ, he invited him and his friends to abandon controversy and defend the Church instead. [33]

Undeterred by the snub, the Liberal Catholics continued their campaign. The reproduction in an Orléans newspaper of a recent scandalous biography of Veuillot was stopped at Dupanloup's request, but on grounds that Veuillot found insulting—not because the presentment was untrue but in deference to " the charity and wisdom of our illustrious and venerable bishop." [34] Falloux attacked Veuillot in a pamphlet,

[31] Lecanuet, iii. 118.
[32] *Ibid.*, 125.
[33] March 17th, 1856. Text in Lecanuet, iii. 128.
[34] Veuillot: *L. Veuillot,* iii. 81.

Le parti catholique, ce qu'il a été, ce qu'il est devenu. Finally, an anonymous publication appeared bearing the title *L'Univers jugé par lui-même.* Its compiler, a certain Abbé Cognat, had brought together a collection of the choicest specimens of the virulences and extravagances of the detested newspaper, with the object of rousing public opinion against it.

Dupanloup had no ostensible part in this production : but it was generally and rightly believed that he and Sibour were behind it. [35] The Ultramontane bishops, on the other hand, strongly resented it : and several of them openly supported Veuillot. Parisis even declared that " the suppression of the *Univers* would be a public misfortune for religion " and described it as " a great Catholic institution." The Pope was of much the same opinion. " *Qu'il persévère dans la voie où il est,*" he is said to have remarked. " *Je lis* L'Univers *et je l'aime.*" [36]

In his indignation Veuillot decided to have recourse to the law. He brought an action against the compiler for defamation of character. The action would almost certainly have had awkward results for Dupanloup and others had not a tragic event caused Veuillot to abandon it. [37] On January 31st, 1857, Archbishop Sibour was stabbed to death in the Church of St. Étienne-du-Mont by a priest whom he had inhibited for immoral conduct.

---

[35] Maurain, 174 n.
[36] Veuillot : *L. Veuillot,* iii. 112.
[37] *Ibid.,* 114ff.

CHAPTER IV

NAPOLEON III. AND THE LIBERATION OF ITALY
1855—1861

I

IT was the misfortune of the Second Empire that it could never overcome the vices of its origin and make up its mind what it stood for. If, from one point of view, it was an autocracy, a vindication of authority and order against anarchy, from another and deeper point of view it was the child and representative of the Revolution. Even as an autocracy it rested in theory and fact on the will of the people, expressed by plebiscite. For this and for other reasons its alliance with the Church—at least with the Church as conceived by the Ultramontanes—could never be anything more than a working arrangement: on the deeper ground of principle the two could only be antagonistic. Veuillot might cozen himself into believing that the consecration of the " principles of 1789 " by the Constitution of 1852 was only a matter of form: but it was in truth fundamental. This was to be proved as soon as the Italian question came on the scene.

It was not only his position as an heir of the Revolution that led Napoleon III. to favour the cause of Italian unity and independence. His family antecedents and personal inclinations drove him in the same direction. His name was Italian; the founder of his dynasty had (if only for a few years) made of Italy a single kingdom; and he himself in his youth had fought in the revolution of 1830 to deprive the Pope of his states. Policy, too, dictated the same line of action. Between France—the representative of the new European order—and Austria—the accredited champion of the old—there was intense rivalry. And it was Austria that upheld the existing political arrangements of Italy. The little kingdom of Piedmont indeed was the hereditary foe of Austria and had led the struggle to throw off the Austrian yoke in 1848. But the rest

74

of northern Italy was under Austrian dominion; the Papal power (though for the moment guaranteed by French arms) was in sympathy and policy much more nearly allied to Austria than to France; while the reactionary government of the kingdom of Naples-Sicily looked to Austria as the bulwark of its existence. If, then, the Austrian hegemony in Italy could be overthrown, what a triumph for France and her Emperor! The only difficulty was the fact that, by his action in 1849 and since, Napoleon had made himself a surety for the integrity of the papal dominions. But this difficulty might be overcome—if indeed it was seriously envisaged at all.

From the beginning of his reign, Napoleon had shown sympathy for Piedmontese aspirations. Early in 1855 this sympathy was to develop into something more tangible. The Crimean War was dragging its difficult course along: and the help of Piedmont, though a small matter, might yet be of value to the Allies in the prosecution of their struggle with Russia. The Piedmontese Prime Minister, Cavour, for his part, was very willing to give this help in the hope of having a voice in the settlement that would follow the conclusion of the war. The offer was accepted: and in January 1855 an alliance was concluded between the Allies and Piedmont. In the following July Napoleon announced officially that Piedmont would share in the profits, as she had shared in the perils, of the war. " Dangers, honours, advantages—all will be shared." [1] At the end of the year Victor Emmanuel and Cavour visited Paris: and Napoleon asked them to tell him what he could do to help the cause of Italy. Cavour's demands included the surrender of the Romagna, a papal possession now in Austrian occupation.

The alliance between France and Piedmont was a matter of deep concern to the Holy See, which knew perfectly well what Piedmont was aiming at and was already in open hostility with her on the ground of her policy towards the Church. Even in the entourage of the Emperor himself it was by no means universally approved. The Empress in particular was anxious to avoid anything that might alienate the Pope.

[1] *Moniteur,* July 12th, 1855.

The war over, the Peace Congress met in Paris. On April 8th, 1856, Walewski, the French Foreign Secretary, acting on the Emperor's instructions, formally raised the Italian question. He expressed the desire of the Government to terminate the French occupation of the papal states at the earliest possible date. The English plenipotentiary, Lord Clarendon, criticized severely the papal administration, describing it as " the most detestable of governments." [2] Before it separated the Congress expressed the wish that liberal institutions might be accorded as soon as possible in those Italian states where they were still lacking, particularly in the papal dominions, and that by this means the foreign occupation of the latter might be brought to an end.

This wish was intimated by the French Government to the Pope. The Pope in reply declared that he had already done as much as the circumstances permitted, and that the demand for reforms was merely a device of the revolutionary party for overthrowing the pontifical government altogether. A more formal demand from the Emperor (June 30th, 1857) met with no better result. Such an attitude was by no means calculated to improve the relations between the French Government and the Holy See. Rayneval, the French Ambassador at Rome and an opponent of the new Italian policy, was recalled : and the Duc de Gramont, who was on good terms with Cavour, took his place. The Government also watched without dissatisfaction a revival in political circles of the old Gallican spirit. In the discussion on a *senatus-consultum* providing for the establishment of a regency in case of the Emperor's death, a determined attempt had been made to impose on the regent (who would presumably be the Empress) an oath to observe not only the Constitution but also the Organic Articles. The attempt was only defeated by a small majority [3] (July 17th, 1856).

The case of the Bishop of Moulins, Dreux-Brézé, created further tension. [4] Dreux-Brézé, a Legitimist and Ultramon-

[2] Lecanuet, iii. 202.
[3] Maurain, 176.
[4] See *ibid.*, 190ff.

tane, had been appointed bishop by Falloux in 1849 and had set himself with energy to reform his difficult diocese and to remodel it on stringently Roman lines. He was soon loathed by his clergy : and two of his curés organized a petition to the Pope against him. The Pope replied that he had no fault to find with the bishop. Dreux-Brézé then took the offensive and inhibited one of the curés, who appealed to " the justice of the Emperor." His appeal was supported by the chief citizens of Moulins, who petitioned the Government against the bishop. The Emperor decided to take action : and informed the Pope that if he did not compel Dreux-Brézé to resign, the bishop must be brought before the Council of State. As the Pope refused to take the step required, the Council of State tried the case and found Dreux-Brézé guilty of *abus* as having infringed the Organic Articles.

The *Correspondant* protested against the verdict and received an *avertissement* for its pains. The *Univers* also protested and received a similar *avertissement*—its first brush with the Government. Veuillot now discovered that Napoleon III. was only a " *Louis Philippe perfectionné* " [5] after all. In the general elections of 1857 Montalembert's candidature was opposed by the imperial administration, and he lost his seat. When the bacchanalian and anti-clerical poet Béranger died in July, the Emperor ordered that he should be given a public funeral. Finally, a seat in the Cour de Cassation was restored to the ex-Orléanist Dupin, [6] a Gallican of the deepest dye who had specially signalized himself by his opposition to the *parti catholique* in the closing years of the July Monarchy.

A serious rupture between Church and State seemed at hand when an event occurred which for the moment appeared to presage a drawing-together of the two antagonists. On January 14th, 1858, an Italian refugee, Orsini, hurled bombs at the Emperor and his wife as they were entering the Paris Opéra. A number of bystanders were killed : but the imperial pair miraculously escaped. The bishops were not slow to point

---

[5] Debidour, 543.

[6] His definition of the word " episcopate " is classic : " a function of the Church exercised in the name and under the control of the State." *Manuel du droit ecclésiastique*, s.v.

out to the Emperor the moral of his deliverance. Henceforth
he must devote himself unreservedly to the cause of the Holy
See and of religion.[7] Veuillot, in a private audience, drove
home the same lesson. For the moment Napoleon seemed
disposed to follow the advice proffered to him. New favours
were showered upon the Church : and in August an imposing
demonstration was staged of the alliance between it and the
Emperor. The Emperor and his consort visited Brittany, the
most Catholic part of France, and greatly edified its inhabitants by their piety. In an address the Bishop of Rennes,
Brossais-Saint-Marc, spoke of Napoleon III. as " of all French
monarchs since St. Louis the most devoted to the Church," [8]
and was rewarded by the erection of his see into an archbishopric. Veuillot accompanied the imperial party on their
tour and wrote an account of it in ecstatic terms.

Actually, however, the effect of the Orsini outrage was the
precise opportunity of what had been anticipated. The Emperor's nerves had been badly shaken by this rude reminder
of his Carbonarist past. It was not the first attempt of the kind
that had been made : nor, unless he took the hint, was it likely
to be the last. The effect on his mobile and impressionable
nature was deepened by a letter, written to him by Orsini
from prison and read at the latter's trial, in which the assailant
adjured him to right the wrong done by him to Italy in 1849
and to restore to her her freedom. If he failed to do so, the
plots against him would be renewed. By the Emperor's orders
the prefect of police visited Orsini in prison and persuaded
him to write a second letter inviting his fellow-revolutionaries
to abandon their violent methods in return for the liberation
of Italy. Immediately afterwards he was executed.

The die was cast. Napoleon now definitely engaged himself to the Italian cause. On July 17th, 1858, he and Cavour
had their famous secret interview at Plombières. It was
agreed that France should unite with Piedmont to drive the
Austrians out of Italy, that the war should begin in the
following spring and that Piedmont should be enlarged to

[7] Maurain, 225.
[8] Ibid., 228.

form a state of ten or twelve million inhabitants. As the price
of her help France was to receive Nice and Savoy. Italy was
to be formed into a confederation under the honorary presidency of the Pope (who would retain his states) but under
the effective hegemony of Piedmont.

.   For the time being the bargain remained a secret. But
the secret would soon be out : and meanwhile it was necessary
to prepare public opinion for its divulgement. With this object
the Government allowed and even encouraged the Liberal
and anticlerical press to demand war on Austria and in particular to attack the pontifical government.   Among such
attacks a series of caustic articles by Edmond About in the
official *Moniteur* engaged particular attention.   The *affaire
Mortara* that occurred at this time played into the hands of
the enemies of the Holy See.   Four years before a Jewish boy
(Mortara by name) had been baptized without the knowledge
of his parents by a Christian servant-girl, who believed him
to be on the point of death and hoped thereby to save his soul.
The boy, however, recovered : and in 1858 the Holy Office,
hearing of the baptism, took him away from his parents to
have him brought up as a Catholic. The parents protested and
the French Government supported their protest. But the Pope
replied that he could not conscientiously give back a Christian
child to Judaism.   The incident created a very bad impression
in France and was exploited to the full by the anticlerical
press. [9]

A similar advantage was made of an apparition of the
Blessed Virgin alleged to have occurred in a grotto in the little
village of Lourdes in the Pyrenees on February 11th, 1858.
Bernadette Soubirous, a girl of fourteen, declared that she had
witnessed the apparition and that the Virgin had said (rather
oddly) : " I am the Immaculate Conception."   At once a
stream of pilgrims began to flow to Lourdes, whereupon the
Government ordered the grotto to be closed.   The mass of
Catholic opinion was sceptical : but the local clergy declared
for the " miracle."   Veuillot, without committing himself as
yet one way or the other, published a series of articles extolling

[9] Maurain, 230ff.

faith in the supernatural. The anticlerical papers of course held up the whole business to ridicule. [10]

Towards the end of the year Montalembert was condemned to fine and imprisonment for an article in the *Correspondant* in which, having just returned from a visit to London, he contrasted " the servile and corrupting miasmas of our own country " with " the purer air of free England " (October 25th). The *Moniteur* of December 2nd, however, intimated that the Emperor had graciously remitted the penalty " *à l'occasion du Deux Décembre* "! [11]

With the advent of 1859 the time had come for Napoleon to drop the mask. On New Year's Day, receiving the Corps Diplomatique, he remarked to the Austrian Ambassador, " I regret that our relations with your Government are not as good as in the past." From this moment public opinion began to envisage definitely the possibility of war. In February appeared a semi-official pamphlet (written by Arthur de la Guéronnière and revised by the Emperor), *L'Empéreur Napoléon III. et l'Italie,* demanding that Italy should be freed from Austrian domination and made into a confederacy under the presidency of the Pope. In return, the Pope was to reform his government, the exclusively clerical character of which was described as constituting " an active cause of discontent and a permanent risk of revolution." [12]

The Catholics were gravely perturbed. The Legitimist press openly attacked the Emperor's Italian policy. Veuillot was of two minds. He sang the praises of Austria and declared that war against her would serve the cause of the Revolution. But he expressed his confidence in the Emperor—though he was far from feeling as confident as he claimed to be. A few priests, including (for the moment) Lacordaire, approved of the war. But all the bishops were against it, as was also the *Correspondant.*

" We shall force Austria to declare war," Cavour had remarked long ago. His prophecy was fulfilled. Goaded by

[10] Maurain, 232ff.
[11] Lecanuet, iii. 183ff.
[12] Maurain, 325.

the provocations of Piedmont, Austria opened hostilities against her. The Emperor had now his *casus belli,* and announced his approaching departure for Italy. On May 10th he set out to join his army. A few days before he had issued a proclamation announcing his purpose " to liberate Italy as far as the Adriatic," and adding that " the authority of the Holy Father would not be disturbed." [13]

The campaign was short. The French and Piedmontese armies swept across northern Italy, defeating the Austrians at Magenta and Solferino. Everywhere they were received with joy by the liberated populations. The revolutionary movement spread to central Italy. Tuscany had driven out its Grand Duke at the end of April; Modena and Parma followed suit; and as soon as the Austrians were across the Po, Romagna rose in revolt against the Pope. A similar attempt was made in Umbria, but was suppressed by the pontifical troops. The whole of the northern half of the peninsula demanded to be annexed to Piedmont.

Suddenly, however, Napoleon's nerve gave way. To hand over Romagna to Piedmont would mean a certain breach with the Holy See. The Catholics of France were indignant : and the conservative element in her political life was deeply disturbed at the onward march of what, after all, was nothing less than the Revolution. These misgivings found an echo in the imperial entourage. Both the Empress and the Foreign Secretary, Walewski, were ill at ease before the turn of events. There was even a possibility that Prussia might intervene on behalf of Austria. Yielding to these considerations, the Emperor concluded the preliminary peace of Villafranca (July 11th). By the terms of this Lombardy was to go to Piedmont; Austria was to retain Venice; the Grand Duke of Tuscany and the Duke of Modena were to be restored to their states; the Pope was to become head of a new Italian confederation and was to grant " such reforms as were indispensable."

Before leaving Italy Napoleon wrote to the Pope, asking him to accept the terms of the peace. He suggested that,

[13] Debidour, 550.

while Romagna would remain his, he should grant to that province a measure of self-government. " In this way," he concluded, " your Holiness will have restored the peace of your states and will be able to dispense with foreign troops " [14] (July 14th).

II

On November 11th, 1859, the preliminaries of Villafranca were converted into a definite peace by the Treaty of Zürich. But would the terms of peace be accepted by those concerned?

Already it was sufficiently clear that they would not. The Pope had at first seemed to be not unwilling to approve the settlement of Villafranca. He accepted in principle the presidency of the proposed Italian confederation and the reforms suggested by the Emperor. He even promised to grant to Romagna a lay administration on condition that the Piedmontese troops were first withdrawn. But he absolutely refused to constitute it a separate province under a governor of its own—to do this might well be the first step towards losing it altogether. [15] The French Government's attempts to move him from this position were in vain, and during the interval between Villafranca and Zürich his attitude grew steadily more and more intransigent. " Il est aveuglé sur sa position," reported Gramont, the French Ambassador to the Holy See. [16]

Romagna, on the other hand, was as determined as ever to achieve its annexation to Piedmont : and this determination was shared by the other liberated states of central Italy. Piedmont, for her part, was only too willing to gratify their wish. The peace of Villafranca had been followed by the withdrawal of her troops and commissioners from the occupied territories : but it was privately intimated that this was by no means intended to bar the taking of active steps to bring about their speedy return. A military league was formed between Tuscany, Modena, Romagna and Parma : and a commissioner (with Garibaldi as his second-in-command) was sent

[14] Debidour, 554.
[15] Maurain, 344.
[16] *Ibid.*, 345.

from Turin to organize its resources. It was indeed not easy to see what could stand in the way of Piedmont's designs. The only effective counter-stroke would be a fresh intervention by Austria : but it was highly improbable that she would attempt anything of the sort after her recent unlucky experience. France was hardly likely to enter the field against her late allies : while England was openly in favour of Italian aspirations.

The treaty of Zürich was thus a dead-letter even before it was signed. In face of this situation, what was to be the attitude of Napoleon III.? Hitherto he had contented himself with pressing on Piedmont the loyal execution of the terms of Villafranca : but it was obvious by this time that nothing was further from her intention. The treaty signed, he next attempted to transfer the responsibility of a decision from his own shoulders to those of Europe in general, and proposed the convening of a Congress of the Powers to settle the fate of Italy. But though the invitations were issued and accepted, there was little likelihood that the project would mature : the views and interests of the Powers were too conflicting to make concerted action possible. Forced thus to take a line of his own, the Emperor more and more inclined to the side of Piedmont. The ex-Carbonarist was still the friend of Italian freedom and unity and had no desire to see the work already accomplished in this direction undone. From a practical point of view, too, the risk of alienating Catholic opinion, at home and abroad, seemed less formidable than that of allowing Italy to remain a hotbed of revolutionary propaganda. The noisy protests of certain French bishops and the Catholic press, so far from intimidating, merely annoyed him. Above all, there was the tempting chance to make capital out of the ambitions of Piedmont by securing for France the cession of Nice and Savoy, which he had not dared to claim at Villafranca. Under the sway of these motives, he allowed the French Liberal press full freedom to urge the Italian cause. A still clearer indication of his intentions was afforded by the publication (on December 22nd) of an anonymous pamphlet entitled *Le Pape et le Congrés*. The actual author of this was again Arthur de la Gueronnière : but it had been drawn up under the imperial eye, and Napoleon made no secret of his approbation. " It is not I who have written it," he said, " but I fully approve of all its ideas." [17]

The pamphlet was certainly explicit enough. The author began by declaring himself a sincere Catholic and the Temporal Power "necessary to the Pope's spiritual authority." But he went on to maintain that, in view of the " paternal " character of the papal sovereignty, its material expression should be severely limited in extent. " The smaller the territory, the greater will be the sovereign." As things are, he said, the Temporal Power is only kept in existence by the French occupation : but as a member of the Italian confederation the Pope will be protected by the federal army. In regard to Romagna the question is posed, How does the Pope propose to retain it ? Persuasion has proved useless : and force is out of the question. Let the Congress then maintain the papal sovereignty in principle : but " the city of Rome is all that really matters "—the rest is of secondary importance. [18]

At Rome the pamphlet was read with rage and consternation. Its significance was not merely noted but exaggerated. Intended simply to justify the cession of Romagna, it was represented as a condemnation of the Temporal Power *per se*. Addressing the officers of the French army of occupation on New Year's Day, the Pope characterized it as " a notable monument of hypocrisy and an ignoble tissue of calumnies," and expressed the hope that the Emperor would disown it.[19] In reporting his words, the *Moniteur* of January 11th declared that they might not have been uttered if the Pope had at the time received a letter of the Emperor dated December 31st. In this letter (the text of which was published) Napoleon advised the Pope to " make the sacrifice of the revolted provinces "— in which event Europe would guarantee to him the remainder of his states. Already, on January 4th, the Emperor had taken the portfolio of Foreign Affairs from Walewski, who was

[17] Maurain, 355. The authority for the remark is the then British Ambassador at Paris, Lord Cowley.

[18] *Ibid.*, 356.

[19] *Ibid.*, 357.

favourable to the Pope, and entrusted it to Thouvenel instead.

The Pope's reply to the imperial suggestion was broadcast to the Catholic world in an Encyclical dated January 19th. In this he declared that " the papal states belong not to any dynastic family but to all Catholics," and that " it is not for [him] to give up what does not belong to " him personally. He affirmed his determination to resist to the uttermost, whatever the price of resistance might prove to be, and called upon the Catholic bishops to " inflame their faithful to an unflinching defence of the Temporal Power." [20]

From this moment the Congress finally vanished from the horizon : and Napoleon faced the task of settling matters for himself. By this time Cavour (who had resigned in despair after Villafranca) was once more in charge of the affairs of Piedmont : and Napoleon entered into formal negotiations with him. A bargain was struck by which the Emperor undertook to abide by the result of a plebiscite of the central Italian states on the question of annexation and was to receive Savoy and Nice in return. As a sop to appearances, he put forward a suggestion that Romagna should be made a vicariate under the King of Sardinia, the Pope still remaining its titular sovereign. But Cavour refused the proposal, which was also repudiated with scorn by the Pope. Ten days later (March 11th—12th) the central states registered an overwhelming vote in favour of annexation : and on March 24th a treaty was signed by which Nice and Savoy were handed over to France. The Pope retorted (March 26th) by a bull excommunicating all those responsible for " the criminal rebellion of the provinces of our states, their fautors, auxiliaries and adherents." [21] As the bull might be thought to involve the Emperor himself, the Government took steps to prevent its publication in France.

In the face of these developments, the French occupation of Rome became more of an anomaly than ever. Napoleon, in fact, was already casting about for a means of bringing it to an end. In reply to Catholic representations in the Corps

[20] *Ibid.*, 357f.
[21] *Ibid.*, 401.

Législatif it was asserted on behalf of the Government that the French troops would not quit Rome until the Pope was in a position to defend himself against his enemies. But the question was, Where was an alternative guarantee of his security to be found? Napoleon suggested that the King of Naples might undertake the duty. But that monarch required all the troops at his command to keep his own tottering throne from falling, and declined the proposal. The Emperor then offered the Holy See an alternative arrangement by which the smaller Catholic powers (Belgium, Bavaria, Spain and Portugal) should provide the Pope with a body of troops. The cost of maintaining them was to be defrayed by a subsidy from all the Catholic states: and the Powers would guarantee what remained of the papal territory. In return he asked the Pope to grant reforms to his subjects. The Pope, however, haughtily replied that he would grant reforms when and as he thought fit, and that to accept a guarantee would be to recognize the loss of Romagna, which he would never do. [22]

The papal entourage, in fact, was already thinking of recruiting an army of its own. The leading spirit in this scheme was a chamberlain of the Pope and brother-in-law of Montalembert, Mgr. Xavier de Mérode, an ex-officer in the Belgian army who had not doffed the military temper when he put on the cassock. Closely allied with him was the papal Nuncio at Paris, Sacconi, who had quarrelled with the French Government and was only too anxious to put a spoke into its wheel. Against this combination the caution of Antonelli, Pius IX's Prime Minister, found itself more and more powerless. At Mérode's suggestion the Pope issued an appeal to the Catholic aristocracy of Europe to enrol its sons under his banner. A considerable number of them answered the call, actuated either by religious zeal or the love of adventure. The rank-and-file of the new army—which amounted to some 15,000 men—consisted of paid mercenaries, some of whom, but by no means all, were inspired by a genuine enthusiasm for the papal cause. To provide the means for their upkeep a further appeal was made to the pockets of the faithful. The

[22] Maurain, 404. Debidour, 561.

ancient *denier de Saint Pierre* was revived in support of the papal necessities : and a loan of fifty million francs was launched on the market. The French Government put no obstacles in the way of either, beyond stipulating that not more than twenty-five millions of the loan should be subscribed in France and forbidding the employment of ecclesiastical pressure either to promote the loan or to extract gifts. [23]

To make all complete, a commander-in-chief for the new army was found in the Breton General Lamoricière, [24] an erstwhile republican who had been exiled from France after the *Coup d'État* of 1851 and had recently returned to the practice of the Catholic religion. He had been allowed to come back to France in 1859 ; but remained irreconcilably opposed to the Government. Mérode made a personal journey to France to secure his consent : and the two reached Rome at the beginning of April, Lamoricière travelling under an assumed name. Antonelli had assured Gramont that the Pope would not nominate Lamoricière without the Emperor's consent : but when Lamoricière declined to apply for this, Pius nominated him all the same (April 3rd). Mérode did not conceal his delight. " *Mais oui,*" he remarked, " it is a little slap we are giving the Emperor." [25] On April 11th he himself was appointed to the post of Minister of Arms.

The time seemed come at last to remove the French troops from Rome, especially as Lamoricière and Mérode expressed their conviction that the new army would suffice for the defence of the papal states. No difficulty was raised on either side : and on May 11th a convention was signed by which the army of occupation was to be withdrawn in three month's time.

Fate, however, decreed otherwise. The chain forged by Napoleon in 1849 was to drag at his ankles to the end. The very day the convention was signed, Garibaldi landed in Sicily. The Revolution had spread from the centre to the south : and the whole Italian situation was changed in a moment.

[23] Circular by Rouland, May 5th, 1860. Maurain, 407.
[24] On Lamoricière's career, see Flornoy : *Lamoricière,* 1903.
[25] Gramont's despatch to Thouvenel, April 10th. Maurain, 407.

In making his sensational descent on the kingdom of Naples-Sicily Garibaldi had acted against Cavour's overt wishes but with his secret connivance. The great Italian statesman had never faltered in his determination to make Italy a united kingdom under the House of Savoy. The sudden *volte-face* of Napoleon III. at Villafranca had been a cruel disappointment of his hopes. But the determination remained. " They have stopped me from making Italy by diplomacy from the north," he said : " but I will make it by the Revolution from the south." [26]   No consideration for Napoleon's interest need be allowed to bar the way. If the Emperor had helped Piedmont to win central Italy, he had extorted Nice and Savoy in return : and the two bargainers were now quits. Moreover, while Naples-Sicily remained, with its traditional dependence on Austria and attachment to the Holy See, the " Roman question " would stay for ever unsettled.

The attempt of Garibaldi had been preceded by an insurrection near Messina at the beginning of April 1860. The insurrection was unsuccessful, and was mercilessly crushed. But before this happened Garibaldi applied to Victor Emmanuel and Cavour for leave to come to its assistance. Cavour dared not flout European opinion by giving a public consent : but he bade Garibaldi go on his own responsibility and provided him with arms for the purpose. Garibaldi leaped at the opportunity and landed at Marsala at the head of his famous red-shirt "Thousand" on May 11th. At the end of two months he was master of the island. He proclaimed himself dictator and announced his intention of crossing to the mainland. Ferdinand II. appealed to the Powers : but they either could not or would not help. Early in August Garibaldi passed the straits. The royal army evacuated Naples at his approach : and the dictator entered the capital in triumph on September 7th. Cavour had for some time been counselling moderation in the hour of success. The triumph of the Revolution, he saw, would be the downfall of the monarchy. But Garibaldi refused to heed. Already he was planning to secure his supreme objective by a march on Rome.

[26] Quoted, Alison Phillips: *Modern Europe*, 379.

The crisis was acute: and Cavour felt that Piedmont had now no alternative but to forestall Garibaldi and " save Italy from madmen." On the day after Garibaldi entered Naples he called on the Pope to dismiss his army. The Pope refused, and next day the Piedmontese army entered the papal states. Garibaldi continued his march northwards: but, fortunately for Cavour, the gallant resistance of the Neapolitan army at the Volturno slackened the speed of his advance. Meanwhile, the Italian army continued its invasion of the states of the Church: and at Castelfidardo (September 18th) Lamoricière's army was finally routed. Master of the papal states except the territory immediately surrounding Rome, Cavour summoned the Italian Parliament. In pursuance of its decision, plebiscites were held in Naples and Sicily, as also in the erstwhile papal provinces of Umbria and the Marches: and an overwhelming majority was recorded in favour of union with Piedmont. The Italian army now pushed forward into the kingdom of Naples, where Garibaldi was still held in check by the royal forces. Ferdinand was forced to retire: and on October 26th at Teano the dictator resigned his authority into the hands of Victor Emmanuel. The Neapolitan army held out for three months at Gaeta, but was at length compelled to surrender.

And what of Napoleon III. meantime? The bold plan of the Piedmontese Prime Minister for arresting Garibaldi's march on Rome could only be carried into effect if France consented to stand aside. With this object Cavour made it his business to satisfy the Emperor that in Piedmont and her army lay the only guarantee for preserving the peace of Europe. Two envoys were despatched to Chambéry in Savoy (where the Emperor happened to be staying) to persuade him to give her a free hand. Napoleon was convinced by their arguments. He declared that, though he could not openly approve the action of Piedmont, he would not oppose it. " Fate presto,"[27] he added. Cavour hardly needed the admonition. The invasion of the papal states followed, with all the other events of which it was the prelude. The French

[27] Maurain, 421. Debidour, 566.

army of occupation remained in Rome to protect the patrimony of St. Peter : but it made no attempt to stay the march of events outside. The Pope complained bitterly of " the fatal and pernicious principle of non-intervention "[28] and even threatened to leave Rome. But the French Government remained unmoved.

At the end of February 1861 Victor Emmanuel was proclaimed King of Italy. A month later Rome was declared the capital of the new kingdom, but with the understanding that France must first give her consent and guarantees be provided for the spiritual independence of the Holy Father.

[28] Maurain, 424.

CHAPTER V

THE IMPERIAL GOVERNMENT, THE CATHOLICS AND THE POPE
1859—1864

THE war of 1859 marks a crucial epoch in the relations between the Second Empire and the Church. The alliance between the two, which in spite of many strains had been preserved up to the present, at least in outward appearance, was now at an end: and the clergy and the more militant Catholics were flung into an attitude of opposition to the Government. In the presence of this hostility, the Gallican tendencies of the latter were to be strongly intensified in the years that followed. Yet it is easy to exaggerate the extent of the change. The tension between Church and State was already acute when the war broke out: the events of 1859 only caused the sudden explosion of a conflict that was in any case preparing. The growth of Ultramontanism and the intransigence of Pius IX. had already revealed the incompatibility of the Church's claims both with the " principles of 1789 " and that Gallicanism which was the traditional policy of French administration and the basis of the Concordat settlement. The war merely brought the incompatibility into the full light of day.

I

Before considering in detail the reaction of Catholic opinion to the Italian policy of the Emperor, it may conduce to greater clearness if we differentiate the various schools of thought existing within the Catholic body in France, especially as regards their attitude to the Government.[1] The opposition between two of these groups—the Liberal Catholics on the one hand, the Ultramontanes on the other—has been already illustrated at length. The Liberal Catholics were in the un-

[1] See Veuillot: *L. Veuillot,* iii. 244f.

fortunate position of being neither on the side of the Emperor (to whom, indeed, they were irreconcilably opposed) nor wholeheartedly on the side of the Pope. Hence their practical impotence, in spite of the brilliant gifts of their chief representatives. Politically they were parliamentary Liberals of the Whig sort—some of them Legitimists of a mild hue, others (the most prominent) partisans of the Orléanist dynasty. The Ultramontanes were more widely divided. Pie of Poitiers, their leading figure in the episcopate, was a strong Legitimist of the extreme reactionary school and only accepted the Empire under compulsion. But the followers of Veuillot had embraced the Napoleonic autocracy with enthusiasm : and it was they in consequence who were to feel most severely the strain imposed by the new orientation of the imperial policy.

A third group was formed by those Catholics who were at once supporters of the Government and opposed to the Ultramontanism of the *Univers.* These included a large proportion of the bishops appointed under the Empire, the policy of which they were naturally concerned to uphold, so far as might be, in both political and ecclesiastical matters. Chief among these in the years that followed was to be Darboy, appointed Bishop of Nancy in 1859 and destined as Archbishop of Paris (1863-1871) to be one of the most notable figures (and perhaps the ablest) in the French episcopate of his time. Finally, there was the group of democratic Catholics —republicans at heart but supporters of the Empire for the time being. Their theology was of a pronouncedly Gallican cast : and their Gallicanism extended no less to their view of the relations between Church and State. Their leader was the learned Dean of the Sorbonne, Maret, who was in close relations with the strongly Gallican Minister of Religions, Rouland, and had openly espoused the Emperor's Italian policy from the beginning.

It is obvious from this analysis that when the imperial policy began to define itself, it was the Liberal Catholics who would find least difficulty in opposing it. They had no loyalty to be strained—indeed, they rather rejoiced in being able to express their distrust and dislike in so good a cause. They had bitterly resented the charge constantly levelled against them by the *Univers* of being lukewarm in support of the Holy See. Now was the chance to give this accusation the lie. It might have been expected perhaps that their alleged devotion to the " principles of 1789 " would have suggested at least the question whether such a government as that of Pius IX. was of a nature to satisfy those principles, and whether it was equitable to compel the subjects of a ruler to endure a yoke so widely abhorred. As " Liberals," in fact, they might have shown some concern for liberty. Lacordaire, indeed, was sufficiently true to his principles to declare his gratitude to the Emperor for taking steps to overthrow the hated power of Austria. But the other members of his group never seem to have paused to examine this side of the question. Montalembert even wrote to Lacordaire a stern letter expressing his *cuisante douleur* at his friend's attitude. [2] Their Liberalism in any case never went very deep : and the chance of impressing the Holy See by a display of their devotion was too good to be missed.

It was, then, Montalembert who, as early as 1856, assumed the defence of the papal administration against the strictures of the English plenipotentiary at the Congress of Paris in his pamphlet *Pie IX. et Lord Palmerston*. When the war broke out, Dupanloup watched its progress with grave misgivings : and the events that followed the Peace of Villafranca turned misgivings into wrath. The proposal of a plebiscite to justify the annexation of Romagna drew from him an indignant *Protestation*, in which "as bishop, as Catholic, as Frenchman" he declaimed against " this miserable result of our victories and of the precious blood of our soldiers." [3] Montalembert again lifted his voice in the *Correspondant* and was once more made the object of police proceedings. The appearance of *Le Pape et le Congrés* furnished the Bishop of Orléans with a further opportunity of plying his copious pen—this time in a *Letter to a Catholic* in refutation of the pamphlet in question.

[2] Lecanuet, iii. 205.
[3] Lagrange, ii. 275ff.

A second *Letter* quickly followed. [4] By this time, Lacordaire had repented of his initial approval of the war, and in February 1860 he too produced a pamphlet in defence of the Temporal Power.

To Veuillot, of course, as to the Ultramontanes who had followed his lead in passionate support of the Empire, the war brought a terrible disillusionment. For some time he had been beginning to wonder whether Napoleon III. was really as trusty a friend of the Church as he had imagined. But now it became all too certain that his blind confidence had been misplaced. For a time he tried to make the best of things, and enjoined his followers to await the issue of events in confident reliance on the Emperor's promise that " all the rights of the Holy See would be respected." But the logic of facts was too strong. The appearance of *Le Pape et le Congrés* was a signal not to be mistaken. The *Univers* attacked it, comparing it to " the kiss of Judas," and recommended an address of sympathy to the Pope, receiving an *avertissement* from the Government in consequence. [5] It also published the Pope's allocution to the French officers in Rome on New Year's Day, 1860. The Government forbade it to do so : but at the last moment the veto was withdrawn through the intervention of the Emperor, who remarked, " I do not want M. Veuillot to die a martyr." [6]

When, however, the *Univers* went on to publish the papal encyclical of January 19th, the Government felt that a drastic step was necessary. The audacious paper was suppressed. On hearing of the suppression, Pius IX. exclaimed, " *Caro Veuillot! Caro Univers!* " [7] and suggested that its publication should be resumed in Belgium or elsewhere. The proprietor soon received permission to revive the *Univers* under the name of the *Monde :* and its policy continued unchanged. But the condition was imposed that Veuillot must not contribute : so that for several years the most brilliant journalist of his time found himself deprived of an organ.

[4] Lagrange, ii. 285, 286.
[5] Maurain, 359.
[6] Veuillot : *L. Veuillot*, iii. 303.
[7] *Ibid.*, 349.

His only consolation was the triumphant reception he received from the Pope when he visited Rome shortly afterwards. Pius IX. issued a brief praising the *Univers* without reserve. On the other hand, Montalembert (who had himself just been prosecuted anew for another attack on the Emperor's policy[8]) did not trouble to control his sense of the justice of the fate that had overtaken the hated journal. " I loudly declare," he wrote to a friend, " that I do not feel the least sympathy for those who certified in advance the justice of the decision which smites them when they wrote (in 1855): ' We grant ourselves the privilege of speaking and writing every day, while we refuse it to others who do not offer the same guarantees as ourselves.' " " The most fitting punishment of the *Univers*," he added, would be " to go on existing and report every day the flagrant lie that events are giving to its theories and practices." [9] Hard words—but scarcely undeserved.

The attitude of the French episcopate to the events of 1859-1860 was, for the most part, cautious and restrained. It is true that certain prelates expressed their disapproval in no measured terms. The protests of Dupanloup have been already recorded. His great rival, Pie of Poitiers, delivered his soul with no less energy. He had never trusted Napoleon III.: and he was devoted heart and soul to the Pope. The " principles of 1789 " were anathema in his eyes. For him (as he wrote to Pius IX.) the papal government was " almost the only refuge left of political orthodoxy." [10] There was, therefore, no reason why he should be other than hostile : nor was he ever afraid to say what he thought. Those bishops (like Salinis) who had shared Veuillot's combination of Ultramontane views with zeal for the Empire now shared his disillusionment and expressed themselves accordingly. If they must choose between Pope and Emperor, there was no doubt what their choice would be.

The bulk of the episcopate, on the other hand, were the

[8] In an article published in the *Correspondant* for October 25th, 1859, entitled *Pie IX. et la France en 1849 et 1859*.
[9] To Mgr. de Mérode, January 1860. Lecanuet, iii. 216.
[10] July 1859. Baunard: *Histoire du Cardinal Pie*, ii. 7.

victims of a divided allegiance and found their situation very difficult. The protests of the Holy See against the danger that threatened the Temporal Power and its appeals for their support could not be a matter of indifference to them. Moreover, the lower clergy, deeply influenced as they were by the *Univers,* exercised a continual pressure on them from below. This pressure was particularly urgent after the appearance of *Le Pape et le Congrés.* Yet, as the nominees of the Government and concerned by the circumstances of their position to avoid a quarrel with it, they shrank from open opposition to its policy. Moreover, it was not easy for them to run counter to the wave of patriotic enthusiasm that was sweeping the country, or to its pride and triumph at the rapid success of its arms. The more moderate-minded of the bishops were therefore in favour of private representations to the Government rather than of open protests. At the same time they counselled their flocks to have confidence in the Emperor.

The papal Encyclical of January 19th made their position more difficult still : and the agitation among the priests and faithful laity became more acute. Attempts were made in concert with the Legitimists to excite public opinion against the Government, so that towards the end of February the latter had to take active steps to suppress them. The bishops, while much less ready than before to counsel confidence in the Government, did nothing for the most part to increase the agitation but rather sought to calm it ; with the result that it very soon came to an end. The bulk of the nation was entirely unaffected by it. So long as worship was not interfered with, the Catholic masses refused to believe that the Church was in danger. The lesson was not lost upon the clergy : and no further attempts of the sort were made under the Empire. [11]

Within the limitations imposed upon them the Catholics did what they could. French recruits joined the papal army and provided a useful stiffening to the decidedly poor material of which it was mainly composed. The *denier de Saint Pierre* was organized in a considerable number of dioceses : and

[11] Maurain, 367—397.

similar steps were taken to stimulate subscriptions to the new papal loan. But the results were on the whole disappointing. The papal recruits did not exceed 400 or 500 in number; the *denier de Saint Pierre* brought in but a small amount compared with the enormous papal expenses; while only seventeen million francs were subscribed out of the twenty-five millions maximum fixed by the Government. [12]

The tidings of Castelfidardo were a fresh blow to the Catholics. It was not relished by the nation either. After all, Lamoricière was a Frenchman, as were the pick of the troops under his command. The cause of Piedmont commanded by this time little sympathy in France, except among avowed republicans. Her methods were regarded as brutal and unscrupulous : and the rôle played by Garibaldi in the evolution of events was alarming to conservative opinion. It was felt, moreover, that the rise of a strong and united Italy on her flank might constitute a serious peril to France in the future—an anticipation which has certainly not been unjustified by the event. But if France as a whole was little in favour of Piedmont, she was even more indifferent to the Pope. It was clear even to the Catholics themselves that there was little chance of making political capital out of his misfortunes. [13]

The effect of Castelfidardo was chiefly visible among the bishops. Even those who had remained faithful to the Government after the annexation of Romagna now lost confidence in it. At first the protests against the fresh despoilment of the Pope by the annexation of Umbria and the Marches were few in number. But soon the example of the more ardent spirits was increasingly followed : and the majority gave vent to their indignation in *mandements* of differing degrees of emphasis. The action of Piedmont was universally condemned : but the responsibility of the Government was variously assessed. From this time, too, the bishops who had abstained from encouraging the *denier de Saint Pierre* began to come into line with their brethren. [14] The situation was

[12] *Ibid.*, 413, 414.
[13] *Ibid.*, 426ff.
[14] Maurain (431) estimates the total French contributions at from three to four million francs a year.

serious enough for the Government to take steps to limit the circulation of episcopal charges as *brochures,* and also to break up associations which had been illegally constituted to collect money for the Pope's needs.

The appearance early in 1861 of a further pamphlet by De la Gueronnière gave occasion for fresh episcopal outbursts. This pamphlet, entitled *Rome, la France et l'Italie,* laid the blame of the religious agitation exclusively at the door of the Liberal Catholics and the Legitimists, whose political disaffection, it was alleged, had made the clergy " the dupe of party spirit." [15]   Dupanloup again rushed into the field with a *brochure* in denial of the assertion : [16] but Pie this time went one better.   In a charge to his flock the audacious prelate dared, in a transparent allusion, to arraign the Emperor himself.   " Wash thy hands, O Pilate," he exclaimed.   " Posterity rejects thy justification.   A man is presented to our gaze nailed to the pillory of the Catholic creed, branded with the stigma of ' slayer of God.'   He is neither Herod, nor Caiaphas, nor Judas : he is Pontius Pilate.   His doom is just.   Herod, Caiaphas, Judas, had their part in the crime : but naught could have befallen without Pilate.   Pilate might have saved Christ, and without Pilate they could not have put Christ to death.   The signal could only come from him." [17]   The matter was brought by the Government before the Council of State : and the Bishop was declared guilty of *abus.*   Pie, however, was undaunted : and encouraged by the warm congratulations of Pius IX. he returned to the attack.   This time the Emperor figured in the rôle not of Pilate but of Herod—" the third Herod " who " does despite to the Church and lays hands on Peter." [18]   The Emperor was extremely annoyed, and asked the Pope to make amends by some public utterance favourable to himself.   But he got little satisfaction.   Further legal proceedings against Pie had to be dropped.

The controversy also had its repercussions in the Senate and the Corps Législatif.   Feeling his need of the support of public

[15] Maurain, 489.
[16] Lagrange, ii. 331.
[17] Baunard : *Histoire du Cardinal Pie,* ii. 116f.
[18] *Ibid.,* 148.

opinion amid the difficulties that beset him, the Emperor by a decree of November 24th, 1860, had given to the two legislative bodies the right of examining each year, by way of address, the policy of the Government. In accordance with this provision a discussion of the Roman question was initiated in the Senate on February 28th, 1861, when two Cardinals joined with the leaders of the Clerical laity in a defence of the Temporal Power. Next day Prince Napoleon ("Plon-plon," the Emperor's cousin) retorted by a speech demanding that it should be restricted to the Leonine city. This speech made a great sensation—the more so as it was believed to express the views of the Emperor: and Persigny, the Minister of the Interior, ordered it to be posted in all the communes of France. The strength of the Clerical opposition, however, was revealed by the voting on a Clerical amendment in favour of the Pope, which was only lost by seventy-nine votes to sixty-one. In the Corps Législatif the Clerical attack won a similar success. An amendment of Jules Favre in favour of the evacuation of Rome was lost by 246 votes to five: and a rival Clerical amendment in favour of the Pope commanded 91 votes against 158. For the first time for ten years the dominant factor in the political life of France was seen to be no longer the imperial Government, but the conflict between the partisans of the Church and the anticlerical democrats. [19]

The growing difficulties of his position made the Emperor more anxious than ever to have done with the ties which bound him to the Pope. A negotiation was begun with Cavour by which France would evacuate Rome in return for a promise that Italy would respect what remained of the papal territory. But the death of Cavour (June 6th) caused the negotiation to be postponed. The Emperor, however, recognized the new kingdom of Italy (June 25th), and appointed as his ambassador at Turin Count Benedetti, a friend of the Italian cause.

The solution of the Roman question thus remained in suspense. For nine years the deadlock persisted; the Italian Government claiming Rome as its capital, the Pope refusing to give up his right to the annexed provinces, the French

[19] Maurain, 494.

Government seeking in vain to reconcile the two and continuing meanwhile its most unwilling occupation of what was left of the papal states. The Emperor's chief hope lay in the death of the Pope : but Pius IX. failed to gratify his wish.

Further attempts were made in 1862 to bring about a settlement : but all was in vain before the obstinacy of Pius and his entourage. This obstinacy found fresh support in a great assembly of Bishops held at Rome in 1862 for the canonization of the Japanese martyrs. An address was voted affirming the inviolability of the papal states. The influence of Dupanloup, however, was exerted to prevent the inclusion of reflections unfavourable to France. [20]

In the same year (1862) Garibaldi, driven to desperation by the delay in giving Italy what she desired, collected an army of volunteers in Sicily and made another dash on Rome from the south. The Italian Government, alarmed at the prospect of embroilment with France, determined to bar the way. Garibaldi was wounded and taken prisoner at Aspromonte (August 29th) : and his small army immediately disbanded.

Such action by no means implied that the Italian Government had abandoned the object that Garibaldi sought to attain, even though it might feel itself compelled to oppose his reckless method of achieving it. On September 10th its Foreign Minister, Durando, declared in a circular that " the entire nation demanded its capital," and that resistance to its wishes would end by " compromising very seriously both the peace of Europe and the religious interests of Catholicism." [21] The French Government, however, turned a deaf ear to these representations. The Clerical influences in the imperial entourage, with the Empress and Walewski at their head, were successfully mobilized for their defeat : and the proximity of the elections of 1863 made it desirable to conciliate Catholic opinion. Thouvenel was dismissed from the Foreign Office. His place was taken by Drouyn de Lhuys, a firm friend of the Pope. One of the new minister's first official acts was to notify to Durando the Government's formal rejection of his pro-

[20] Lagrange, ii. 359f.
[21] Debidour, 578.

posal. The Senate in its address of January 1863 warmly congratulated the Emperor on his attitude: and the Corps Législatif also expressed its satisfaction.

A further result of the imminence of the elections was to bring about a *rapprochement* between the Clerical champions in the Corps Législatif and the former heads of the Liberal-Catholic party. These latter in their turn joined hands with the Orléanist and Legitimist leaders, who now decided to abandon their policy of " abstention " and take their place once more in the political *mêlée*. Chief among the Orléanists was Thiers, who, anxious to secure Catholic support and genuinely alarmed at the danger to France created by the emergence of the new Italian kingdom, set the maintenance of the Temporal Power in the forefront of his programme. The miscellaneous character of the anti-imperial alliance was oddly heightened by the adhesion of the democrats and republicans, who shared their associates' detestation of the Empire, if nothing else. [22] This so-called *union libérale* was severely criticized in the Catholic press; and was implicitly condemned in a letter bearing the signature of seven bishops (with Dupanloup at their head), exhorting the Catholics to vote for those candidates, governmental or not, who were most favourable to the Church. [23] But it was not unsuccessful in its object, especially as the local clergy, generally speaking, used their influence in support of the opposition candidate, unless he was frankly anticlerical. The election returns showed a strong majority in favour of the Government, but the opposition (which included Thiers but not Montalembert) was formidable and distinguished. Henceforth, too, even the Government's supporters felt themselves at liberty to exercise a greater independence of it, especially in regard to religious questions.

In the reconstruction of the Cabinet that followed the Emperor sought to conciliate the various elements that made up the opposition. The Clericals saw with satisfaction the disappearance of the ministers most repugnant to them : and this, combined with the temporary abatement of their anxiety

[22] Debidour, 579.
[23] Maurain, 639.

respecting the Temporal Power, made them somewhat more friendly to the Government. But the Pope remained as intransigent as before. He obstinately maintained his claim to the whole of his former dominions, and equally his refusal to grant reforms in what remained. His ungracious attitude deeply mortified Napoleon, whose animosity against the Holy See rekindled. At this time, too, as the result of his mishandling of the great European questions of the time (the Polish rebellion and the Danish war) the Emperor found himself practically isolated in Europe and saw in Italy his only possible ally. The negotiations of 1862 were therefore resumed. The Italian Government expressed its willingness to accept Florence as its capital instead of Rome, at least for the time being : but it demanded, as some compensation for the national disappointment, that the French troops should evacuate Rome, in return for a pledge on its part that the city should not be attacked. The guarantee was not very convincing : but Napoleon's situation forbade him to examine it too closely. On September 5th, 1864, a convention was signed by which France undertook to withdraw her troops within two years, while Victor Emmanuel promised not only not to attack the Pope, but to defend him. The transfer of the capital from Turin to Florence was made the subject of a secret article.

The arrangement (as Bismarck said of his almost contemporaneous Treaty of Gastein) was no more than " a papering over the cracks." The Italian Government had undertaken not to attack the Pope : but it made it clear that in case of a rebellion against his authority it would not hesitate to occupy Rome under the pretext of " restoring order." Nor did the convention enjoy any popularity outside those whose immediate purpose it served. In Italy it was intensely resented : and it brought about the immediate fall of the Cabinet that had made it. The French Catholics regarded it as a barely disguised abandonment of the Pope, and their distrust of the Emperor waxed stronger than ever. The Pope himself made no open protest : but three months later, in the Encyclical of December 8th, 1864, he was to fling down the gauntlet to every principle which had conspired to bring modern Italy, and indeed modern Europe, to the birth.

II

The growing hostility of militant Catholic opinion to the imperial regime from 1859 onwards could not but be reciprocated in a corresponding coolness on the part of the Government towards the Church. The relations between the Church and the Empire had not been too harmonious even in the years that preceded: but now the rift was to grow steadily wider. From 1860 onwards a definite change is visible in the ecclesiastical policy of the Government. This change found a willing agent in the Minister of Religions, Rouland. Appointed in 1856, Rouland had hitherto been compelled to put a curb on his sturdy Gallicanism: but now the circumstances permitted him to give it freer rein, if not always to the extent that he would have desired. In April 1860 he presented to the Emperor a memorandum in which the main features of the new policy were clearly outlined. [24]

The memorandum began with an introduction defining the ecclesiastical situation as it had developed in France, in a sense very unfavourable to the Ultramontanes. Rouland pointed out that the attitude of the Church under the *ancien régime* had been firmly Gallican and that the clergy had then combined with the civil power to resist the pretensions of the Holy See. But during the nineteenth century the tendency of the French clergy to favour the Ultramontane doctrine had steadily increased. In the hope of seeing in Napoleon III. " a new Charlemagne," *episcopus ab extra,* it had warmly espoused his authority. Of course the Emperor had no intention of filling the rôle assigned to him or of handing over the State to the Church. But the clergy hoped that he would, and had taken advantage of the imperial favour to extend their influence as widely as possible over the lay society of France.

The strength of clerical influence was specially visible in the sphere of education. The primary education of France was

[24] Analysed in Maurain, 451ff.

largely in the hands of the teaching congregations : and the secondary schools controlled by them attracted a large proportion of the children of the upper and middle classes. Other religious orders had directed the operations of Catholic charity to the same end—the domination of the Roman Catholic Church. If the bishops and secular clergy showed any signs of resisting the Ultramontane penetration, they were at once made the target of the diatribes and calumnies of " the lay Pope of the Gauls," M. Veuillot, and of unfavourable reports to Rome by the papal Nuncio. The policy of the Holy See was consistently to impair the bishops' authority in their dioceses, and so to compel them to become Ultramontane as the only means of conciliating the papal favour. These tactics had been employed with particular success in bringing the bishops to heel on the question of the Temporal Power. " Henceforth Rome dominates the clergy and the Church of France, and through the Church aspires to dominate the country." A considerable part of the clergy is opposed at heart to Ultramontanism and genuinely fears a rupture with the Government.

After this conspectus the Minister proceeds to outline the steps that should be taken to counter the clerical menace :

(1) No new houses of male unauthorized congregations to be established " except to meet unquestionable local needs."

(2) Extreme strictness to be exercised in *authorizing* female congregations.

(3) A similar strictness to be displayed by the Council of State in regard to gifts and legacies made to authorized congregations.

(4) To maintain as far as possible "lay" primary education. With this object it was desirable not to recognise in future any male congregation for primary instruction as an *établissement d'utilité publique*.

(5) To support energetically State education, " *car c'est l'enseignement vraiment national,*" and to give to State schools adequate financial provision for their proper equipment. Since there must be competition, " let us fortify and favour the education given by the State."

(6) To make as full use as circumstances permit of the Organic Articles in resisting the papal encroachments : and in particular to allow no correspondence with the bishops nor influence in the choice of bishops on the part of the papal Nuncio ; to allow no act of the Roman Curia to be received or published in France without Government authorization ; to choose as bishops only ecclesiastics " known to be attached to the Emperor " ; to suppress the religious journals and to encourage the public study of " the ancient French liberties."

(7) To protect loyally the interests of the clergy, especially by an increase in the stipends of the inferior clergy.

(8) To control the activity of the great associations of the Catholic laity (e.g. the Society of St. Vincent de Paul), " which are really in the hands of the clergy and the Legitimist party."

The authenticity of Rouland's memorandum has been called in question : but there seem to be no valid reasons for denying it.[25] In any case, the policy it recommends fairly represents the ecclesiastical policy of the French Government from 1860 onwards. That policy centred round three cardinal points in particular : (1) the nomination of bishops, which was at once the easiest and the most effective instrument in the hands of the Government for resisting the growth of Ultra-montanism in the higher councils of the Church of France ; (2) the favouring of the lay education provided by the State as against the " free " education controlled by the Church ; (3) the discouragement of the religious congregations and of the great lay associations that were so largely under their control.

1. The question of the Government's right to appoint to bishoprics irrespective of the preferences of the Holy See was raised almost immediately. The see of Vannes falling vacant, Rouland, in May 1860, nominated the Abbé Maret to fill it. At once the Nuncio, Sacconi, asked the Minister to postpone the publication of the decree, alleging Maret's deafness as likely to prove an obstacle to his preconisation by the Pope. Rouland, while regarding the objection as no more than a pretext, consented to the postponement, but informed the

---

[25] The question is discussed in Maurain, 46off.

Holy See that Maret's deafness was not serious enough to hamper him in the performance of his duties. Meanwhile, the Nuncio was attempting to excite Catholic opinion against the Government's nominee, and the Ultramontanes seconded his efforts. The Pope now alleged a further objection of a technical character against Maret, but refused to admit that the real difficulty was his notorious Gallicanism. The Government persisted, and on June 25th the nomination was made public by the Emperor's express command. The Pope still refused to preconise Maret, and ended by acknowledging that Maret's Gallicanism was the true ground of his opposition after all. The deadlock dragged on until early in 1861, when Maret, unwilling to be a bone of contention, intimated to the Government his readiness to withdraw his acceptance. Rouland held out for some time longer, but finally consented to the appointment of Maret as a bishop *in partibus,* with the title of Bishop of Sura. [26]

A further conflict broke out later in 1860 in connection with the nomination of the Abbé Mouniq as Bishop of Martinique. The appointment was extremely distasteful to the strongly Ultramontane *Congrégation du Saint Esprit,* which under the previous Bishop had acquired a preponderent influence in the island. In this case the Pope was in a stronger position, inasmuch as he was able to raise objection to the moral character of the Government's nominee. He brought pressure to bear on Mouniq privately to induce him to withdraw his acceptance. Mouniq, however, declined to do so : and the Government continued to press the matter, insisting that Mouniq's guilt must be proved before he was condemned. The Pope persisted in his refusal : and the see of Martinique remained unfilled until the fall of the Empire. [27]

In these two cases, then, the Holy See offered a successful resistance to the wishes of the Government. But otherwise it accepted its choices, however distasteful they might often be. When the Pope, in a personal letter to Napoleon III., [28]

[26] Maurain, 475ff, 540f.
[27] Maurain, 480ff, 540ff.
[28] Dated Dec. 25th, 1860. Maurain, 483f.

suggested that the Government should confer with him as to the suitability of its nominees before the decrees of nomination were published, he received a tart reply, in which the Emperor informed the Holy See that in view of its unfriendly attitude he proposed to make what choices he thought fit.

2. In regard to education, Rouland systematically pursued the policy outlined in his memorandum of encouraging the State schools at the expense of those controlled by the clergy. The Government refused to permit the opening of any new secondary school by an unauthorized congregation or to allow voluntary secondary schools to assume the title of " college." The handing over of municipal colleges to the clergy was stopped, and a number of these that had been suppressed were re-established. In the same way the transfer of State primary schools to the care of the teaching congregations was sternly resisted : and the control of the civil authority over the teachers in voluntary primary schools was tightened up. Restrictions were placed on the endowment of Catholic schools by gifts and legacies; while on the other hand the financial provision for State schools was increased. These measures were entirely successful. Whereas from 1850 to 1862 the congregational schools had gained rapidly on the State schools, after 1862 the process was reversed.[29]

3. The unfriendly attitude of the Government towards the teaching congregations was evinced towards the religious orders in general. Obstacles were put in the way of the founding of new houses by unauthorized congregations, the Jesuits and Capuchins especially. In two cases charges of illegally enticing young Jewish girls from the faith and homes of their families were pursued into the Courts.[30] A number of religious houses were suppressed on various grounds, including charges of immorality. The policy of " hushing up " hitherto acquiesced in by the Government in regard to scandals in the clerical order generally was now at an end.[31] The associations of Catholic lay folk which had so

[29] Maurain, 58off.
[30] *Ibid.*, 466, 533, 575.
[31] *Ibid.*, 534ff.

powerfully served the Catholic cause in the last decade shared with the congregations in the governmental suspicion and disfavour. A circular of Persigny, the Minister of the Interior, dated October 18th, 1861, while paying homage to the charitable activities of these associations, complained of their continued failure to furnish themselves with the legal authorization required by the law. [32] " The time is come," it said, " to regularize a situation of which time has only aggravated the inconveniences."

The association particularly aimed at was the Society of Saint Vincent de Paul, which by this time possessed 4,000 conferences (1,500 in France) under the control of a *Conseil Général* at Paris and administrating a budget of five million francs. " Such an organization," Persigny premised (and not without truth) " cannot be explained by the interest of charity alone." The prefects were therefore instructed to see that all charitable associations in their departments (Masonic lodges as well as conferences of the Society of St. Vincent de Paul) which had not yet sought the authorization of the Government should take steps to do so. In regard to the *Conseil Général* of the Society of St. Vincent de Paul, it was further insisted that its President must be nominated by the Emperor. The Government's demands were received with a storm of protests in episcopal charges and elsewhere; the assimilation of the conferences to Masonic lodges being specially resented. The majority of the conferences, however, at once sought the authorization required. Some 300 refused to do so and declared themselves dissolved. The *Conseil Général,* declining to accept the Emperor's choice of a President, though he was a Cardinal (Donnet), was also dissolved (January 1862).

The dismissal of Thouvenel in October 1862 signalized a temporary change in the attitude of the Government in regard to the Temporal Power : but this did not involve any change in its general ecclesiastical policy. When the archbishopric of Paris fell vacant by the death of Cardinal Morlot, Rouland appointed as his successor Darboy, Bishop of Nancy, a strong Gallican and no less firm supporter of the Empire (January

[32] Maurain, 557ff. Debidour, 572.

1863). The nomination was little to the taste of the Pope, who however preconised Darboy without difficulty. To succeed him at Nancy Rouland appointed another governmental Gallican, Lavigerie. The two prelates were to be the chief ecclesiastical advisers of the Government until the fall of the Empire.

In the reconstruction of the Cabinet that followed the elections of 1863 Rouland was one of the ministers who were sacrificed. His successor, Baroche, however, was firmly Gallican too : and the ecclesiastical policy of the Government was much the same as before, if somewhat less rigorous in its mode of expression. [33] Baroche's nominations to vacant sees passed without protest at Rome. But friction arose over a decision of the Cardinal-Archbishop of Lyons (Bonald) to introduce the Roman liturgy into his diocese—one of the few in which it had not yet been received. When practically the whole of the clergy of the diocese signed a protest to the Holy See in favour of its existing rite, the Government vigorously supported them : and when Pius IX. notwithstanding issued a brief (dated March 17th, 1864) enjoining the gradual acceptance of the Roman liturgy, it forbade its publication. The brief was, none the less, put into execution. [34]

[33] Maurain, 672.
[34] *Ibid.*, 695ff.

CHAPTER VI

THE CONGRESS OF MALINES, THE SYLLABUS AND THE
ROMAN QUESTION, 1863—1870

THERE is little likelihood that an Englishman of to-day will feel much sympathy with the conception of human society for which Pius IX. and his Ultramontane stalwarts battled in the great conflict that reached its climax in the 'sixties of the last century. It is not easy for him even to understand it, so entirely has it ceased to be a directive force in the world we know. Yet he must make the effort to understand, if he would be fair to those who held it—and all the more because of its august past, its logical consistency and the passionate loyalty it was able to inspire.

In its essence the conflict of the time was a phase of the age-long conflict between authority and liberty. That conflict still goes on : and the problem of reconciling the two principles seems as far from solution as ever. In many European countries the freedom so painfully won in the nineteenth century appears now to be lightly esteemed : and men are once more choosing to be ruled rather than to rule themselves. But the ultimate ideas and sanctions that lie behind the modern authoritarian conception of society are different from those which found their champion in the great reactionary Pope. The difference lies here—that the modern conception of authority has abandoned the *supernatural* foundation on which the old conception rested. The latter was a survival of the Middle Ages, and assumed as its basis the Christian revelation in the form in which it found expression in the medieval Church. According to this view,[1] God has made known the truth concerning Himself and the relations of men to Him and to one another in an infallible revelation, and has entrusted the

---

[1] It is stated with great clearness and authority in Baunard, *Histoire du Cardinal Pie,* ii. 204ff. Mgr. Baunard, Rector of the celebrated Catholic Institute of Lille, was one of the most notable exponents of the " traditionalist " position in these matters.

custody of this revelation to the Church. Not only is the Church the guardian of the Divine revelation, but it is also its interpreter, endowed with the authority to settle infallibly disputed questions as they arise—an authority concentrated in the Roman pontiff, the Vicar and mouthpiece of Christ, the Son of God, on earth. This being so, it is obviously inadmissible that men should claim the right to think for themselves on matters concerning which the Pope has decided or may decide. When God has spoken, men must be content to be silent and obey. From the same premises it follows that, inasmuch as the province of the spiritual authority is to guide the nations according to the revealed will of God, the temporal rulers of those nations must be ready to act in subordination to it and so assist it in the accomplishment of its divine mission. As God has appointed the Pope to be supreme in the spiritual sphere, so He has appointed monarchs to be supreme in the temporal sphere : but always with the understanding that their rule shall be in harmony with the Divine revelation, and that the material force at their disposal shall be exercised to defend the Church and to vindicate its rulings against every kind of opposition. On the further question as to the degree in which the subjects of a monarch are permitted to influence the exercise of his sovereignty there was diversity of opinion. But the prevailing view was that, freedom being always dangerous, a paternal absolutism was the safest expedient. In any case, the sovereignty of the temporal ruler, whether absolute or limited, must always be strictly subordinated to the Divine infallible *magisterium* of the Church and the Vicar of Christ.

The social doctrine outlined above was not, of course, universally accepted even in the Middle Ages. The Church and the Holy See never ceased to proclaim it : but to hold up an ideal was one thing, to turn it into practice was quite another. Not only was its theoretical basis attacked by a number of writers more or less heretical (as e.g. Marsiglio of Padua and Wyclif), but its practical application in the temporal sphere was governed less by sincere belief than by motives of self-interest. The secular rulers acted on it when it was to their advantage to do so, and ignored it when it was not. With

the coming of the Reformation the ideal ceased to command
even in theory the allegiance of a large part of Europe. In
the countries that remained loyal to the Holy See the
medieval situation persisted by which the temporal rulers used
the theory so far as it ministered to their own ends : and the
State and the Church remained in an uneasy alliance. The
French Revolution, however, put an end to the alliance, and
brought into existence an entirely new doctrine of society that
was altogether divorced from the supernatural basis of the old.
The watchword of the new order was no longer authority, but
freedom. So far as authority existed, its source was neither
Divine revelation, Pope or King, but the will of the sovereign
people, of which all government was the agent and delegate.

It is indeed hardly an exaggeration to say that the French
Revolution meant the coming of a new religion into the world
—if that can be called a religion which has no outlook and no
sanctions outside the temporal order. We can only understand
the religious conflict in Roman Catholic countries by realizing
that there " the Revolution " means not merely a historic
event or a political movement, but a whole system of ideas
that are in radical opposition to Christianity in its traditional
form. It is this fact that gives to the conflict its internecine
and irreconcilable character. For an Englishman like Gladstone there was no necessary incompatibility between his
Churchmanship and what he understood as " Liberalism."
But that was because " Liberalism " here meant something
quite different from what it meant to a continental Catholic.
For the latter Liberalism was simply " the Revolution." It was
in this sense that Newman used the word when he said in his
biglietto speech at the time of his receiving the Cardinalate in
1879 : [2] " For thirty, forty, fifty years I have resisted to the
utmost of my power the spirit of Liberalism in religion. . . .
Liberalism in religion is the doctrine that there is no positive
truth in religion, but that one creed is as good as another. It
is inconsistent with any conception of religion as *true*. It
teaches that all are to be tolerated, for all are matters of
opinion. . . . Revealed religion is not a truth but a sentiment

[2] See Ward : *Life of John Henry Cardinal Newman*, ii. 459ff.

and a taste; not an objective fact, not miraculous; and it is in the right of the individual to make it say just what suits his fancy." And again, "Hitherto the civil power has been Christian. Now everywhere the goodly framework of society which is the creation of Christianity is throwing off Christianity. . . . For great working principles to take the place of religion it provides—the broad, fundamental ethical truths, of justice, benevolence, veracity and the like; proved experience; and those natural laws which exist and act spontaneously in society and in social matters, whether physical or psychological."

In a world organized on such a basis, the Catholic Church could have no claim to anything but toleration. The Christian State was no more: henceforth the State was indifferent and treated all religions alike. A man was free to practise the religion he chose as long as he claimed no right to interfere with others on the strength of it. In the situation thus created Catholics had perforce to acquiesce. But as time went on there came to be two schools of thought regarding the principle underlying such acquiescence. The Holy See and the Ultramontanes who championed its claims held that acquiescence was merely a practical condescension to the necessities of the situation and involved no surrender of the traditional doctrine. A distinction came to be formulated between the " thesis " and the " hypothesis." [3] The thesis remained, and must ever remain, unaltered. The true basis of society is still " the reign of Jesus Christ " as exercised through the Church and its Divinely accredited Head. This is the ideal—an ideal which the Church must never cease to proclaim and to direct all its efforts to re-establishing in practice as circumstances permit. But the " hypothesis " permits the Church, as a matter of practical policy, to accept and turn to the best account the freedom that is all that the new order allows it, pending the time when the " thesis " can once more be enthroned as the

---

[3] The distinction appears to have been first formulated clearly in the *Civiltà Cattolica* of October 17th, 1863. It was given classic expression in Leo XIII's Encyclical, *Immortale Dei*, of 1885 (*v. infra* p. 215). See Lecanuet iii. 359ff. Also Baunard, *loc. cit.*, with its criticism of the Liberal Catholic position.

basis of human society. In other words, the Church will accept toleration—and not only accept but demand it—so long as it can get nothing better. But it will persecute again as soon as it gets the chance—always, of course, in the name of Jesus Christ.

As opposed to this, the traditionalist, view a rival attitude manifested itself in France in the years following 1830 and under the influence of those who had partnered Lamennais in his *Avenir* venture but had declined to share his apostasy. These men—Montalembert, Lacordaire and the rest—were themselves faithful sons of the Church : but they were willing to believe that God fulfils Himself in many ways, and that the French Revolution might not be the wholly " Satanic " thing that the traditionalists imagined. With the " Revolution " as a rival religion to Christianity they had, of course, no sympathy whatever. But it seemed to them that the " principles of 1789," taken at their face value, might furnish a basis for the Church's status and mission which it was lawful for it to recognize, not simply as a deplorable *pis-aller,* but as something not repugnant to the will of its Divine Head. They did not go so far as to condemn the traditional conception. They regarded it as even necessary in its day, if the Church was to carry out its work of Christianizing and civilizing the young nations of Europe. But that day was past; the nations had grown to manhood; and now the Church might fully and frankly accept a regime that left it free to pursue its mission in reliance on the inherent truth and preciousness of its message and without aid from the arm of the flesh. In this view they were confirmed by the surprising renaissance of Catholic life and activity which in practice the Church was able to achieve on the basis of simple freedom and religious equality, even in the unsympathetic atmosphere of the July Monarchy.

I

This\ " liberal " view as to the place of the Church in the modern world had already for some years found utterance in the pages of the *Correspondant* and elsewhere. It was now to be proclaimed to a wider public from a more imposing

platform.   The occasion was a Congress of Catholics that had
been invited to meet at Malines in August 1863.   The soil of
Belgium was particularly suitable for the enunciation of the
view in question, for in that country more than anywhere else
it had been proved that liberal institutions were compatible
with a vigorous and aggressive Catholicism.   It was indeed as
the result of an alliance between Liberals and Catholics that
Belgium had been brought into existence as an independent
state in 1830.   The Chief Justice of the Cour de Cassation,
Baron de Gerlache, issued the invitations to the Congress : and
a future Prime Minister, M. Dechamps, brother of a future
Cardinal Archbishop of Malines, was the most active mover
in the proceedings.   The president was Cardinal Stercx, Archbishop of Malines :   and among the prelates supporting him
was the English Cardinal Wiseman.

Chief of those invited to address the Congress was Montalembert.   The invitation was couched in the most pressing
and flattering terms.   " A resounding tribune is offered to
you," wrote M. Dechamps.   " This tribune you must use for
the benefit of our common cause.   It is of the utmost importance that the result shall be liberal and that the programme which issues from it shall be yours—Catholicism and
liberty.   If you fail us, the object of the Congress will be
defeated." [4]   Montalembert hesitated long, but finally decided to accept and to " declare his whole mind."   " I will
make in public," he said, " *mon testament politique.*"

On his appearance at the Congress the whole assembly rose
to its feet with shouts of " *Vive le fils des croisés!   Vive le
Comte de Montalembert!* "   The two speeches in which he
delivered his message rank as perhaps the most eloquent of his
life, despite the sitting posture that his growing infirmities
compelled him to adopt.   In the first [5] (August 20th) he began
by drawing a contrast between the self-reliant activity of
Catholics in Belgium and their political impotence elsewhere.
This impotence he attributed to their refusal to take part in
the great revolution that had brought modern society to the

[4] Lecanuet, iii. 347.
[5] Analysed *ibid.*, 349ff.

birth. Many of them still clung to the *ancien régime*. But the *ancien régime* was dead; while the new society— democracy—existed and alone was strong and alive. Let Catholics, then, face it with courage and plant within it the banner of their faith. Thus only could democracy find its true equilibrium instead of being tossed continually (as at present) between the Revolution and despotism. The age of privilege is past for the Church. Its most precious possession is freedom : and this it can only enjoy if freedom belongs to all. Every attempt to prop the Altar on the Throne has failed. On the other hand, wherever the Church has boldly accepted the new order it has vanquished its enemies. In no other way, too, can it hope to conjure the perils that threaten democracy— the revolutionary spirit with its exaggerated claim for equality and its excessive centralization, and, above all, the menace of modern materialism and irreligion. Universal suffrage, equality before the law, liberty of association, of education, of the press—" there is not one of these which Catholics do not stand in need of even more than democrats."

In the second [6] of his Congress speeches (delivered next day) Montalembert dealt with the most difficult and delicate of the problems confronting him—liberty of conscience. He begins by repudiating with horror " the ridiculous doctrine that all religions are equally true in themselves or that spiritual authority does not bind the conscience." He accepts the distinction between dogmatic intolerance and civil toleration. Further, he claims to speak not as a theologian but only " as a politician dominated by the feeling of what is possible and what is no longer so." Nor does he wish to condemn the past. None the less, he asserts that liberty of conscience " is in his opinion most precious, sacred, legitimate and necessary." He denies that the Church has anything to lose by it—on the contrary, experience proves that it has everything to gain : nor can it claim freedom for itself except by conceding it to others. He concludes, then (1) that the Church may perfectly well make friends with the modern State, which is founded on freedom of conscience; (2) that anyone is at liberty to con-

[6] Analysed Lecanuet, iii. 353ff.

sider the modern State preferable to the old. For himself he did so prefer it; though he did not deny the orthodoxy of those who took the opposite view. In burning words he expressed his horror at the enormities perpetrated in the name of religion in the past. " The fires lit by a Catholic hand appal me not less than the scaffolds on which Protestants have immolated so many martyrs. . . . . The Spanish inquisitor who says to the heretic ' The truth or death! ' is as odious as the French Terrorist who said to my grandfather ' Liberty, fraternity or death! ' " In his peroration the speaker hailed the new age that was dawning, called by him " the age of the liberty of the Church," and drew a picture of " the mild and imposing majesty " of its sway, " when, set free from every bondage to party or dynasty, it shall appear amid the tossing waves of democracy as the sole force that is unshakable and sure of itself and of God, opening wide its maternal arms to all that is legitimate, suffering, innocent and repentant in every camp and in every country." In conclusion, he submitted all that he had said to the infallible authority of the Church.

Both speeches were greeted with rapturous applause. At the close of the second the Cardinal-President said to the orator, " Your discourse is excellent. It was no use your saying that you didn't wish to talk theology : you have spoken as a perfect theologian." But certain English Catholics present looked askance; and Montalembert's reception by the Nuncio at Brussels was icy.[7] " *Incedo per ignes,*" he had quoted as he began the most dangerous part of his subject. But he hardly realized how scorching the flame was to be, or how complete was the repudiation he was to incur.

To what extent, if at all, Montalembert had erred from Catholic orthodoxy is still matter of dispute. The eminent Mgr. d'Hulst, writing some thirty years later, expressed the opinion that it would be difficult to " extract from his pages a single proposition contrary to the pontifical utterances."[8] The question is not made less difficult by the fact that Montalembert's exposition of his attitude is more eloquent than clear.

---

[7] Lecanuet, iii. 357f.
[8] In *Correspondant,* September 25th, 1891.

He rejects the traditionalist view : but he does not reject the principle on which it is founded—that the voice of the Church is the voice of God. How, then, can a system which repudiates this principle be " preferable " to a system which postulates it? He refuses to condemn the past : yet he *does* condemn it. But even his Catholic defenders are forced to admit that his language is extremely unguarded : and the title he gave to his speeches on publication—*The Free Church in the Free State*—was more provocative still. For the phrase was Cavour's ; and on his lips expressed a view which no Catholic could admit. It was, however, the feud between the French Ultramontanes and the Liberal Catholics that constituted the real peril of Montalembert's situation. His enemies were on the watch : and now he seemed to have delivered himself into their hands.

The *Monde* not only failed to publish the speeches but spoke of them in terms carefully calculated to excite suspicion and alarm. A few weeks later it had the satisfaction of announcing that they were being made the subject of " a thorough examination at Rome, at the request, it is said, of various members of the French episcopate." [9] In truth, the sleuth-hound of orthodoxy, the Bishop of Poitiers, was hot on Montalembert's trail. In a letter to the Pope he urgently demanded his condemnation : and he despatched his vicar-general to Rome to back up the request. At the same time he issued his *Third Synodal Letter* in which he denounced " naturalism, rationalism, and Liberal Catholicism " as the supreme dangers of the time. [10] Pie's representations were supported by a number of other bishops, including several English ones : and the Jesuits at Rome joined in the hue and cry. To one who told Pius IX. that the condemnation of Montalembert would give great pleasure to the Protestants, the Pope replied, " I know Catholics to whom it would give greater pleasure still." [11]

To do him justice, Pius was not too anxious to condemn Montalembert, recognizing his signal services to the Catholic

[9] Lecanuet, iii. 362.
[10] Baunard, *Cardinal Pie,* ii. 222.
[11] Lecanuet, iii. 364.

cause. In a conversation with the offender's brother-in-law
he remarked : " I should have preferred not to say anything,
but I shall probably be obliged to. . . . In any case, I will
look into the matter. He went much too far. One can't
admit all he said." He added, " It is a sin not to believe that
outside the Church there is no salvation." [12] Montalembert, on
these words being reported to him, was acutely distressed. In
a letter in reply (which its recipient read to the Pope) he
warmly denied that he had said anything to contradict the
proposition in question—in fact he had expressly stated that
" dogmatic intolerance is inseparable from eternal truth." He
went on to make a pathetic plea for mercy. A condemnation
would be a fatal blow to his work for the Church, both in the
past and in the future. He also wrote to Antonelli to the same
effect, explaining—? or explaining away—what he had
said at Malines. He had no thought of enunciating an
" absolute and universal principle," but only of suggesting an
accommodation to the circumstances of the time. [13] His
friends used their influence at Rome to avert the blow.
Cardinal Stercx, several French Bishops and the Paris Jesuits
all wrote in his favour. Dupanloup actually went to Rome to
plead his friend's cause. [14] Even Antonelli was averse from a
condemnation, fearing the effect on public opinion.

For a moment these efforts seemed to promise success. The
Papal Nuncio at Paris, Mgr. Chigi, told Montalembert that
the questions he had raised were merely a matter for discussion in the Catholic journals of different shades of opinion.
" Il ne doit y avoir autre chose." [15] But in the end Pius yielded
to the Ultramontane pressure. He decided to condemn
Montalembert, though only in a private letter written by the
hand of Antonelli. The letter was to the effect that the
Malines speeches were " reprehensible as being in conflict with
the teaching of the Church and with the acts of various
Sovereign Pontiffs," especially one of Pius VI. describing " as
plane exitiosum et pestilens the edict of Nantes so highly

[12] Ibid., 365.
[13] Ibid., 365ff.
[14] Lagrange, ii. 436f.
[15] Lecanuet, iii. 371.

praised " in the speeches referred to. It concluded by inviting
Montalembert to devote himself to " dissipating the sad effects
resulting from " what he had said. [16]
The letter cut Montalembert to the heart. In his reply he
expressed his " astonishment and affliction," but also his
deference to the Church and its august Head. [17] His grief was
not lessened by the congratulations bestowed by the Pope the
following July on a Belgian nobody who had written a
pamphlet—significantly entitled *Free Error in the Free State*
—in which Montalembert was virulently attacked in seventy-
five pages out of ninety-three.

II

If the Pope had abstained from condemning Montalembert
except privately and by implication, he could the better afford
to do so because he was contemplating a solemn utterance that
would indicate, in the most unmistakable way, the Church's
uncompromising hostility to most of the leading ideas on
which modern society rests. The real answer to the " heresies "
of Malines was the famous Encyclical *Quanta Cura* of
December 8th, 1864. [18]
The Encyclical had been in preparation for some ten
years. [19] A committee of theologians entrusted with the task
of drawing up an explicit condemnation of modern " errors "
was appointed in 1854. But the work proceeded slowly until
Gerbet, Bishop of Perpignan, issued in 1860 a pastoral instruction formulating and condemning eighty-five propositions in
which contemporary writers had put forward the errors of the
time. The Pope was profoundly impressed : and Gerbet's
propositions were made the basis of a revised and extended list
prepared by the Roman theologians. The list was submitted

[16] Lecanuet, iii. 373. The text of the letter remained a secret until
Lecanuet published it in 1902, nearly forty years later.
[17] *Ibid.*, 375.
[18] Printed with the accompanying Syllabus in Debidour 719, with the
note : " The text here given is . . . the French translation of these
documents, published, opposite the Latin text, by Adrien Leclere, printer
to the Pope." It may therefore be regarded as authorized.
[19] See Nielsen : *History of the Papacy in the Nineteenth Century*
(English translation, 1906), ii. 261f.

to the Bishops assembled at Rome for the canonization of the Japanese martyrs in 1862. But Dupanloup and other French prelates were averse from its publication at present.[20] The Congress of Malines, however, made the Pope more convinced than ever that some overt action was needed : and the success in Ultramontane circles of Pie's *Third Synodal Instruction* encouraged him to undertake it. It was, however, the Convention of September 15th that really precipitated the publication of the Encyclical. Against the principles in the name of which he had been despoiled the Pope might be powerless : but he would at least let the world know what he thought of them.

The Encyclical begins by declaring that the Holy Father has already condemned the *"monstruosa opinionum portenta"* of the time, but that now a further condemnation has become necessary. The root of the evil lies in the " impious and absurd principle of naturalism," which maintains that "human society should be constituted and governed without regard to religion, or at least without distinction between true religion and false." In accordance with this idea it is asserted that " liberty of conscience and worship is a right proper to every man and that citizens have the right to manifest their opinions publicly, by word or the press, without restraint by the ecclesiastical authority." Such liberty is described by the Encyclical as a " liberty of perdition." Further, men declare that " the will of the people is the supreme law, and that in the temporal order accomplished facts are legitimated by the mere fact of their being accomplished." In the unbridled pursuit of riches and enjoyment, they persecute the religious orders and restrain the operations of Catholic charity. " Professing the fatal error of socialism and communism," they violate the rights of the family and seek to deprave the younger generation by taking away the right of education from the clergy, who are regarded as " the enemies of enlightenment, civilization and progress." Again, it is maintained that the laws of the Church have no binding force on the conscience except when promulgated by the civil power and that the Church has no right to inflict

[20] Lagrange, ii. 455.

temporal penalties for their violation. Such errors it is impossible to pass over in silence. They are therefore " reprobated, prescribed and condemned " by virtue of the Apostolic authority.

To the Encyclical was appended a *Syllabus Errorum,* holding up to execration eighty propositions (arranged under ten headings) which include, among a number of things that every Christian at least is bound to reprobate, not a few of the principles which the great majority of civilized mankind have come to regard as axiomatic. Having given a résumé (§ I.) of the main errors of Pantheism, Naturalism and Absolute Rationalism, the Syllabus goes on to condemn what it calls " Tempered Rationalism " (§ II.) including the view that " the methods and principles of the ancient scholastic doctors are no longer in harmony with the needs of our time and the progress of knowledge." (13) [This was aimed at Döllinger, who had recently criticized Scholasticism with severity as a " one-eyed " science, on the ground of its indifference to history.] The section (§ III.) headed " Indifferentism, Latitudinarianism " condemns the view that "it is open to every man to profess the religion that his reason leads him to consider true " (15), and that " men may find eternal salvation in the practice of any religion " (16). In § IV., Socialism, Communism, Secret Societies, Bible Societies and Libero-Catholic Societies (supporting Cavour's doctrine of " a free Church in a free State ") are all lumped together and condemned. The following section (§ V.) deals with " the Church and its Rights." It condemns all claims made on behalf of the civil power to limit the authority of the Church, as also the view that " the Church has no right to employ force " (24). In § VI. (dealing with " Civil Society ") the view is condemned that " the State, being the source of all rights, enjoys a right uncircumscribed by any limit " (39), and that " in case of a legal conflict between the two powers " (i.e. the civil and spiritual) " the civil jurisdiction must prevail " (42). In addition, it is forbidden to hold that " the good constitution of civil society demands that popular schools open to children of every class and institutions for higher education shall be freed from all authority of the Church " (47), and that " the Church ought to be separated from the State and the State from the Church " (55).   § VII. (" Natural and Christian Morality ") condemns the view that " philosophical and moral science may and should be set free from divine and ecclesiastical authority " (57), as also the principle of non-intervention (62) and the right of subjects to refuse obedience to their legitimate princes (63).   In § VIII. (" Christian Marriage") it is forbidden to assert the dissolubility of marriage (67) and the possibility of true Christian marriage in virtue of a purely civil contract (73)—as also to maintain that " matrimonial cases by their very nature belong to the civil jurisdiction " (74).   In § IX. (" The Civil Principate of the Roman Pontiff ") the view is condemned that " the abrogation of the Temporal Power would serve the liberty and well-being of the Church " (76).   The last section (X., " Modern Liberalism," i.e. Liberal Catholicism) is perhaps the most challenging of all. It repudiates the view that " at the present day it is no longer advantageous that the Catholic religion should be considered as the sole State religion to the exclusion of other religions " (77); and sweeps to a staggering climax in denying that " the Roman Pontiff can and ought to effect a reconciliation and alliance with progress, liberalism and modern civilization " (80).

It is obvious that, if once the Ultramontane thesis is admitted, the condemnations of the Encyclical and Syllabus follow as a matter of sheer logical consistency.   The Church may " condescend " to make the best of a bad job in an unkind age : but its principles remain unaltered.   Further, the Syllabus made it clear, by appending to each proposition condemned a reference to a previous condemnation of it by the reigning Pontiff, that its attitude was no new departure but merely a reaffirmation of a position held all along.   The concentration, however, within a single document of so imposing a body of condemnations produced a staggering effect on public opinion.   The enemies of the Church were thrown into ecstasies of joy at seeing papal intransigence so imprudently unmasked : and the Syllabus remains to this day one

of their choicest weapons. Among Catholics, the Ultramontanes rejoiced no less than the anticlericals: but the
more moderate spirits and those who genuinely desired that
the Church should make friends with the new order were
filled with dismay.

Montalembert was appalled. He and Broglie proposed that
the control of the *Correspondant*[21] should be surrendered at
once into other hands. But their colleagues were against this.
The Encyclical, they urged, was not as bad as it appeared.
To prove this, Dupanloup stepped into the breach with yet
another pamphlet, bearing the title *La Convention du 15
septembre et l'Encyclique du 8 décembre* (Jan., 1865).[22] In
the first part he dealt with the Convention, attacking it with
vehemence and exposing its ambiguities and the opening it
left for Piedmont's designs. In the second he passed to the
Encyclical. The anticlericals maintained that so uncompromising a defiance to the modern world amply justified the
Convention. But, said Dupanloup, this was to misunderstand
its purport. In explanation of the Pope's refusal to " reconcile
himself with modern civilization " he wrote as follows: " In
what our enemies designate by the vague name of modern
civilization there is something good, something indifferent and
something bad. With what is good or indifferent in it the
Pope has no need to be reconciled. With what is bad the
Pope neither must nor can accept reconciliation or alliance."
The Encyclical condemns only " a *certain* progress, a
certain civilization." Again, in condemning philosophic
freedom the Pope only has in view the *abuse* of reason—the
spirit that says " Reason is everything: faith is nothing." As
to liberty of conscience, political liberty and the freedom of
the press, the Church has never condemned toleration and
political liberty of worship. It will not indeed proclaim these
liberties as an absolute right and an universal ideal: but it
orders its children to accept sincerely the constitution and
liberties of their countries. To say that Catholics demand
liberty when they are weak and refuse to grant it when they

[21] Lecanuet, iii. 384.
[22] Analysed in Lagrange, ii. 458ff. See also Lecanuet, iii. 386f.

are strong is a calumny.   The Church rejects no form of government, but accepts all so long as they are just.

Dupanloup's pamphlet had a great reception from those who disliked the Encyclical and from those who feared its repercussion on public opinion.   Six hundred and thirty bishops wrote to congratulate the author.   On the other hand the Ultramontanes dubbed it " Anti-Syllabus " : and Veuillot described it to a friend as " a bad action and a wicked performance."   The Pope wrote to Dupanloup a laudatory letter.   But was there not a sting in its tail when he expressed the hope that the bishop " would devote himself the more energetically to explaining the true meaning of the Encyclical as he had more vehemently refuted erroneous interpretations of it ? " [23]   His enemies were saying, in truth, that he had said less what the Encyclical was than what it was not.

III

Dupanloup's explanations may or may not have been acceptable to Pius IX. : but they were at least couched in terms of intense respect for his authority.   It was reserved for a stronger and perhaps abler man to stand up and administer what was practically a rebuke to the Sovereign Pontiff for an act that profoundly alienated the public opinion of the time.

The author of this rebuke—Archbishop Darboy of Paris [24] —was to play so important a part in the ecclesiastical history of the next few years that it may be well to attempt a brief sketch of his personality.   His cruel death at the hands of the Commune in 1871 would in any case engage our sympathy :

[23] Lagrange, ii. 474.
[24] Two biographies of Darboy exist—Guillermin, *Vie de Mgr. Darboy,* 1888, and (Cardinal) Foulon (Archbishop of Besançon), *Histoire de la vie et des œuvres de Mgr. Darboy,* 1889. Both have been severely criticized. Foulon's gives a touching account of the Archbishop's tragic last days and a sufficiently clear idea of his personality : but its apologetic purpose makes it seriously defective from the historian's point of view.   The most striking feature of Darboy's career—his unflinching opposition to Pius IX. —is minimized to an almost comical extent : and the crucial documents are either suppressed altogether or mutilated and relegated to the footnotes.   Reference should therefore be made to Darboy's own papers published in the *Revue d'histoire et de littérature réligieuses,* 1907, under the title, *Mgr. Darboy et le Saint-Siège.*   There is an admirable character-sketch of Darboy in Ollivier, *Concile du Vatican,* i. 416ff.

but his life no less than his death commands respect. He was always a somewhat lonely figure—reserved, cautious, rather abstract in thought and expression, well liked by those who knew him well but easily misunderstood by those who did not. From both of the great rival schools of theological thought in his time he stood apart. Like Veuillot he backed the Empire, which he at least served faithfully to the end. But in their theological attitude he and the fanatics of the *Univers* stood poles apart. In the case of the Liberal Catholics the situation was reversed. He shared their opposition to the Ultramontane exaggerations of the papal authority: but he had small sympathy for their *political* Liberalism. He set more store by order than by liberty: he genuinely feared the passions of the people and was never tired of proclaiming the need of " respect." This strong conservatism no doubt explains his acceptance of the Empire. He was grateful for what promised to be a " strong " government and one friendly to the Church. He was the favourite ecclesiastic of Napoleon III., and honours rained upon him. But the Emperor himself said that he never flattered him, nor did he hesitate to castigate the vices of the hectic Parisian society of his time. In the discharge of his multifarious duties he never spared himself, in spite of his wretched health. In certain ways perhaps he was an Erastian: but his Erastianism was of the more defensible sort. He dreaded the theocratic aspirations of the Ultramontane school, knowing that it could not challenge with impunity the whole spirit of the age. If the Church was sacred, so was the State. His was a layman's mind rather than an ecclesiastic's: he was less interested in dogma than in morality. He disliked extremes and never lost sight of the possibilities of a situation. Altogether a man who tried to turn to the best account the difficult position in which he stood. His world was always the real world: and he dealt with it as such and in the best way he could.

The pronounced Gallicanism of Darboy made his translation to the see of Paris in 1863 by no means to the Pope's liking. His action as Archbishop was soon to make Pius like him even less. From the very outset he showed his determination to take his own line, whether the Holy See were pleased or displeased. He postponed the establishment of the Roman liturgy in his diocese. He appointed Père Hyacinthe, an eloquent Carmelite of very liberal views, to preach the Advent Conferences of 1864 at Notre-Dame. He insisted on visiting canonically a Jesuit College in Paris despite the protest of the Superior, who claimed exemption. The Pope addressed a letter to him severely rebuking his conduct and also reproaching him with the liberal opinions of the younger generation of Catholics. Darboy took some time to reply, and then in a strain that was not too respectful. He declared that the " regular clergy " were his " inferiors and not his equals " and that " no religious house existing in Paris at present enjoyed a canonical right of exemption." To withdraw the religious orders from episcopal visitation would be to submit France to the immediate jurisdiction of the Pope. He went on to declare his intention of maintaining the rights of the episcopate, if necessary by an appeal to public opinion and to the co-operation of his colleagues. [25] The Pope must have been intensely annoyed by Darboy's tone, but in his reply he made no comment on his letter. He had already said that he would never make the Archbishop of Paris a Cardinal.

About the same time a further dispute between Darboy and the Holy See became serious enough to provoke the intervention of the Government. [26] The curé of Neuilly, Roy, had for some time lived in the same house with his sister-in-law, who was living apart from her husband. At the bidding of Darboy's predecessor, Cardinal Morlot, the arrangement ceased : but Roy continued to pay the lady frequent visits. When he declined to break off their relations, Morlot deprived the curé and appointed someone else to administer his parish. Roy appealed to the Council of State and also to the Congregation of the Council at Rome. The latter requested Darboy, soon after his translation, to go back on his predecessor's sentence. Darboy refused : whereupon the Pope ordered the case to be retried in Rome. In August, 1864, the

[25] Maurain, 724f.
[26] *Ibid.*, 726f.

Congregation of the Council quashed Morlot's sentence and ordered Roy to be reinstated. Darboy complained to the Pope, but suggested as a compromise that Roy should resign. In this he was supported by Baroche, the Minister of Religions, who maintained that Roy's reinstatement would have a bad effect on public opinion. In the following December a decree of the Council of State ordered the execution of Morlot's sentence on its civil side despite the decree of the Roman congregation, which, according to Darboy and the Government, was, by the terms of the Organic Articles, without binding force in France.

Darboy had thus already given full proof of his independent attitude towards the Holy See when the Encyclical *Quanta Cura* appeared. To a man of his stamp—a hater of extremes and at the same time a realist and passionately convinced of the duty of the Church to conciliate and not needlessly to estrange the better public opinion of the time—so reckless an utterance must have appeared as wellnigh madness. In his Lenten charge of 1865 he made a gallant attempt to minimize its rigours : and he followed this up by a pastoral instruction in the course of which he addressed the Pope by name and implored him to take up a more sympathetic attitude towards the modern world. " Your reproof is mighty," he wrote, " but your blessing is mightier still. . . . Turn now your eyes to what is great and honourable in the present time and support it in its generous efforts by the grace of your prayers as well as by the authority of your counsels. . . . It is to you that it is given to reconcile reason with faith, liberty with authority and the world of politics with the Church. . . . Call forth from your large pontiff's heart one of those words that forgive the past, reassure the present and open out the horizons of the future." [27]

The addressing of these words to the Pope being rhetorical and not personal, the object of them could only keep silence for the moment. But the pontifical temper was not improved,

<hr/>

[27] This apostrophe is quoted at length in Ollivier, *L'Église et l'État au Concile du Vatican*, i. 423. Ollivier well speaks of " *ces superbes paroles que j'inscris comme une épitaphe glorieuse sur sa pierre sépulchrale.*"

and very soon an opportunity came of making the audacious prelate feel the weight of it. On October 26th, 1865, the Pope addressed to Darboy a letter of crushing severity. In this he censured a speech delivered by the Archbishop in the Senate the previous March, in which he had ascribed " a certain authority and respect " to the Organic Articles and opposed appeals to the Holy See. He was also rebuked for ordering an archidiaconal visitation of the Jesuit and Capuchin houses in his diocese, and for being present at the funeral of General Magnan, at which the insignia of Free-masonry had been displayed. The position taken up by Darboy in his letter of September, 1864, was unsparingly condemned. " We cannot but be afflicted," wrote the Pope, " at seeing you favour the false and erroneous doctrines of Febronius, which the Holy See has condemned. When you say that the power of the Holy See over dioceses is not ordinary, you ignore a decision of the Fourth Lateran Council which runs : ' The Roman Church according to the Divine disposition has over all others a sovereign right *(principatum)* of ordinary authority, for it is the mother and mistress of all the faithful of Christ.' " [28]

Darboy wrote in reply a letter couched in respectful terms but containing no retractation of his position. He also main-tained his refusal to reinstate the Abbé Roy : and the dispute remained unsettled until the end of the Empire.

The Pope's letter had an interesting sequel some three years later. In 1868, Napoleon III. was strongly pressing the appointment of Darboy as a *Cardinal de Couronne.* The Pope resisted, and by way of justifying his resistance com-municated to the Government his letter of 1865. The effect, however, was only to stiffen the determination of the Govern-ment. A few months later the letter was published in a Canadian newspaper, and from a printing press at Geneva copies of it were distributed all over France. When Darboy complained bitterly of the breach of confidence, the Pope told the French ambassador that " it had not come from Rome " : but he refused to publish the disavowal. [29]

[28] Maurain, 782f.   [29] *Ibid.,* 890f.

IV

The appearance of the Syllabus was a powerful reinforcement of the anticlerical propaganda against religion which, picking up the papal challenge, now became bolder and more aggressive than ever. Nor did the Government take any very active steps to restrain it, except when (as particularly among the students of Paris) it was allied with revolutionary opinions. In 1862 it had suspended the brilliant lectures of the new professor of Hebrew at the Collège de France, Ernest Renan, on the ground of their anti-Christian tendency. Next year, when the appearance of Renan's famous *Vie de Jésus* sent a shudder of horror through the Catholic, and indeed the Christian, world, the Emperor, in a letter to Parisis (which the latter published), expressed his reprobation of the book. Soon afterwards the Government deprived Renan of his post. But after the September Convention and the Syllabus the Emperor fell temporarily under the influence of his cousin, Prince Napoleon, who was no lover of the Church and whose sister, Princess Mathilde, held a *salon* that was a favourite rendezvous of the brilliant free-thinking writers of the time. Early in 1865 he nominated Sainte-Beuve to the Senate : and a little later the Government restored Taine to a post of which he had been deprived through clerical influence.

It was, however, the presence of Duruy at the Ministry of Public Instruction that for the time being constituted the most serious stumbling-block to the Clerical party. Duruy was an avowed free-thinker and anticlerical, an enthusiastic *universitaire* and champion of the education given by the State. In February, 1865, he presented to the Emperor a memorandum in support of compulsory free education in primary schools. The Emperor appeared to favour the proposal : and Duruy's memorandum was published in the *Moniteur*. But soon afterwards an official notice intimated that it represented merely Duruy's personal opinion. The Minister, however, continued to encourage by every means in his power the State system of education as against the Catholic schools; and in this way drew upon himself more and more the suspicion and dislike of the clergy.

In Duruy's view it was even more important to restrain the activity of the Church in the sphere of secondary than in that of primary education. In particular, he was anxious that the State should supply better facilities for the secondary education of girls—a field in which the religious congregations had largely had matters in their own hands. With this object he instituted in 1867 a scheme for providing courses of lectures in the municipalities for girls of the educated class; the lectures to be given by professors of the Université and embracing a wide range of subjects. The clergy at once sounded the alarm: and Dupanloup lifted his voice in still another pamphlet, *M. Duruy et l'éducation des filles*. He expressed his horror and that of all good Catholics that the daughters of France should sit at the feet of those who, besides being *universitaires* and therefore inclined to free-thinking opinions, were also males and in many cases young males at that. The bishops responded to his lead with gusto: and Duruy soon found practically the whole of the episcopal body arrayed against him. Attempts were made to secure his resignation: but the Emperor declined to sacrifice him. The success of the lectures, however, was seriously prejudiced. [30] In the following year a petition signed by 2,000 *pères de famille* and directed against the atheistic teaching given in the École de Médicine received powerful support in the Senate, but was eventually rejected.

At this period Napoleon III. oscillated continually between influences friendly and unfriendly to the Church. The favour of Prince Napoleon came abruptly to an end in May, 1865, in consequence of a speech delivered by him at Ajaccio, in which he said that " Napoleon I. was religious in a general and elevated way, but it is difficult to connect his opinions with a formulated religion," and commended his suppression of the Temporal Power. [31] The Emperor reprimanded him in a letter that he caused to be published in the *Moniteur*. The Prince's disgrace and the death shortly before of the Emperor's half-brother, the Duc de Morny, President of the

[30] Lagrange, iii. 98f.; Maurain, 840f.
[31] Maurain, 735.

Corps Législatif, removed the two influences in the imperial entourage in favour of a Liberalizing policy for the Empire. In Morny's place the Emperor appointed Walewski, a Clerical. The disappearance of Prince Napoleon from the political scene increased the rival influence of the Empress, who was always favourable to the Pope. Her influence was the more to be reckoned with in view of the Emperor's ill-health: for in the event of his death she would be Regent through a long minority.

A *rapprochement* between the French Government and the Holy See followed, and was made easier by a less intransigent attitude on the part of the latter. Mérode was dismissed: and, in view of the withdrawal of the French army of occupation that was now gradually taking place, the Pope deigned to accept the services of a French Foreign Legion which was being assembled at Antibes in readiness for its transfer to Rome after the withdrawal had begun. At the same time the Government sought fresh guarantees from the Italian Government that it would not attack Rome.

The withdrawal of the French army of occupation from Rome was a bitter disappointment to the Clericals, who had continued to hope that it might at least be postponed. The bishops asked prayers for the Pope, and redoubled their efforts to raise money for his necessities. The lower clergy were disturbed and angry. The embarrassments created by the Roman Question were increased by the consequences of the war of 1866, which crowned the coalition of Prussia and Italy against Austria with success. The Emperor's plans to make capital out of the European situation had gone badly astray: and France, having helped to achieve the unity of Italy, now stood confronted with the prospect of a united Germany that was certain to prove a greater menace still. In Mexico, too, the Emperor had been forced to abandon his support of the ill-starred adventure of the Emperor Maximilian and to bow to the enforcement of the " Monroe doctrine " against him by the United States. The loss of his prestige made it more necessary than ever to avoid offending Conservative and Clerical opinion. The Gallican policy of the Government underwent some modification. Significant of this was the permission given to Veuillot to revive the *Univers* under his own editorship. It reappeared for the first time on April 16th, 1867, and soon enjoyed its old success.

Such was the situation when in September, 1867, Garibaldi made known his intention of making yet another dash on Rome. The Italian Government put its *enfant terrible* out of harm's way in the prison-isle of Caprera : but his followers continued their preparations with its connivance and almost immediately invaded the pontifical dominions. In October, Garibaldi escaped from Caprera, and joined his soldiers almost in sight of Rome. The Emperor at once despatched an expeditionary force to the Pope's assistance; while the Italian Government occupied part of the papal territory. On November 3rd the Garibaldians met a column formed of papal and French troops at Mentana and were put to flight. Antonelli now wanted to attack the Italian forces : but the French general forbade this, saying that " it would be madness." The Italian Government withdrew its troops : and war was avoided.

The victory of Mentana merely increased Napoleon's difficulties. Once again he suggested a conference of the Powers for a final settlement of the Roman Question : but they all declined to help him. The Clericals harried the Government in the Senate, and—still more effectively—in the Corps Législatif. In the latter they were reinforced by Thiers, who made great play with the dangers threatening France in consequence of the Emperor's misguided policy and declared that the fall of the Temporal Power was the greatest danger that she had to fear. The profound impression caused by his speech led the Prime Minister, Rouher, to pronounce (December 5th) his famous "*Jamais*." "We declare in the name of the French government," he said, " Italy shall never gain possession of Rome. *Never, never* will France endure this violence done to its honour and to Catholicism ! " [32] The declaration mortally offended Italy, who henceforth, with hatred in her heart, awaited the day when the collapse

[32] Maurain, 829.

of the Empire should give the signal for her to force the gates of Rome.

That day indeed might well seem to be not far off. The prestige of the Empire, at home and abroad, was sinking lower and lower. And meanwhile the republican cause—closely allied as it was with enmity to the Church and even to religion—was advancing by leaps and bounds. The one chance of saving the situation seemed to lie in a concentration of all the forces of conservatism in support of the imperial regime. This could only be effected by conciliating the clergy and their allies. Thus when the elections of 1869 came round it was seen that the situation of 1849 had reproduced itself. A republicanism hostile to the Church stood face to face with the old party of order in alliance with it.[33] The elections gave the victory to the latter: but a strong democratic opposition was returned, including some thirty republicans, who set the separation of Church and State in the forefront of their programme. In the hope of staying the further progress of republicanism, and also to meet the wishes of the conservatives, who thought thus to fortify their independent position, the Emperor remodelled the constitution of the Empire on constitutional lines. The short lived " Liberal Empire " thus came into existence. After a few months of transition the appointment (January 2nd, 1870) of Émile Ollivier as Premier of a Cabinet preponderantly Clerical, with all its incalculable consequences both in the ecclesiastical and the political sphere, set the seal upon the alliance of the dying Empire and the Conservative-Clericals.

[33] Maurain, 936.

CHAPTER VII

THE VATICAN COUNCIL

1869—1870

" THE two great events of modern history," it has been well said, " the Reformation and the Revolution, have made the Papacy what it is—the Reformation by forcibly driving the Catholic half of Christendom into centralization, the Revolution by removing the last remaining independent power in the Church, viz. the Gallican Church with the Sorbonne and Parlement." [1] From the early years of the nineteenth century the progress of Ultramontanism had been steadily maintained —not least in France, which in days past had offered the stoutest opposition to its doctrines. In Pius IX. it had found the ideal Pope for its purposes. And now the Vatican Council, by making belief in papal infallibility henceforth a necessary part of the faith of the Roman Catholic Church, was to crown with triumph the work for which both the Pope and his votaries had laboured with such unflagging zeal.

I

There seems reason to believe that Pius IX. had entertained the idea of summoning a General Council from the very outset of his reign. But it was only at the end of 1864 that active steps began to be taken towards carrying the idea into effect. [2]

[1] Quirinus, Letters from Rome on the Council [Eng. tr. 1870] 696. This famous book is now understood to have been written by Döllinger on information supplied from Rome by his allies, Friedrich, Acton and others. It is a superb piece of polemical journalism and (as might be expected from its author) displays much learning and acumen in a general way. But as an account of the proceedings of the Council itself it is based merely on second-hand information, while its spirit is bitterly partisan. It should therefore be used with great caution.
[2] The best account of the Vatican Council in English is in [Abbot] Butler, The Vatican Council: the story told from inside in Bishop Ullathorne's letters, 2 vols., 1930. Written by a distinguished Roman Catholic scholar, this book is marked by great fairness and moderation both of view and statement, and is based on a careful study of the sources. It is thus a valuable corrective of the accounts given in most Anglican and Protestant writers, who have relied too much on the ex

135

Two days before the issue of the Encyclical *Quanta Cura*—on December 6th, 1864—the Pope asked twenty-one Cardinals for their written opinion as to the advisability of such a step. Nineteen of these Cardinals answered in the affirmative and only two in the negative. On March 1st of the following year a "Directing" Commission of Cardinals was appointed to consider the practical questions involved in the holding of a Council : and in April confidential letters were addressed to thirty-four bishops (including Dupanloup) consulting them as to the subjects that might be brought up for discussion at it. Dupanloup showed little zeal for the project : [3] but the majority were favourable. Two years later—on June 26th, 1867—in connection with the celebration of the centenary of St. Peter, the Pope publicly intimated his intention to hold the Council. It was received with enthusiasm by the five hundred Archbishops and Bishops present. On July 1st the Pope announced that he would summon the Council to meet on the Feast of the Immaculate Conception, but did not state in what year.

Prominent among the bishops assembled at Rome was Dupanloup, who by this time had changed his mind. [4] He took a leading part in the drawing up of the Address of the Bishops in response to the papal allocution of June 26th : and the moment the assembly broke up he hastened back to France to be the first to announce, in a pastoral letter, the coming Council. At the third Congress of Malines (1867), held soon afterwards, Falloux hailed the prospect of what he described

parte version of such anti-infallibilists as Quirinus, Pomponio Leto and Friedrich. In French, Émile Ollivier, *L'Église et l'État au Concile du Vatican*, 2 vols., 1877, still holds pride of place. It is particularly valuable on the diplomatic side and on events outside the Council itself. [See also Mourret, *Le Concile du Vatican*, 1919.] The story of the Council was written from the anti-infallibilist standpoint at great length by Friedrich, *Geschichte des Vatikanischen Konzils*, 3 vols., 1877—1887. The reply to Friedrich was made in Fr. Theodore Granderath, S.J., *Geschichte des Vatikanischen Konzils*, 3 vols., 1903-6 [Fr. tr. 1908-19] —but, says Abbot Butler, "Granderath shows himself almost as decided a partisan as Friedrich." The complete record of the proceedings of the Council is now published in Mansi, *Acta Conciliorum*, vol. xlix.—liii., 1923-7; it fills 6,000 folio columns.
[3] His reply is printed in Mansi, xlix. 118f.
[4] Lagrange, iii. 53ff.

as " the most comprehensive, the freest discussion concerning the most important interests of mankind." [5] But the news of the Council was not received everywhere with the same enthusiasm. The question was, What was it going to do? Many believed that what was really in mind was a declaration of the papal infallibility. It was known that the Jesuits in Rome were working strongly for this end. Not a few, too, of the Catholic bishops ardently desired it. While attending the centenary celebrations at Rome, Archbishop Manning, of Westminster, and Senestrey, Bishop of Ratisbon, had bound themselves by a secret vow " to do all in their power to obtain the definition of the papal infallibility." [6] But the sequel was to show that this enthusiasm was by no means universally shared. Even if the Pope *were* infallible, it might be far from desirable in existing circumstances to say so. And might not, in consequence, the Council serve to reveal rather the disunion than the unity of the Church?

In the presence of these possibilities, Dupanloup and his friends began to feel uncomfortable. Early in February 1868, the Bishop wrote to the Pope to urge that the summoning of the Council should not be long delayed, and a month later, encouraged by the Pope's kindly reply, he wrote again, hinting in the delicate terms that the situation demanded, that the Bull of summons should be framed in such a way as to offend nobody. [7] Meanwhile, five commissions had been set up at Rome to give preliminary consideration to the various classes of questions with which the Council might be called upon to deal.

On June 29th, 1868, the Bull of Indiction [8] at last made its appearance. It fixed December 8th, 1869 as the date on which the Council should assemble. To the great relief of those who had feared a definition of Infallibility as the Council's prime purpose, it made no mention of the subject : though it is possible to see in its opening phrases an implicit

---

[5] Falloux, *Mémoires,* ii. 414.
[6] Purcell, *Life of Cardinal Manning,* ii. 420.
[7] March 16th, 1868. Letter printed in full in Lagrange, iii. 110f.
[8] Text in Mansi, *Collectio Conciliorum,* l. 193* (= xlix. 1249ff.).

declaration of the doctrine.[9] It was observed, too, that a departure was made from the Bulls by which previous Councils had been summoned in that no invitation was addressed to Roman Catholic sovereigns to send *oratores* to represent them at the Council. The omission was largely due (as Antonelli explained privately to the French Ambassador at Rome) to the difficulty of including in such an invitation the King of Italy, who at this time lay under excommunication.[10] It was understood, however, that if the Governments chose to send representatives, they were at liberty to do so. After the issue of the Bull letters were sent to the Oriental Churches and to the Protestants inviting them to take part in the Council. But as neither could hope to be received save as wearing the white sheet of penitence, the invitation was not taken up.

The failure to invite the Catholic sovereigns created an unfavourable impression in France. The future Premier, Émile Ollivier, speaking in the Chamber of Deputies (July 10th) declared that it amounted to " the separation of the Church and the State operated by the Pope himself."[11] The Government, in reply, said that it was still uncertain whether it would or would not use its incontrovertible right of being represented at the Council, and that in any case it reserved its full liberty of action in regard to the decisions taken there. The Liberal Catholics, too, were much concerned. Was this not a fresh manifestation of Rome's incurable resolve to flout and defy modern society? Their misgivings were not lessened by a declaration of Veuillot's that " the Church does not expel the sovereigns, but it proves that they are outside her." The State, affirmed the *Univers,* has become " a chaos, a sink " : and good Catholics " have no longer a place within it."[12]

In the face of such extravagances Dupanloup could hardly be expected to refrain from making yet another pronounce-

[9] *Ego Pius catholicae Ecclesiae episcopus . . . coeli janitor ac ligandorum solvendorumque arbiter, mansura etiam in coelis judiciorum suorum definitione.* See Ollivier, i. 27.

[10] Ollivier, i. 508.

[11] Text of speech in Ollivier, i. 397ff.

[12] *Univers,* July 11th, 1868 (signed L. Veuillot): quoted Lagrange, iii. 115.

ment. But before making it he wished first to consult his colleagues of the episcopate, not only in France but elsewhere. With this object he went first to Malines and had an interview with Archbishop Dechamps, one of the foremost protagonists of the Infallibility. From thence he went into Germany—to Aix-la-Chapelle and Cologne. On his return he wrote a pastoral letter, in which he expressed the conviction that by its " work of illumination and pacification " the Council would put an end to the misunderstanding between the nations and the Church. [13]

Meanwhile, at Rome, the preparations for the Council were being pushed forward. The constitution of the five departmental commissions, and of the *congregazione dirrettrice* charged with the general management of the Council, was not too reassuring to those who feared an ulterior motive in its convocation. Well known theologians from all over the Catholic world had been invited to take part in the important work of preparing the business of the Council : but it was commented that their selection appeared in many cases to be dictated less by their scientific attainments than by their devotion to the Infallibility. [14] This Infallibilist preponderance was specially marked in the case of the crucial dogmatic commission. [15] Newman was among those asked to assist in this way : but after consideration he decided to decline the Pope's invitation, [16] as also a later invitation by Dupanloup to accompany him to the Council as his " theologian." Contrary to precedent, no bishops were asked to take part in the business of preparing for the Council : but a number of rather unimportant questions on ecclesiastical discipline were addressed to the episcopate.

Hitherto, the possibility of a definition of the papal infallibility by the Council had been freely canvassed in private, both among the bishops and elsewhere, and had been a subject for hope or misgiving as the case might be. But the question had

[13] Eng. tr. : *The Future Œcumenical Council,* 1869.
[14] Quirinus, 8.
[15] Nielsen, *History of the Papacy in the XIXth Century,* ii. 298.
[16] For the motives of this refusal see Abbot Butler, *Life and Times of Bishop Ullathorne,* 1926, ii. 46.

not yet entered the field of public discussion. Early in 1869, however, a wide-flung controversy was initiated that was to continue with ever-increasing intensity up to and beyond the meeting of the Council itself. The spark which set the controversy alight was an article that appeared in the organ of the Roman Jesuits, the *Civiltà Cattolica,* on February 6th. [17] The article was presumably no more than a *ballon d'essai* sent up to test in what direction the wind of Catholic opinion was blowing : but the close connection between the Roman Jesuits and the Vatican gave it significance. It took the form of a " letter from France " and prophesied that the Council would be short, would proclaim the doctrines of the Syllabus in a positive instead of a negative form and would declare the Pope infallible by acclamation, i.e. unanimously and without serious discussion.

Immediately after the appearance of the article Antonelli disclaimed all responsibility for it, and the Pope declared privately that the *Civiltà* was in no sense the organ of the Holy See. Two months later the *Civiltà* itself disclaimed responsibility for the contents of the " letter." But the sensation was profound, and the misgivings of the opponents of Infallibility were deepened. Dupanloup at once published two articles in his new journal, the *Français,* strongly deprecating all such attempts to anticipate the findings of the Council. [18] It was in Germany, however, that the infallibilist designs provoked the most formidable counter-attack. From March 10th to 15th Döllinger published a series of articles in the *Allgemeine Zeitung* of Augsburg in which he foreshadowed the disastrous results that a proclamation of the Infallibility would produce in the Catholic world. His attitude was shared by a large body of German Catholics. The German bishops, while including a certain number of Infallibilists, were on the whole opposed to the idea of a definition. In particular, the most erudite of them all, Hefele, Bishop of Rottenburg, the eminent historian of past councils and regarded as, with Döllinger, the chief light of German Catholic learning, shared to the full the attitude of the great Münich scholar.

[17] Text in Ollivier, i. 404.   [18] Lagrange, iii. 125.

It was, however, the influence of Döllinger and his friends with the Bavarian Government that constituted the chief danger of their opposition. There had always been a fear that the European Governments might intervene in regard to the proceedings of the Council: and now for a moment there appeared a possibility that this fear might be realized. On April 9th the Bavarian Foreign Minister, Prince Hohenlohe, alarmed at the developments of the last two months and responding to pressure from Döllinger and others, issued to the Bavarian foreign representatives a circular despatch requesting them to call the attention of the various Governments to the Council, and to suggest joint action in view of the menace to modern ideas and State-rights involved in its possible decisions. [19]

The suggestion, however, met with no success. Austria declined from fear of appearing to threaten the freedom of the Council. Prussia also declined: in her opinion the question of Infallibility was a purely spiritual matter. Belgium, Italy, Spain and Portugal followed suit. The French Government asked for time to consider. Even the Gallican Baroche shrank from a step that might have such far-reaching consequences; while the Emperor was anxious not to alienate the clerical party. The result of the elections of 1869 increased this unwillingness. At length, on October 19th, the new Foreign Minister, Prince de la Tour d'Auvergne, informed the French ambassador at Rome [20] that the Government had no intention of sending an ambassador to the Council. Communication would be made *"par les organes habituels."* On purely spiritual questions it had no opinion to express. But in view of the Ultramontane tendency to " increase the prerogatives of the Roman pontiff to an exaggerated extent *(démesurement)* " and thus " to make the power of the bishops almost purely nominal," it declared its determination to stand firmly by the Concordat. Any interference, too, with " our political and

---

[19] Ollivier, i. 511f. English translation of Hohenlohe's despatch *in extenso* in Butler, *op. cit.*, i. 97. The original documents relating to the attitudes of the Governments in 1869 are all printed in full in *Collectio Lacensis Conciliorum recentiorum*, vii. 1199-1253.

[20] Complete text of despatch in Ollivier, 519ff.

social settlement " might have serious consequences. " The
government of the Empire is founded on the modern ideas of
progress, liberty and toleration." If a declaration was to be
made on the subject of Infallibility it hoped that its terms
would be " framed with an extreme moderation." No difficulty was made about according permission to the French
bishops to attend the Council : and on November 29th the
Emperor, in his opening speech of the legislative session, expressed his conviction that " from the assembly at Rome of
the bishops of the Catholic world nothing but a work of
prudence and conciliation should be expected." [21]

Meanwhile the controversy on the Infallibility had been
growing more and more animated on both sides. In Germany
the laity had begun to move. At Coblentz on May 18th a
" laymen's address " was drawn up for presentation to the
Bishop of Trier and the Archbishop of Cologne, deprecating
the revival of the theocratic aspirations of the Middle Ages,
and expressing the hope that the bishops would rather concentrate on a revival of the ancient national, provincial and
diocesan synods and the establishment of better relations
between the Church and the State. The address delighted
Montalembert, who wrote an enthusiastic letter of congratulation to the promoters on their " glorious manifestation of the
conscience and reason of the Catholics of old time," which
he described as " a light in the midst of darkness." [22] Veuillot
thereupon accused him of having " passed over to the Volsci."
The excitement was increased by the publication at the end of
July of the famous book called *The Pope and the Council,* [23]
in which Döllinger, under the pseudonym of " Janus," recast
his articles of the previous March into a devastating attack
on the Infallibility from a historical point of view.

Soon afterwards the German bishops came into the field.
It was arranged that they should meet at Fulda early in
September to deliberate on the line to be adopted by them at
the Council. Hearing of this, Dupanloup at once wrote them

[21] Ollivier, i. 531.
[22] July 1869. Lecanuet, iii. 437.
[23] English translation, 1869.

a short note designed to facilitate joint action on the part of the more moderate members of the French and German episcopates. [24] He also paid visits to various German bishops and incidentally met Döllinger, much to the scandal of the Ultramontanes. On September 6th the German bishops assembled at Fulda issued a pastoral letter declaring their conviction that the Council would neither promulgate new dogmas nor attack in any way the existing constitution of society. They also addressed a secret memorandum to the Pope (not, however, signed by all of them) in which they urged that a declaration of the Infallibility at the moment would be altogether inopportune, and expressed the hope that the Holy Father would not entertain the idea. The letter naturally gave great offence at Rome.

In France the controversy was exacerbated by the appearance (in September) of a book by Maret, *Du Concile général et de la paix réligieuse*. While not absolutely denying the Infallibility, he maintained that it could not exist without the consent (express or tacit) of the episcopate: otherwise a monarchy tempered by aristocracy would be converted into an absolute monarchy. [25] The book was furiously attacked by the *Univers*, which received the support of several bishops.

At this moment an unfortunate incident put into the hands of the Ultramontanes a weapon which they rejoiced to use to the uttermost. The eloquent Carmelite, Père Hyacinthe, who had been installed by Darboy in the pulpit of Notre Dame and was on terms of intimate friendship with Montalembert, declared his intention to quit his Order. For some time his faith in the Church had been wavering: and now the dark possibilities of the Council gave it its deathblow. Montalembert and Dupanloup had sought to bring him back to submission, but in vain. When the final step was taken the former addressed to him a heartbroken letter of bitterest reproach telling him that " by betraying his friends " he had " betrayed our cause, the cause of liberty." [26] From all sides

[24] Lagrange, iii. 130.
[25] Ollivier, i. 408f.
[26] Printed *in extenso,* Lecanuet, iii. 449ff.

abuse and curses rained upon the unhappy renegade. But one utterance stands out amid the fierce uncharity of the time. Darboy, when asked to condemn him, replied, " Père Hyacinthe must be suffering greatly at present. It is not kind to trample on those who suffer." [27]

As for Dupanloup, the incident would appear to have at once hardened his determination and roused his temper. On October 3rd he had a secret interview with the Emperor at St. Cloud. What happened he never told : but it was generally believed that the monitory tone of Prince de la Tour d'Auvergne's despatch on October 17th was the result of this colloquy, in which presumably the Bishop set himself to excite Napoleon against the designs of the Ultramontanes. Meanwhile the *Univers* was organizing a vast petition of Catholics, priests and laity, praying the Council to proclaim the Infallibility. By way of reassuring moderate opinion Darboy issued a pastoral (October 28th), in which he declared that " both good sense and history protested " against such a step. The Council, he said, would " only define things generally admitted " : nor were modern liberties in danger. [28] On November 10th Dupanloup in turn published a pastoral, in which he promised that the Council would effect a work of " unity, truth and charity." [29] But his *Observations sur la controverse soulevée rélativement à la définition de l'infaillibilité*, published soon afterwards, were pitched in a very different key.[30] In these, while not calling in question the Infallibility itself, he declared in the strongest terms against the opportuneness of its definition at the present time, and animadverted severely on two recent pastorals by Archbishop Deschamps and Manning, the latter of whom had been tactless enough to appeal to the French bishops to " stand forth to lead the voices of the episcopate " in demanding it. [31] The controversy was continued at Rome during the Council. Even Falloux and others of his friends were of opinion that the

[27] Foulon, *Histoire de Mgr. Darboy*, 311.
[28] *Ibid.*, 438.
[29] Lagrange, iii. 140ff.
[30] *Ibid.*, 143.
[31] Butler, i. 146, 149.

Bishop would have done better to reserve his remarks for the Council itself. [32] As for the *Univers,* it leaped joyfully on its prey. Dupanloup then lost his temper completely and addressed to Veuillot personally a withering *Avertissement,* [33] in which he assailed his " deplorable taste for irritating questions and dangerous solutions." " No one," he wrote, " has merited more than you the severe word of the sacred Scriptures, *Accusator fratrum.* Above all I reproach you with making the Church participate in your violences by giving as its doctrines with rare audacity your most personal ideas."

Bitter however as was Dupanloup's animosity against the Ultramontanes, that of the now dying Montalembert was more bitter still. Towards the end of 1868 the outbreak of the Revolution in Spain had provoked him to write a lengthy article for the *Correspondant,* in which he once again proclaimed defiantly the doctrines of Malines and upbraided the Jesuits of the *Civiltà* for their hatred of liberty. The article was so outspoken that his colleagues refused to insert it. Whereupon Montalembert resigned his collaboration. "Henceforth," he wrote, " I know the *Correspondant* no more." [34] Condemned to silence, he liberated his soul in countless letters in all directions.

II

It is impossible within the limits of the present book to give a full account of the complicated happenings of the Council of 1869-70. All that can be attempted is to present a brief account of the more important stages of its history, with special reference to the part played by the French bishops and (in the background) by the French Government.

The bishops who attended the Council from all over the world were divided into three parties. There was, first, an Infallibilist majority, the leaders of which were two Archbishops, Deschamps of Malines and Manning of Westminster. Among the French bishops, the most important members of

---

[32] Falloux, *Mémoires,* ii. 422.
[33] Printed by Veuillot himself in the appendix to his *Rome pendant le Concile,* 551ff.
[34] Lecanuet, iii. 440ff.

this group were Pie of Poitiers, Plantier of Nîmes, and Cardinal Donnet of Bordeaux. Next came an Anti-infallibilist (or more properly Inopportunist) minority. Of this the leading figures were, among the German bishops, Cardinals Rauscher of Vienna and Schwarzenberg of Prague, Hefele, Bishop of Rottenburg, Haynald, Bishop of Colocza (Hungary), and Strossmayer, Bishop of Bosnia-Sirmium; and among the French bishops, Dupanloup, Darboy, Mathieu (Cardinal Archbishop of Besançon) and Ginouhliac of Grenoble.[35] To these two main groups was added what Ollivier calls a *tiers parti*, composed of French bishops, such as Cardinal Bonne-chose (Rouen), Guibert (Tours), Lavigerie (Algiers), and Forcade (Nevers). This group was to play an important part in the evolution of events.

The number of Cardinals, Bishops, Abbots and heads of religious Orders present at the opening of the Council in St. Peter's on December 8th, 1869, was 679; and rose by January 6th to 750. Of the total, well over 200 were Italian. This preponderance of the Italian bishops (Infallibilist almost to a man) was, however inevitable, a very sore point to the minority. "In Church matters," it was complained, "twenty German bishops count for less than one Italian."[36]

The method of procedure had been laid down by the Pope himself in a *regolamento, Multiplices inter,* dated November 27th.[37] This was a deliberate departure from the precedent of the Council of Trent, which had helped to settle its own procedure. The Pope explicitly abrogated not only the pontifical constitutions contrary to the present dispositions, but also the canons of previous General Councils. As Ollivier remarks, "This was more than to claim the sovereign power: it was to exercise it."

In addition to those of the commissions that were to prepare the *schemata,* or draft-projects, the meetings of the Council were to be of two kinds—general congregations and public

[35] Ginouhliac was promoted to the Archbishopric of Lyons during the Council.
[36] Quirinus, 141. The calculation was not very accurate. Six to one would have been nearer the mark.
[37] Printed in Mansi, l. 215* (= xlix. 1271)ff. Ollivier, i. 493f.

sessions. Only to the latter was the public to be admitted. The *schemata* prepared by the theologians in secret were to be distributed to the bishops some days before the general congregation at which they were to be discussed. If a *schema* were found in discussion to require recasting, it was to be referred to one of four permanent "deputations" to be elected by the Council, with (in each case) a president nominated by the Pope. This was to go on until the Council was satisfied. The decree stated that the right of proposal belonged in strictness to the Pope, but it was graciously permitted to bishops to suggest written proposals, which must, however, be referred to a congregation of initiative or *postulata*, which would examine them and report to the Pope. The Pope would then decide. Strict silence was imposed on all concerned as regards both *schemata* and discussions: but this injunction was more honoured in the breach than in the observance. All Rome buzzed with the doings of the Council, and even the ladies did their share. Veuillot nicknamed the latter " *les commères du Concile.*" [38]

The election of the four deputations mentioned above provided the opposing factions with an immediate opportunity of testing their strength. The results brought little comfort to the minority. The all-important congregation of *postulata*— nominated by the Pope himself—was the first to have its composition made known (December 10th). It was preponderantly infallibilist. Manning, Deschamps and Bonnechose were among those nominated. A few days later the result of the election of the pivotal deputation *de Fide* revealed the fact that not a single member of the opposition had been chosen, apart from one elected by mistake. [39] In the deputation on discipline the minority was but feebly represented. Well might Veuillot exclaim, " The Council is Ultramontane! "

Just before the opening of the Council the bishops of the minority had appointed an international committee in order to secure unity of action. The president of this was Cardinal

---

[38] Purcell, *Life of Manning,* ii. 428.
[39] Abbot Butler considers this " the one serious blot " on the Council's doings. The responsibility was apparently Manning's. The Pope himself did not wish it. Butler, i. 172f. Cf. ii. 52.

Rauscher: and Darboy and Dupanloup were among the prelates included. The first idea was to attack the Pope's *regolamento*. But this was abandoned, and the bishops contented themselves with complaining of certain details. It was also decided to attack the first *schema de Fide*, which was to be brought up for discussion at the general congregation of December 28th. The discussion was lively and lasted several days. It had been hoped that the *schema* might be accepted in time for its promulgation at the public session on January 6th. But the criticism to which it was subjected (notably by Strossmayer) made this impossible. The session of January 6th thus found itself with nothing to do, apart from the tedious performance of 750 prelates making each a separate profession of the Tridentine confession of faith to the Pope in person.

If the extreme papalist party in the Council had ever entertained a hope that the Infallibility might be proclaimed quickly and "by acclamation,"[40] it was tolerably clear by the beginning of January that the minority was at least strong and determined enough to put such an eventuality out of the question. It was necessary, therefore, to fall back on the slower and less spectacular procedure permitted by the papal *regolamento*. The Pope, though convinced of his own infallibility, was determined at all costs to avoid taking the initiative himself: for (as Ollivier says) " to have asked the Council to decree his infallibility would, *ipso facto,* have destroyed it, by recognizing the superiority of the episcopate."[41]   What, therefore, the Pope could not do for himself his partisans must do for him. On January 3rd Manning and other Infallibilists circulated a *postulatum* in favour of Infallibility with a view to collecting signatures in its support.

Having succeeded in their first attempt, the minority continued their " blocking " process—the only resource that seemed available in view of the large majority arrayed against them. The discussion of the first *schema de Fide* was prolonged till January 10th, when it was referred back to the de-

---

[40] On this see Butler, ii. 34. Undoubtedly, as Butler says, the fear of it " haunted the minds of the minority like a bogy."
[41] Ollivier, i. 535.

putation with instructions to prepare a new text. The same fate also befell thee other *schemata* which came up in turn for discussion—(1) on the Episcopal Office (January 14th—25th), designed to make the episcopate still more dependent on the Holy See; (2) on the Clerical Life (January 25th—February 8th), and (3) on the Little Catechism (February 10th —22nd). Dupanloup spoke on the first and third of these, in his second speech strongly opposing a scheme that seemed designed to use a universal catechism imposed by Rome as a means of propagatingUltramontanism throughout the Church.

It was clear by this time that the papal *regolamento* had failed to achieve its purpose of expediting the discussions, which at this rate might drag on indefinitely. The Pope therefore had already instructed the presiding Cardinals to take counsel with the congregation of *postulata* with a view to drawing up a new procedure. The new *regolamento* appeared on February 22nd.

A further effect of these debates was to kill the theory of " inopportunity." " *Quod dixerunt inopportunum,*" it was said, " *fecerunt necessarium.*" [42] The strength of this feeling was shown by the fact that the *postulatum* for Infallibility collected some 380 signatures, as against only 140 in favour of a counter-*postulatum* circulated by the opposition.

The Council itself seemed for the moment to have come to a standstill. But outside events were moving. The text of the *postulatum* of January 3rd in favour of the definition of Infallibility got abroad, and was published in the *Allgemeine Zeitung* on January 21st. Döllinger, abandoning his anonymity, at once made a protest in its columns against the attempt to impose on Catholics under anathema a doctrine which the Church as a whole had never believed or taught. [43] His protest was widely approved in Germany, where he became almost a popular hero. A similar intervention was made in France by the saintly Oratorian and Academician, Père Gratry, the philosopher of the Liberal Catholic group. For

[42] *Ibid.,* ii. 66. Cf. a letter of Ullathorne's dated February 4th in Butler, *Life of Bishop Ullathorne,* ii. 60 (also 69f).
[43] Part of the article is quoted in Butler, i. 207.

over twenty years Gratry, like Maret, had sought to vindicate the claims of a "reasonable faith" against the traditionalism and scorn of human reason characteristic of Ultramontane thought. From a different angle he now, in three successive letters, assailed "the school of lies and error" which flouted history by ignoring the indubitable fact that at least one Pope, Honorius, had been declared guilty of heresy, and had in the past resorted to "forgeries" and "fabricated documents" in support of its position. [44] From his deathbed Montalembert sent an enthusiastic congratulation to the "eloquent and intrepid priest."

A graver development was the renewal of the danger of diplomatic intervention by France. This was the more to be feared because the Council was in a sense at its mercy: for only the French army of occupation kept the Italians out of Rome. On January 2nd the Ollivier ministry had come into office. Ollivier himself was strong for complete abstention— in his eyes the Infallibility was a purely spiritual question. But the Foreign Minister, Comte Daru, who was a Liberal Catholic and had been closely associated with Montalembert and his group, was in favour of intervention if necessary. The Emperor was inclined to the same view, but was willing to go with Ollivier and the majority of the ministry. The Cabinet decided not to intervene as long as the Concordat was not violated: and Daru on January 11th defended this attitude in the Senate.

The French minority bishops, however, continued to hope that an intervention might take place, as the only means of checkmating the minority. Darboy determined to make a personal appeal to the Emperor. It was he and not the noisy Dupanloup who was the real leader of the French anti-infallibilists in the Council. It seems probable too that, unlike Dupanloup, he not only held the definition of Infallibility to be inopportune but disbelieved in the Infallibility itself. Already in the congregation of January 14th he had made a scathing attack on the limitation of the powers of the epis-copate involved in the *schema de Sede Episcopali*. Twelve

[44] Ollivier, ii. 55ff.

days later (January 26th) he wrote a letter to Napoleon III., [45]
in which he made strong representation of the limits imposed
on the Council's freedom by the papal *regolamento* and incidentally complained of the acoustics of the Council Aula,
which (he said) made much of the discussions practically
nugatory. He urged that the Imperial Government should do
at least something to back up the minority—if only by way of
a warning in the Corps Législatif. Ollivier, however, decided to
do nothing in the matter, and was confirmed in his resolution
by an interview between the Minister of Worship and Lavigerie, who was paying a flying visit to Paris. "An immense
majority," said the Archbishop, " is assured to the Infallibility.
Quoiqu'on tente elle aura lieu! " [46]   The policy of abstention
was therefore maintained, especially as Daru had already
(January 17th) instructed the French ambassador at Rome,
de Banneville, to express to Antonelli his " apprehensions "
and the need of moderation. [47]

A fresh leakage of the conciliar proceedings seemed likely
for a moment to change the situation.   On February 10th the
Allgemeine Zeitung was able to publish the text of the *schema
de Ecclesia* with its accompanying twenty-one canons imposed
under anathema. [48]   It laid down that the government of the
Church belongs in perpetuity to the Bishop of Rome, and that
this government is " not merely an office of inspection and
direction but a full and supreme power over the Universal
Church "—" an ordinary and immediate jurisdiction over
each and all the Churches " (canon 16).   It condemned the
principles that " the Church should tolerate all religions " (6),
and that " it has the right only to persuade rebels and sinners,
not to compel them by exterior penalties " (12), as also any
subjection whatever of the Church to the secular power. This
appeared to be the Syllabus over again. The Austrian

---

[45] Printed in Ollivier, ii. 91ff. Of it Cardinal Foulon says: "*Notre
impartialitè nous fait un devoir de ne point passer sous silence cette lettre,
qui incontestablement donne lieu à de graves réserves* "! (p. 461).

[46] Ollivier, ii. 96.

[47] Text of despatch in *ibid.,* 89f.

[48] Text in Mansi, li. 539—53. See also Ollivier's analysis of it, *ibid.,*
102ff.

Premier informed Antonelli of his " inquietude " and declared
that he would forbid the publication of any act " contrary to
the majesty of the law." [49]   As for Ollivier, while recognizing
the gravity of the canons concerning Church and State, he
was still of opinion that intervention was unnecessary : the
situation could be dealt with in other ways. [50]

Daru took a different view.   He prepared a despatch to
de Banneville which he submitted to the Emperor, but not to
Ollivier.   The despatch declared that the *schema* would make
the Church supreme over the State and constitute the infallible
Pope the arbiter of political and social rights.   After it had
been sent off (February 20th) he told the Cabinet what he had
said.   His colleagues thought that his note had been too
strongly worded.   It was therefore recalled and, as the result
of criticism and discussion by the Cabinet, considerably toned
down—" *émondée, édulcorée, énervée,*" [51] to use Ollivier's
own expression.   In its revised form [52] it still complained of
the *schema* as a challenge to the civil power, but ended tamely
by merely asking for the communication of documents and
the right to make observations.   Daru personally desired to
send an Ambassador Extraordinary to the Council as the
channel by which such observations should be made, and expressed himself in this sense to the foreign governments in
communicating his note.   But Ollivier was against this and
persuaded the Emperor to share his views.   He also let it be
known that no " *acte sérieux* " would follow. [53]   The foreign
governments, while consenting as a matter of courtesy to ask
Rome to consider Daru's note, declined to demand representation at the Council.   Thus, in replying to Daru's note
(March 19th) Antonelli, who knew all about the disagreement
in the French Cabinet, felt himself in a position to take a high
line. [54]   He expressed his surprise that the *schema* should have
excited such alarm and intimated that there was no valid

[49] Ollivier, ii. 102.   Butler, ii. 4.
[50] Ollivier, ii. 124.
[51] *Ibid.,* 126.
[52] Complete text *ibid.,* 551ff.
[53] *Ibid.,* 131.
[54] Text in *ibid.,* 195f.

reason why it should be withdrawn. It merely represented, he said, the traditional doctrine of the Church.

Meanwhile at the Council the new papal *regolamento*[55] of February 22nd, designed to shorten the debates, had come into operation. It laid down that the bishops instead of making speeches were to present to the competent deputation, some time before the discussion came on, their written observations on the proposals submitted to them. The deputation was to examine these observations and revise the proposals accordingly; then on bringing forward the revised proposals to indicate the objections alleged. The real discussion was only then to begin. It was to follow a fixed order and might be terminated by the closure, if the majority signified its desire to that effect. It was also laid down that at the final votings in a general congregation three kinds of vote were to be permitted : *Placet, Non placet* and *Placet juxta modum*. Those who voted in the last form were to give their reasons for doing so in writing to the commission, in order that their objections might be weighed before the project was submitted to the public session, at which the voting must be either *Placet* or *Non placet*. It was also decreed that ordinarily a simple majority was sufficient and that therefore the " moral unanimity " demanded by the opposition was not required.

These changes in the procedure of the Council were much resented by the minority. They believed that they were aimed at themselves, and saw how much they would hinder that policy of obstruction which seemed their only resource within the Council itself. At once five groups of bishops (the French group numbered thirty) drew up separate protests against the new *regolamento* ; the total number who signed amounting to ninety. But the protest was without practical effect.

III

On March 6th, in response to the *postulatum* of two months before, the *schema* on Infallibility was distributed to the Fathers as a supplement to the chapters on the Roman Primacy

[55] Printed in Mansi, li. 13f. See also Ollivier, ii. 79ff.

in the *schema de Ecclesia*. An accompanying *monitum* informed the bishops that very many *(plurimi)* had prayed the Pope to bring the Infallibility before the Council and required them to send in their observations on the new *schema* before March 17th. [56]

Six days later (March 12th) the Pope left no room for further doubt as to the side on which his own sympathies were engaged. In a letter to Dom Guéranger congratulating him on his book, *De la Monarchie pontificale* (written in answer to Maret's book of the previous September), " the tricks, the calumnies, the sophisms " of the opponents of Infallibility were denounced in a fine flow of vituperation. [57] The temper of the Holy Father had not been improved by a letter of Montalembert's [58] (published at the writer's request in the *Gazette de France* on March 7th) in which he expressed to his correspondent, a M. Lallemand, his detestation of those who " began by treating as naught *(faire litière de)* all our liberties, all our principles, all our ideas of days gone by, before Napoleon III., only at last to immolate justice and truth, reason and history, as a holocaust to the idol that has been set up in the Vatican."

Within a week of the publication of this letter Montalembert was dead (March 12th). But the wrath of Pius IX. was not appeased. On hearing the news he remarked, " A man is dead who had rendered great services to the Church. . . . But that man had a great enemy—pride." When Montalembert's brother-in-law, Mérode, arranged for a solemn service in his memory at the Ara Cœli, the Cardinal Vicar of Rome forbade it. Some days later, however, the Pope ordered a service at Santa Maria Transpontina (the parish church of the Vatican), without saying for whom, and was present himself behind a grille. [59] It should be added that Montalembert had

---

[56] Mansi, li. 543, 701. For purposes of comparison see Butler, ii. 133, where the three official Infallibility formulæ: (1) that circulated March 6th, (2) that circulated May 9th, (3) that finally adopted, are tabulated in parallel columns.

[57] Quoted in Ollivier, ii. 170.

[58] The whole letter is printed in Lecanuet, iii. 466ff.

[59] Lecanuet, iii. 475.

always said that, if the Infallibility were voted, he would accept it not merely *extérieurement* but *ex animo*. [60]

The definite emergence of the Infallibility at the Council and the reply of Antonelli to Daru's note of February 20th raised afresh the question of diplomatic intervention by France. The three sections of the French episcopate sent each its representatives to Paris. The infallibilists assured the Government that there was no ground for alarm, the anti-infallibilists pressed for intervention, while the *tiers parti* (represented by Forcade of Nevers) thought that the situation would be sufficiently met by the appointment of a prelate committed to neither party as "protector of the crown of France." [61] The Government, after due consideration, decided (in deference to Daru's wishes) to send a memorandum to the Pope with a request that he would communicate it to the Council. The memorandum [62] gave renewed expression to the misgivings enunciated in the note. But the Government adhered to its opinion (without saying so, however) that the Infallibility was a purely spiritual question: and the memorandum ended by stating that "the declaration of the principles contemplated could not entail any serious consequences. . . . The necessity of the time will condemn such decrees to remain in the status of a dead letter." No mention was made of withdrawing the French troops from Rome. The memorandum was despatched on April 6th: and it was at the same time communicated to the foreign governments with a request that they would support it diplomatically.

Forcade at once returned to Rome to ask the Pope and Antonelli, on behalf of the Government, to give favourable consideration to the memorandum. The other Cabinets without exception supported it. But when the French ambassador presented it to the Pope on April 22nd, the latter replied that he could not bring such a document before the Council. [63] He knew by this time that the memorandum was more than ever a *brutum fulmen*. On April 11th Daru had

[60] *Ibid.*, 471.
[61] Ollivier, ii. 201ff.
[62] Full text in *ibid.*, 558ff.
[63] *Ibid.*, 220.

resigned, and Ollivier took his place temporarily as Foreign Minister. At once a telegram was sent off to Rome: " Daru resigns, Ollivier takes his place, the Council is free." [64] Even so, however, the *Univers* refused to be satisfied. A plebiscite was imminent in France : and the Ultramontanes sought to obtain from the Government, in return for their support, a disavowal of the memorandum and a declaration that the French troops should never leave Rome. Ollivier refused the bargain ; whereupon the *Univers* advised its readers to abstain from voting. [65] At the same time the Government was blamed from the other side for not having made the memorandum strong enough. Ollivier himself admits " the disproportion between the premises and the conclusion." [66] The Emperor for his part would have liked to take a stronger line. When Gratry in June urged him to this effect, he replied : " I sympathize with you : but what am I to do in face of an episcopate of which the majority repudiates my intervention ? " [67]

Meanwhile the debates in the Council were proceeding. The discussion of the now much revised *schema de Fide* was begun on March 18th. An exciting scene occurred on March 22nd, when Strossmayer aroused the disapproval of the majority by defending Protestantism against the charge of being the parent of Rationalism, and was nearly howled down when he went on to declare that nothing less than " moral unanimity " could bind the consciences of Catholics. In the end the President told him to stand down. [68] The *schema* was passed on April 11th, eighty-three Fathers voting *placet juxta modum* but none *non placet*. Having undergone certain further modifications it was finally voted unanimously at the third public session on April 24th. [69]

What was to be done next ? For more than a month the

[64] Ollivier, ii. 225.
[65] *Ibid.*, 226f.
[66] *Ibid.*, 212.
[67] *Ibid.*, 238.
[68] For an account of this incident (summarized from Mansi, li. 72) see Butler, i. 270f. The author calls it the one real " scene " in the Council.
[69] The Constitution as voted is printed (Latin text with English translation opposite) in Butler, ii. 248ff.

majority had been trying by means of a series of petitions to the Pope to get the question of Infallibility brought on at once. The minority counter-petitioned against this : and on April 23rd Dupanloup wrote a personal letter [70] to the Pope, urging that " nothing could be more dangerous." The Pope, however, decided to accede to the majority's wishes : and on April 29th an announcement was made to this effect. Circumstances, however, compelled the revised *schema* on the Little Catechism to be dealt with first. This was carried on May 4th.

Outside the Council the controversy on Infallibility continued unabated. The Comte de Chambord delighted the French Ultramontanes by intimating to the Pope his attachment to the " infallible representative of Jesus Christ." [71] Far more important was the publication in March of a private letter [72] (dated January 28th) which Newman had written to his friend and diocesan, Bishop Ullathorne of Birmingham, condemning the agitation for Infallibility and asking " why an aggressive and insolent faction should be allowed to make the hearts of the just to mourn whom the Lord has not made sorrowful." A new sensation was created a little later by the publication in Paris of a book called *Ce qui se passe au Concile*, denouncing in lurid language the partial way in which the proceedings of the Council had been conducted.

The time was now come for the Council itself to debate the Infallibility. On May 9th the revised *schema de Ecclesia* was distributed to the Fathers. It was only a part of the original *schema*; the portions dealing with the relations between Church and State being omitted and deferred for later consideration, as likely to cause complications and delay. The new version dealt exclusively with the authority of the Pope.

[70] Eng. tr. (with the Pope's reply) in Butler, ii. 40 from original in Mourret, *Concile du Vatican*, 270.

[71] Ollivier, ii. 265.

[72] Letter printed in full in Ward, *Life of Cardinal Newman*, ii. 287f. For the circumstances of its divulgement see Ullathorne's own letter to Newman in Butler, *Life of Bishop Ullathorne*, ii. 61f. Newman regarded the Infallibility as " practically certain " (*ibid.*, 47), but opposed its definition as likely to create fresh difficulties in the way of non-Catholics joining the Church. His view was thus the same as that of the minority —Inopportunist.

It consisted of a proem and four chapters. The first three dealt with the Primacy of the Roman Pontiff; while in the fourth the Infallibility was clearly set out. The debate was opened on May 13th by Pie, speaking as a member of the deputation *de Fide*. In the course of this he was inspired to bring forward a new argument for Infallibility based on the legendary story of the manner of St. Peter's death. Not only was he crucified, not beheaded, as a sign of the indissoluble union between the Church and its Head, but he was crucified *head downwards,* to show that the Pope as Head bears up the whole Church. [73] This remarkable utterance evoked the warm felicitations of the Pope.

The discussion thus initiated lasted till June 3rd, when it was ended by the closure at the behest of a large majority. Some eighty French and German bishops protested against the closure, but in vain. Of the speeches made, those of Manning (defending the definition) and Darboy [74] (against it) were the most important. The minority (as Ollivier remarks [75]) would have been in a stronger position if, following the Gallican Articles, they had taken their stand on the Council of Constance and maintained that the question had there been settled for good and all. Darboy would probably have been prepared to take this line: but he knew that, if he did, the minority as a whole would refuse to follow him. He did, however, what he could. Besides speaking against the definition he wrote again to the Emperor (May 21st), urging that the Government should take some overt step to "give a moral support" to the minority and suggesting the recall of the French ambassador to the Holy See as a suitable expedient. [76] But Ollivier's mind was finally made up.

The Council next gave itself to a particular discussion of the several sections of the *schema*—the "committee stage," so to speak. The chapters on the Primacy were considered first (June 6th—14th): then, on June 15th, the debate on the

---

[73] Complete speech in Mansi, lii. 35f.
[74] French translation in Ollivier, ii. 284ff. English tr. in Quirinus, Appendix i., p. 819ff.
[75] Ollivier, ii. 308f.
[76] Letter printed in *ibid.,* ii. 236f.

Infallibility began. The minority continued their opposition. If (as now seemed the case) it was impossible to prevent the definition, at least it might be feasible to mitigate its terms. Their efforts received an unexpected reinforcement in a speech of the learned Dominican Cardinal Guidi, in which he propounded a canon affirming that the Pope, in defining matters of faith and morals, " acts not *ex arbitrio* and by himself . . . but by the counsel of the bishops as manifesting the tradition of the Churches." [77] For this the Cardinal was summoned into the Pope's presence and angrily rebuked. His speech was stigmatized as " unworthy and heretical." When Guidi defended himself by appealing to tradition, the Pope retorted " *La tradizione son'io.*" [78]

By this time Pius IX. (to apply Randolph Churchill's famous jibe at Gladstone) was " an old man in a hurry." In the early days of the Council he had said to Cardinal Schwarzenberg : " I, Gian Mastai, I believe in Infallibility ; as Pope, I have nothing to ask of the Council ; the Holy Spirit will enlighten it." [79] The time was now come to assist the Spirit's working by broadcasting his personal conviction to the world. Every device of cajolery, of congratulation, of rebuke was resorted to in order to make the pontifical wishes known and to hasten the definition. Already the Pope had publicly congratulated Veuillot (May 19th), [80] and addressed letters of thanks to the clergy of various French bishops of the minority for their zeal for his prerogatives. [81] He now went on to dismiss the erudite Jesuit, Theiner, from his post as keeper of the papal archives on a charge of aiding and abetting the opposition. He supported the clergy of Marseilles in their resistance to their anti-infallibilist bishop. He praised the lower clergy of France for their enthusiastic support of his Infallibility. [82] When attempts were made to

[77] Butler, ii. 96.
[78] Ollivier, ii. 326. Mourret, 299, quoting Dupanloup's diary.
[79] Ollivier, i. 535.
[80] Text in *ibid.*, ii. 311.
[81] Texts in *ibid.*, 312.
[82] See *ibid.*, 326 ; also 609f. Butler regards this personal intervention of the Pope as "very regrettable "—and also (with truth) as " quite unnecessary." ii. 204.

induce him to adjourn the Council till the autumn, on the ground that the heat of Rome in summer was making many of the bishops ill, he flatly refused. The Council, he said, would go on till the *schema* was voted. Veuillot was delighted and exclaimed ecstatically, " *On grillera.*" [83]

By the first week in July everyone was weary of the debate —the minority included. The phrase " *Il faut en finir* " was heard on all lips. Even the knowledge that war between France and Germany was imminent, and might compel the adjournment of the Council by forcing the bishops of those countries to return home, was insufficient to reanimate the minority, while it increased the resolve of the majority to achieve a final settlement at once. Negotiations were set on foot between the two parties for a closure of the discussion by agreement. Dupanloup was furious : but the compact was made. On June 11th the deputation *de Fide* proposed a new draft of the constitution, designed to give some satisfaction to the minority by making it clear that the Infallibility was official and not personal and had never been used but to preserve the *depositum fidei*—not to promulgate new doctrines. The minority would have desired more : but the majority would make no further concessions. Two days later the Council voted on the whole *schema*. The voting was as follows : *Placet* 451, *Non placet* 88, *Placet juxta modum* 62. In accordance with the *regolamento* of February 22nd, the *schema* was referred back to the deputation with a view to meeting the wishes of those who had given a qualified approval. [84] It emerged with an important addition, and one most distasteful to the minority. To the declaration that the Pope's decisions were irreformable " *ex sese* " was added the phrase " *non autem ex consensu Ecclesiæ.*"

The night before the revised formula was to come before the general congregation for a final vote, a deputation of the minority, with Darboy as spokesman, visited the Pope and implored him to allow the inclusion of some such phrase as

[83] Quirinus, 733.
[84] Half of these desired the strengthening of the Definition, half that it should be toned down. Butler, ii. 154.

" *innixus testimonio Ecclesiæ.*" Ketteler of Mainz even fell on
his knees and wept. The Pope asked Darboy to put the wishes
of the minority into writing. This was done next day : but
the Pope was of opinion that it was too late to make any
change now. The same day (July 16th) the deputation's
formula was voted. It was then announced that the public
session for the final vote on the Infallibility would take place
on July 18th.

What were the minority to do now? Haynald declared
boldly for a *Non placet* vote and at first carried the rest with
him. But Dupanloup then came in and urged abstention
instead. [85] Finally it was agreed to compose a joint letter to the
Pope in which the signatories said that " out of filial love and
reverence " they would not vote *Non placet,* but would absent
themselves from the public session and go back to their flocks.
Only fifty-five bishops signed the document. [86] Next day, as
Dupanloup and Haynald were sitting in the same compart-
ment waiting for the train to start that would carry them away
from Rome, the latter remarked to his companion :
"Monseigneur, we have made a great mistake." [87] It was too
late to mend the mistake now. Nevertheless the pertinacity
of the minority had been by no means in vain. The designs
of the extreme infallibilists had been thwarted : and the
Definition emerged from the long battle in a moderate and
carefully limited shape. [88]

At the public session of July 18th the constitution *Pastor
Aeternus* [89] was finally voted, including the definition of the
Infallibility in the following form : " The Roman Pontiff,
when he speaks *ex cathedra* and when, in the exercise of his
office as pastor and teacher of all Christians, he defines by
virtue of his supreme apostolic authority the doctrine concerning faith and morals to be held by the universal Church,
is, by the divine assistance promised to him in the person of

---

[85] Mourret, *Concile du Vatican,* 307.
[86] Text in Ollivier, ii. 344f.
[87] Lagrange, iii. 184.
[88] See Ward, *W. G. Ward and the Catholic Revival,* 260ff. Cf. Ollivier,
ii., 371.
[89] Complete text [Latin and English] in Butler, ii. 276ff.

S. Peter, possessed of that infallibility wherewith the Divine Redeemer willed that His Church should be endowed [90] in defining doctrine concerning faith and morals : and that for this cause such definitions are irreformable of themselves and not because of the consent of the Church. And if any (which God forbid) should presume to contradict this our definition, let him be anathema."

Only two bishops voted *Non placet,* as against a majority of 533 in favour of the constitution. The voting took place to the accompaniment of a terrific thunderstorm, which was variously interpreted as a repetition of the approving thunders of Sinai or as the protest of heaven against human presumption, according to the view of the commentator.

The Council stood adjourned *sine die.* Next day France formally declared war on Germany. The French army of occupation was withdrawn early in August : and on September 20th the Italian troops entered Rome.

[90] This phrase was adopted because the precise scope of the Church's infallibility still remained to be defined at a later stage of the Council. This stage, however, was never reached. See Butler, ii. 142f.

CHAPTER VIII

THE NATIONAL ASSEMBLY AND THE CHURCH

1870—1876

AFTER the epoch-making events of the 'sixties, alike in the secular and the ecclesiastical sphere, the 'seventies come as somewhat of an anti-climax. Or it would be truer to say that they represent the process of settling down after the upheavals that preceded them—the slow return of Europe to a state of comparative equilibrium which, however unstable, was not to be seriously disturbed till 1914. By 1871 the welding of Germany through " blood and iron " into a single and mighty whole was an accomplished fact—a fact instrumented and sealed by a crushing victory over her age-long foe. Italy, too, was now one and free, and had won Rome at last for her capital through the (as it seemed) final extinction of the papal sovereignty. As for France, which for twenty years—if with ever diminishing effectiveness—had posed as the arbiter of Europe, the cruel defeat of 1870-1 had humbled her pride in the dust and shorn her of two of her fairest provinces. The Second Empire had collapsed in ruin and disgrace, and for several years the problem of her form of government was to remain unsettled. The Government of National Defence organized in 1870 in face of the crowning disaster of Sedan gave way early in 1871 to a quasi-republican regime which, in view of the strongly conservative and Clerical character of the Assembly that for the moment held the destinies of France in its hands, might well have given place to a restored Bourbon monarchy. But the monarchists misused and wasted their opportunity; the hostile eyes of Germany and Italy frowned upon their endeavours; and as time went on it became increasingly clear that a republic and not a monarchy was the Government that the nation as a whole really desired.

In the ecclesiastical sphere the sense of anti-climax is still more marked. The secular politics of the time, if less exciting and dramatic than those of the preceding decade, were big

with consequences for the future. But in the closing years of
Pius IX. the gaze of Rome seemed to be fixed entirely on the
past. Her invincible hostility to modern ideas was more in
evidence than ever. The long battle between Ultramontanism
and Gallicanism had been decided for good and all at the
Vatican Council. All that remained to do was to gather in the
spoils of victory : and this was done without much trouble. In
Germany the followers of Döllinger (but not Döllinger himself, albeit excommunicate) formed a schismatic body, the
" Old Catholics " : but in France not even this occurred.
The bishops who had been most anxious to prevent the definition of infallibility hastened to accept the *fait accompli*.
Ultramontanism became the order of the day among bishops
and lower clergy alike. The political circumstances of the
tim̭e assisted in this development : for as time went on the
incompatibility between the claims of the Church and the
rising Republic became ever more clearly marked, and there
seemed to be less and less room for a *via media*. Meanwhile,
the octogenarian Pope maintained his claim to the Temporal
Power, and angrily repudiating every offer of the Italian
Government assumed the rôle of the " prisoner of the
Vatican." The Powers and the Catholic world were besieged
by his repeated protestations; but without practical effect except to make the relations between France and her neighbours
more difficult. For the moment Rome, like her aged pontiff,
seemed to have sunk into the self-willed torpor of old age.
Visiting Rome in 1876, Cardinal Manning thus recorded his
impressions : " At this moment the Holy See seems to be
reduced very low in its counsellors and men of action. . . .
Six years have passed since 1870, and its organization has been
dying out year by year. I find some looking for miracles,
some for inaction and some for action. The inactive unite
with the first class in doing nothing, letting everything get
worse and speaking against those who would act as *con-
ciliatori*. . . . Are we to shut ourselves in like Noë and wait?
Or are we to act upon the world, as all the Pontiffs from Leo
the Great? " [1]

[1] Purcell, *Life of Manning*, ii. 575.

I [2]

It has been seen how in the closing days of the Vatican Council the profound interest excited throughout Europe by its deliberations suddenly gave way before the oncoming of an event which by its immense and tragic significance eclipsed every other topic of the time. The day after the voting of the Infallibility, France, her pride goaded to desperation by Bismarck's famous " Ems telegram," declared war on Germany (July 19th, 1870). The French and German bishops who had fought shoulder to shoulder at the Council to defeat the Infallibilist designs now found themselves ranged in opposing camps as the champions and hearteners of their respective nations. As is customary under such circumstances, the official representatives of religion in each country were profoundly convinced that its cause was just, and that God might be safely assumed to be fighting on its side.

The first of the French bishops to make a pronouncement was, as usual, Dupanloup. Immediately on his return from Rome he poured forth his soul in a pastoral letter [3] in which he appealed to the Almighty to " secure the triumph of justice by the hands of France." His fellow-bishops hastened to

---

[2] The story of the Church in France from 1870 to 1903 (the date of Leo XIII's death) has been admirably and fully told by the Oratorian biographer of Montalembert, Lecanuet, *L'Église de France sous la IIIme République*. There are four volumes: i. *Les dernières années du Pontificat de Pie IX.*, 1906. ii. *Les premières années du Pontificat de Léon XIII.*, 1910. iii. *Les signes avant-coureurs de la Séparation*. iv. *La Vie de l'Église sous Léon XIII.*, 1930. The work is interesting, full of information, amply documented and extremely moderate in tone. It supplies a valuable and needful corrective to the account of the same period written by the anticlerical historian, Debidour, *L'Église catholique et l'État sous la IIIme République*, Vol. i., 1906; Vol. ii., 1910. This work, like its predecessor, is brilliantly written and reliable enough so far as facts are concerned, but is again disfigured by a fanatical hatred of the Church. It appeared soon after the passing of the Separation Law; and was intended to justify the anticlerical campaign. The leading authority for the general history of France in the '70's is G. Hanotaux's great work, *Histoire de la France contemporaine*, 1903. Of this only four volumes were written, ending with Gambetta's death in 1882. Falloux, *Mémoires d'un royaliste;* Lagrange, *Dupanloup;* Veuillot, *Louis Veuillot;* and Baunard, *Cardinal Pie*, are again valuable —also Weill, *Histoire du catholicisme libéral*. Other books are referred to in the notes. For Leo XIII.'s reign see also Soderini, *Il Pontificato di Leone XIII.*, 3 vols., 1933, especially vol. ii.

[3] Printed in Lagrange, iii. 189.

follow his example. Not content with words, the members of the episcopate vied with one another in their endeavours to give practical assistance to their country in its extremity. Nor were their priests at all behind them in patriotic ardour. The record of the whole French clerical body in the terrible days of 1870-1 is a noble one. The bishops made strenuous and often successful efforts to protect their conquered flocks against the harshness and exactions of the Prussians. The priests volunteered in large numbers to serve as *aumôniers* in the army, and many of them performed prodigies of valour on the field. The religious, both male and female, and the members of the lay teaching orders showed an equal heroism. The French *Zouaves Pontificaux,* released from their watch on Rome, were among the bravest of the defenders of France. [4]

But all the efforts of French valour were powerless to stay the victorious march of the invader. The disaster of Sedan (September 2nd) and the surrender of Napoleon III. on the field were followed immediately by the collapse of the Empire. A Government of National Defence was set up in Paris with General Trochu at its head and Gambetta as Minister of the Interior. The attitude of the new Government towards the Church was by no means unfriendly : and the Church was ready to reciprocate its good will. " It is better," wrote Darboy in his diary, " in the interests of religion and of France, to give the Government a loyal co-operation." [5] The archbishop ordered the *Domine salvam fac Republicam* to be sung in the churches of his diocese. The majority of the episcopate had certainly little love for the republican idea in itself : but they had few tears to shed over the Empire either. Pie, who was never unwilling to display his intimate knowledge of the Divine counsels, unhesitatingly proclaimed that the misfortunes of France were the chastisement of heaven on Napoleon III.'s base betrayal of the papal cause. [6]

The patriotism of the clergy and the pacific attitude of the Church towards the new regime combined with the tempo-

[4] Lecanuet, *Les dernières années du Pontificat de Pie IX.,* 6off.
[5] Foulon, *Vie de Mgr. Darboy,* 479.
[6] Lecanuet, *ibid.,* 59.

rary revival of spiritual fervour which, in France as in other countries, is liable to occur in moments of national stress to procure that in the country generally religion should be treated with respect. The chief exceptions to this were seen in the poorer parts of Paris. Here the anti-religious frenzy of the coming Commune was already at work in the later months of 1870. The maire of the eleventh *arrondissement,* M. Mottu, took upon himself to close the Catholic schools within his jurisdiction: and the Government, though they removed him from office, did not dare to undo his work. In truth they were afraid of the Jacobin clubs which now, as in 1789 and 1848, lifted their heads and openly inveighed against all authority, human and divine. A counter-government was thus allowed to organize itself that was to give birth to the Commune.

The march of the German forces on Paris made it necessary to transfer the seat of the Government to some less dangerous spot. Three of its members therefore went to Tours, where they were lodged in the palace of the Archbishop. Gambetta remained for the moment: but on October 7th, when the investment of Paris was complete, he escaped to Tours in a balloon and set himself to reorganize the defence of the still unconquered parts of the country. For the moment France rallied valiantly to the call of the new dictator. But the surrender of the great fortress of Metz with 170,000 troops (October 27th) was a new and deadly blow, and despite the valour of the French arms, the resistance in the south quickly collapsed. The siege of Paris dragged on till January 28th, 1871, when the great city capitulated. An armistice was signed with the expressed object of making possible the election of a National Assembly that should decide on the question of peace or war. The elections took place on February 8th: and on February 12th the new Assembly was formally opened at Bordeaux and elected Thiers as Head of the State. Thiers immediately set out for Paris: and on February 26th the terms of peace were signed.

The one all-absorbing issue on which the Assembly had been elected was, as we have said, the question of peace or war. But the lines of cleavage in national opinion on this point followed, as it happened, those of the general political situation : and for this reason the elections of 1871 determined far more than the issue they were primarily designed to settle. The fall of the Empire had put the political future of France into the melting pot : and it was the new Assembly that was going to decide (if it could) what should come out of it. The Republicans had been in favour of war *à l'outrance*. But this attitude was by no means to the taste of the mass of Conservative better-class opinion, especially in the provinces. For one thing, the representatives of the latter had far more to lose by the prolongation of a resistance which almost from the beginning seemed to be little more than a forlorn hope. Again, they had a wholesome dread of the evils of dictatorship. They had had enough of autocratic methods under the Empire, and desired for the most part a government on constitutional and parliamentary lines. Nor was there anything in the antecedents of the Dictator, if Dictator there should be— Gambetta—to disarm their misgivings. In consequence, while the great towns returned Republicans, the country constituencies, still largely controlled as they were by the lesser aristocracy, voted in favour of the Conservatives. The destinies of France were thus to be for some years in the hands of an Assembly in which Conservatives at the outset exceeded Republicans by a majority of two to one. The Conservative majority was at once inclined to a monarchical restoration and favourable to the Church. Thus M. Hanotaux is right in saying that " if one wishes to go to the bottom of things, one sees that the real division of the country was made on the religious question—Catholicism and free thought." [7]

The extremities to which this division could go were to find immediate and tragic expression. No part of France had suffered so severely from the war as Paris. The trials of the rest of the country had been short and sharp : but to the capital was given the protracted agony of the siege. Hunger, bombardment, rage against the fallen Empire that it was so easy to make the scapegoat of the national misfortunes—all

[7] Hanotaux, *Histoire de la France contemporaine,* i. 36.

these had done their work : and to them was added the sense of isolation and desertion when the Government sought a safer refuge. Under such circumstances men easily fall a prey to desperate counsels. Throughout the siege the forces of revolution had been steadily and openly organizing themselves under their *Comité Central* : and an absent Government could do nothing to restrain them. The clubs rang with fierce and often insane denunciations of the established order, and of the principles of religion on which it claimed to rest. The termination of hostilities and the complexion of the new Assembly combined to precipitate the catastrophe. The hot-heads of Paris now felt themselves free to act—and were the more ready to do so in that the fate of France was in the hands of a body which represented everything they were out to destroy. Their hatred and fear of the Assembly was reciprocated by it to the full. The distrust of the capital that marked its whole career was manifested from the beginning. [8] No heed was paid to its desires or interests : and when the chosen representatives of the nation decided to move from Bordeaux in March, it was not in the Palais Bourbon that they installed themselves but eleven miles away at Versailles. In truth, as Hanotaux says, " *Paris leur faisait peur.*" [9] The resentment of Paris showed itself in the municipal elections of March 26th. The *Comité Central* triumphed, and the Commune was definitely established.

The violently anticlerical character of the Communist regime was visible at once. On April 1st a decree proclaimed the separation of Church and State and ordered the sequestration of all ecclesiastical property. The churches were pillaged and profaned : and not a few of them witnessed a repetition of the sacrilegious scenes of the Terror. Early in April, on the charge that the clergy had in various ways impeded the execution of the municipal decrees, a number of ecclesiastics were arrested and put into prison. Chief among them was the Archbishop of Paris. [10] In the course of his interrogation at

[8] Debidour, *L'Église catholique et l'État sous la IIIme République,* i. 31.
[9] Hanotaux, *op. cit.,* i. 132.
[10] For an account of Darboy's last days see Foulon, *op. cit.,* 512ff.

the Hôtel de Ville, Darboy addressed his judges as " *mes en-fants.*" The presiding magistrate rudely interrupted him :
" There are no children here, there are only magistrates. For
1800 years you have talked to us about fraternity ; it is time
that all that came to an end." [11] By this time the Government
of Versailles was engaged in a second siege of the capital : and
on April 5th, in revenge for the execution of Communist
prisoners by its military chiefs, the Commune passed the
notorious *décret des ôtages*—declaring that they regarded the
imprisoned ecclesiastics as hostages and that if further execu-
tions took place three times as many of these hostages would
be put to death. A little later a proposal was made to the
Versailles Government that Darboy and certain others should
be handed over in exchange for the surrender of the old revolutionary conspirator, Blanqui, who was in its hands. Darboy
was persuaded to send a letter in support of this request. But
after ten days' delay Thiers declined the proffered bargain.

Meanwhile the bombardment of Paris by the army of
Versailles continued : and on May 21st it succeeded in
entering Paris. The Communist troops retreated before it
step by step. The struggle was waged without quarter on
either side, and the most frightful atrocities were committed.
The avenging forces of order made innumerable prisoners,
innocent as well as guilty : and many of these were executed
without mercy and after the merest mockery of a trial.

It is not surprising that the Commune should have meditated reprisals for a butchery so ferocious and undiscrimin-
ating. On May 22nd it ordered the transfer of Darboy and
his companions from the prison of Mazas to that of
La Roquette. Here its corporate and official responsibility
ended : [12] for it never met again as a body after the day the
decree was signed. On May 24th, however, one of its members,
delivering judgment at the *mairie* of the eleventh *arrondissement* in response to the demand of a battalion of the National
Guard, ordered six of the prisoners, including Darboy, to be
shot. The execution took place at La Roquette the same

[11] Debidour, i. 34.
[12] *Ibid.*, 46.

evening. Further massacres followed on the three following
days—of five Dominicans and a number of their servitors in
the Avenue d'Italie on May 25th, of eleven priests and religious (including three Jesuits) in the Rue Haxo on May 26th,
and of three priests in the Faubourg S. Antoine on May 27th.
The last two groups of victims fell at the hands of the mob.
Next day (May 28th) the resistance of the rebels finally
petered out: and the Government of Versailles was in full
possession of the city.

Its vengeance was appalling. The execution of prisoners
continued for days on a more bloodthirsty scale than ever :
and it is estimated that altogether not less than 20,000 men
and women perished in this way. [13] In addition, thousands
of prisoners were to remain in captivity, at home or in the
penal settlements abroad, for years to come. To Darboy, on
the other hand, was accorded a magnificent funeral at Notre
Dame in the presence of the whole body of civil and military
authorities. In his place the Government chose Mgr. Guibert,
the Archbishop of Tours. It would have liked to appoint
Dupanloup : but it knew that Rome would never consent. It
is consoling, however, to reflect that (according to Cardinal
Manning) when Pius IX. heard of the tragic fate of the
murdered Archbishop of Paris, he felt justified in saying that
" Mgr. Darboy has washed out his errors with his blood." [14]
The concession was the easier to make in that the Archbishop
had written to the Pope at the beginning of March expressing
his " pure and simple " adhesion to the Vatican decrees. [15]

II

The Commune finally stamped out, the Assembly set itself
in earnest to the task of evolving a new constitution for France
in place of the fallen Empire. It is true that the Republicans
denied to it the rôle of " *Constituante.*" In their eyes its
mandate extended to deciding the question of peace or war
and went no further. But the Assembly was in possession, and

[13] *Ibid.,* 49.
[14] Purcell, *Life of Cardinal Manning,* ii. 468.
[15] Foulon, 502ff.

intended to use its position to give France the form of government that the majority in it desiderated.

This was unquestionably a restored Bourbon monarchy of some sort. It is true that Thiers, elected by it as *Chef du Pouvoir Exécutif*, deemed a monarchy impracticable for the present. Indeed he had neither the desire nor the intention of handing over the headship of the State to anyone else if he could help it. But he had pledged himself by the so-called *pacte de Bordeaux* to take no steps towards settling the constitutional question without the full cognizance of the Assembly. Nor did the Conservative *politiques* entertain any scruples or anticipate any difficulties in regard to getting rid of him, when once he had served his immediate purpose of acting as the negotiator of a humiliating and unpopular peace. [16]

To desire a restoration was, however, one thing; to effect it quite another. Agreed as to their objective, the Conservatives were deeply divided as to how or in whose favour it was to be carried out. Setting aside the numerically insignificant Bonapartist element, which could hardly hope to achieve its plans except by a fresh *coup d'État*, the partisans of Monarchy were divided into two main groups—the Legitimists and the Orléanists, pressing the claims of the elder and the younger Bourbon line respectively. The candidate of the first was the Comte de Chambord, grandson of Charles X. and now living in exile at Frohsdorf in Austria; of the second, the Comte de Paris, eldest grandson of Louis Philippe. The fact, however, that Chambord was childless seemed to make possible an adjustment of the rival claims. The Comte de Chambord might become King of France for his lifetime, and on his death the Comte de Paris would succeed as his nearest male heir.

Here again, however, there was a stumbling block. Chambord and his entourage had a profound aversion for the House of Orléans, which, both in 1789 and again in 1830, had played false to the elder line. But the division went much deeper than mere personal feeling. The House of Orléans had always been Liberal in its sentiments, and the Comte de

[16] Debidour, i. 28f.

Paris represented this hereditary attitude in combination with marked intellectual gifts and much charm of character and of manners. But the Comte de Chambord was a reactionary of the blackest dye. [17]   His devotion to the principles of divine right and absolute government was positively mystical in its fervour. In him, as Hanotaux says, "*l'idée dominante est l'idée religieuse—tout est là.*" He was in truth an *exalté,* a visionary, an illuminist, who regarded the cause of God and the cause of the monarchy as identical, and held that to him, as the Anointed of the Lord, was given a responsibility for his personal action that none could share or control—not even the Vicar of Christ himself. He was King by the inalienable right of his birth : and he must be received as such without demur or conditions. For him, too, the only possible monarchy was *la monarchie chrétienne*—with the teachings of the Church enthroned as the guide and norm of all its action. This attitude was shared by the men of his confidence—both within the Assembly and without. On the other hand it was clear to the majority of the Conservatives in the Assembly—to moderate Legitimists and Orléanists alike—that there was no hope of monarchy finding favour with France as a whole except on the understanding, first, that the King would consent to receive his crown at her hands, and secondly, that he would accept a constitution on parliamentary lines that would guarantee the liberties that the modern social order had come to postulate. A regime founded on divine right and the Syllabus would never have a moment's chance of success.

Somehow or other, then, these incompatible points of view must be reconciled. And as a first step it was necessary to effect a " fusion " of the claims of the rival dynasties. The Comte de Paris must recognize the Comte de Chambord as the head of the House of Bourbon and the rightful representative of the monarchical principle in France; while Chambord in return must recognize him as his heir. At once steps were taken to bring such " fusion " about. In this task no one bestirred himself more actively than Dupanloup. The Bishop of Orléans had always been a close personal friend of the

[17] See Hanotaux's portrait of him, i. 136.

Orléans family and a warm supporter of its interests. He had been elected a member of the Assembly in 1871 despite the sneering opposition of Veuillot, who now and hereafter was to hamper his efforts within it on behalf of the nation and the Church in every possible way. The Comte de Paris was persuaded without difficulty to express his willingness to pay a visit to his cousin, who was now in France at the Château de Chambord in Touraine, and to make the "recognition" asked of him. But Chambord coldly informed him—in the third person—that he could not receive him until he himself had made a public declaration on "some reserved questions." [18]

Of these the most important—for its symbolical if not for its practical significance—was the question of the tricolour. It was felt that France would never consent to abandon the use of her national flag, adorned as it was with the laurels of so many famous victories. To Chambord, on the other hand, it was the symbol of the Revolution, and to consent to its retention would be to condone by implication the revolutionary idea. The moderate Legitimists and Dupanloup went to Chambord and implored the Prince to modify his position, but without success. "Never have I seen," said the Bishop on his return, "so absolute a moral blindness." [19] Immediately afterwards Chambord published (July 5th, 1871) a manifesto in which he declared that "the flag that had floated over his cradle"—the white flag of the Bourbons—"would overshadow his tomb." [20] "It is the suicide of the Comte de Chambord," exclaimed the Legitimist Falloux. [21] But Pie and the *Univers* were ecstatic over the noble firmness of the pretender.

Meanwhile the Catholics and ultra-Royalists continued their propaganda on behalf of him whom they represented as the Messiah who alone could save France. The friends of compromise for their part began to consider the possibility of appointing a lieutenant-general of the kingdom to function

[18] Letter printed in Falloux, *Mémoires,* ii. 473.
[19] *Ibid.,* 479.
[20] Printed *in extenso, ibid.,* 479ff.
[21] Lagrange, *Dupanloup,* iii. 232.

during Chambord's lifetime. The Duc d'Aumale, a brother of the Comte de Paris, was designed for the position. But Chambord spiked their guns by a second manifesto declaring that he would never abdicate nor prove unfaithful to his principles. " I will never consent," he said, " to be the legitimate King of the Revolution." [22] At length on January 25th, 1873, Dupanloup determined to make a final appeal to the Prince (who had now returned to Frohsdorf) in a letter [23] imploring him not to refuse " to sick and dying France all sacrifices that are possible." Chambord's reply (February 8th, 1873) was scathing and final. " I have neither sacrifices to make nor conditions to receive. I expect little from the cleverness of men and much from the justice of God." [24] Two days before writing his letter to Chambord, Dupanloup had also written to the Pope [25] to ask him to help to remove the scruples of the Prince. But the Pope either could not or would not help—it is uncertain which.

The difficulties in the way of a restoration seemed to be almost insuperable. It was becoming increasingly clear too that the feeling of France in general was turning in quite another direction. The Republicans had never ceased their propaganda, and about this time Gambetta, styling himself the *commis voyageur* of the Republican idea, was conducting a campaign all over the country in its behalf. " There is no need to speak of the old parties," he said. " One party remains—the enemy of all independence, of all light, of all stability. That party is Clericalism." Whenever elections occurred, Republicans were practically always chosen. Thiers now openly abandoned his neutrality and declared that a Republic was the only possible government for France. The Assembly, incensed, retorted by appointing a Commission of Thirty to prepare a constitutional settlement. When Thiers changed the ministry in a Republican direction, the Conservatives defeated it and so compelled the President to resign (March 24th, 1873). In his place Marshal MacMahon was

---

[22] Debidour, i. 77.
[23] Published for the first time in full in Lecanuet, 192f.
[24] Printed in full, *ibid.* 281f.
[25] *Ibid.*, 278.

elected : and the Duc de Broglie became head of a Government pledged to " *le rétablissement de l'ordre moral.*"

Things had evidently come to a crisis for the friends of monarchy. It was now or never. The Church openly stepped into the arena and preached a veritable crusade. All over France pilgrimages were made to famous shrines. The most imposing of these demonstrations were those held at Chartres on May 26th, when Pie harangued 40,000 pilgrims, and at Paray-le-Monial during June. It was at Paray that the nun, Marguerite Marie Alacocque, had seen in 1689 a vision of the Sacred Heart and had been charged to bid Louis XIV. dedicate his kingdom to it. Louis had paid no heed : but the Royalists believed the time now come to fulfil the divine behest and so win from heaven the triumph of the *roi chrétien.* At the close of the pilgrimage a group of members of the Assembly was present, bearing a banner of the Sacred Heart given by 150 of their colleagues. Their spokesman, M. de Belcastel, dedicated his country to the Sacred Heart " in the measure of the powers of " those in whose name he spoke. A further triumph of the Clericals was the vote of the Assembly on July 24th, 1873, declaring " of public utility " the project for the erection of a great basilica of the Sacred Heart on Montmartre in expiation of the sins of the nation and in supplication of the mercy of heaven on its woes.

For a moment these prayers seemed to be answered. Early in August " fusion " became an accomplished fact. The Comte de Paris went to Frohsdorf and recognized his cousin as " the sole representative of the monarchical principle " in France. At once the various Royalist groups got together and formed a Commission of Nine to arrange the terms of a settlement. A *projet* was drawn up by agreement for presentation to the Assembly. The Comte de Chambord was formally called to the throne : and the main outlines of a settlement on constitutional lines were laid down. It was asserted that without the retention of the tricolour monarchy was impossible : but the formal solution of the question was left until after the return of the King.

Would the Comte de Chambord accept this settlement? A

leading member of the Right, M. Chesnelong, was sent to Frohsdorf to find out. After much parleying he obtained a promise that the Prince would demand no change in the flag until after his return, when he would submit to the national representatives " a solution compatible with his honour that he thought would satisfy the nation." [26] The monarchists were in raptures. But in a moment all was at an end. On October 27th the Prince addressed to Chesnelong a letter [27] declaring his determination not to accept the tricolour, and his surprise that any guarantees should be asked of him seeing that he was " the necessary pilot who alone can bring the ship to port."

The Royalists were dumbfounded. The Pope himself did not conceal his disappointment. " What! " he exclaimed, " Henry IV. thought that Paris was worth a Mass : and Henry V. thinks that France is not worth *une serviette*." [28] But Pie and the *Univers* expressed a satisfaction without reserve.

Henceforth the cause of monarchy was for all practical purposes dead and buried. Orléanists like Broglie and Dupanloup might still delude themselves with the belief that what could not be done for the Comte de Chambord might be done for the Comte de Paris, and, with this aim in view, secure the passing of the *Septennat,* prolonging the powers of MacMahon as President for seven years (November 20th, 1873). But it was a forlorn hope at best. For France was showing more and more unmistakably that it was not a monarchy she desired but the Republic. The steady infiltration of Republicans into the legislature continued : and by an unhallowed combination of the Extreme Right and the Left Broglie was driven from power on May 16th, 1874. After his fall the control of the Assembly passed to the Centre—not without the approval of Gambetta, who thought that " something might be done with it on these terms." [29] His previsions were not unjustified by the event. The *loi sur les pouvoirs publics* of February 25th, 1875, definitively constituted the Republic : and when at the close of the year the Assembly at last ended its chequered existence the elections

[26] Falloux, *Mémoires,* ii. 575.
[27] Printed in full, *ibid.,* 577ff.
[28] Lecanuet, 219.
[29] Hanotaux, iii. 4.

of February 1876 returned a majority of 200 for the Republicans in the lower house; though the Senate showed a slight majority for their opponents.

III

The Assembly had thus failed to achieve that triumph of the monarchical principle which Catholics, then as for many years to come, regarded as the only effective guarantee of the claims and interests of religion. But at least, while it lasted, it had done its best to defend and increase the prestige and the privileges of the Church, and so to set up a barrier against the rising tide of unbelief and secularity that threatened to overwhelm her in the conditions of the modern world.

It was with this object that steps were taken in the years following 1870 to restore that unity of Catholic action which had been lacking since the passing of the Loi Falloux in 1850. A *comité catholique* was formed in Paris in 1871 : and similar committees quickly sprung up in the provinces. The work of these committees received a great extension in 1873 when, under the auspices of M. Chesnelong, a *Comité Central* was set up to assume general control of the Catholic forward movement and, under its direction, nine permanent committees were charged with the furtherance of the various branches of Catholic activity. A Congress of all the *comités* was to be held every year. Unfortunately, however, the old divisions in the Catholic body persisted. It was the Liberal Catholics (with Broglie and Dupanloup at their head) who took the lead in the Assembly : and to them belongs the credit of what it was able to achieve on behalf of the Church. But they were continually hampered by the opposition of the Catholic intransigents, with their obstinate refusal to face the practical possibilities of the situation. It was they, as we have seen, who were largely responsible for the failure of the attempt to restore the monarchy, by encouraging the Comte de Chambord to refuse the accommodations suggested to him by their hated rivals. The same opposition created similar difficulties in other directions as well—difficulties which the attitude of the Holy See did nothing to allay.

Among the preoccupations of Catholics the plight of the
Holy Father held a leading place. The prisoner of the
Vatican was by no means content to suffer in silence, and
called loudly for help on his spiritual children all over the
world. The Catholics of France generally would gladly have
done something ; for the Pope seemed specially to rely on them,
and was not France the eldest daughter of the Church? But
it was obvious to all sensible men that any effective intervention on her part was out of the question. France was no longer
the arbiter of Europe ; but was defeated, humiliated, occupied
in a large part of her territory, with Germany and Italy watch-
ing her every movement and ready to pounce on the slightest
provocation. The attitude of the Government towards the
Holy See was, indeed, one of studied respect. Even the
Government of National Defence, while declaring itself unable
to recognize the Temporal Power, had consented to reserve the
question concerning it to a more favourable time. It even
offered Pius IX. a refuge in Corsica after the occupation of
Rome, and dispatched the frigate *Orénoque* to Civita Vecchia
to wait at his disposal. The Government of Versailles was not
likely to be less sympathetic. It decided, despite the scowls of
Italy, to send an ambassador, the Comte d'Harcourt, to the
Holy See. The Pope, on his part, abounded in sentiments
and declarations favourable to France. During the celebrations marking the twenty-fifth year of his pontificate he thus
addressed the French pilgrims (June 18th, 1871): " I love
France, I have always loved her and will love her to the end."
The effect of his speech was, however, rather spoiled for some
of his audience when he went on : " But I must tell France
the truth. There is in that country an evil more to be feared
even than the Commune. I mean Liberal Catholicism, which
is *un véritable fléau* " ! [30]

The intransigent Catholics, however, wanted more than
platonic demonstrations of respect from the rulers of France
to their afflicted Father. The *Univers,* in particular, called
upon the Assembly to take some definite action. All over
France petitions were organized, demanding at least a diplo-

[30] Lecanuet, 146.

matic intervention. The bishops—many of them against their better judgment—were carried away by the stream. The Comte de Chambord issued a declaration on May 8th, 1871 : " The independence of the Pope is dear to me and I am determined to obtain effective guarantees for it." [31] Italian opinion at once took alarm, and the Republicans accused the Catholics of wanting war. The situation was indeed perilous. Already the first steps were being taken in the process that was soon to link Germany and Italy together in the bonds of the Triple Alliance.

The Catholics refused to heed. Their petitions were brought before the Assembly in July : and despite Thiers' entreaties for moderate counsels that body decided that they should be referred to the Minister for Foreign Affairs. The Minister in question, Jules Favre, resigned shortly afterwards.

Even so, the *Univers* refused to be satisfied. The Italian Government having transferred its seat to Rome on July 1st, 1871, it organized a further petition. On March 2nd, 1872, Thiers deprecated a discussion of this : and the Assembly voted an adjournment. The wrath of the *Univers* was expressed in such violent terms that even the Pope thought it necessary to intervene and rebuked the Catholic journal for its " want of charity." This, however, did not prevent an outbreak of ill-temper on his part when Thiers ordered the officers of the *Orénoque* to pay their respects at the Quirinal as well as the Vatican the following New Year's Day. The Pope declared that in that case he would not receive them at all. The French Ambassador to the Holy See, Baron de Bourgoign, resigned as a protest against his Government's action.

With the appointment of MacMahon as President instead of Thiers the hopes of the Catholics rose high. Unfortunately, its effect was also to increase distrust of France on the part of Germany and Italy, which were now on closer terms than ever. Italy believed that if " Henry V." became King of France, he would speedily take overt action to restore the Temporal Power. Germany shared these misgivings. Bismarck was at present deeply engaged in his struggle with

[31] Lecanuet, 149.

the Catholic Church called the *Kulturkampf;* and was determined to prevent anything that might increase the strength of his opponent, even to the extent of threatening France with war. When the French bishops lifted their voices in encouragement of their persecuted German brethren the Iron Chancellor demanded that the Government should take steps to punish them openly. The Government was on the point of refusing and taking the consequences when a fresh indiscretion of the *Univers* in publishing an anti-German-Italian pastoral of the Bishop of Périgueux made possible an alternative solution. The Government suspended the *Univers* for two months : and Bismarck was for the moment satisfied. The Pope, however, wrote to Veuillot expressing his sympathy.

Having climbed down to Germany, the Government had next to climb down to Italy. The Italian Government demanded the recall of the *Orénoque.* The ministry obeyed; though it stationed another vessel, the *Kléber,* off Corsica at the Holy Father's disposal (October 1874).

In the defence of the Holy See, then, the Assembly could hardly be said to have exerted itself to any striking practical effect. But in the sphere of internal affairs its action on behalf of the Church was more successful, though (as we shall see) its principal achievements were to prove but short-lived.

The most striking of these concerned education. By two important legislative measures changes were made in the existing educational system of France. The first—passed on March 19th, 1873—modified the constitution of the *Conseil Supérieur de l'Instruction Publique.* By the law of 1850, it may be remembered, this was to include, besides representatives of the Université, a majority of elected representatives (a) of the episcopate and of the non-Catholic religious bodies, (b) of the Council of State, the Supreme Court of Appeal and the Institut. In 1852, however, a decree of the Empire ordained that henceforth the *Conseil* should be entirely nominated by the Government. This was the arrangement that was brought to an end by the law of 1873, which restored to the *Conseil* a constitution similar to that laid down by the *Loi Falloux.*

More important still was the law of 1875 concerning higher
education.   In the passing of this the Bishop of Orléans
played so important a part that it might well be called the
" Loi Dupanloup."   What the *Loi Falloux* had done for
Catholicism in the sphere of primary and secondary education
it sought to do in the sphere of the higher studies.   In 1849,
and again in 1868-9, steps had been taken towards securing
for Catholics the right to found Faculties of their own on a
level with the State Universities.   But these attempts were
ineffectual—to the grave disappointment of the Catholics, who
were much concerned at the materialistic teaching given in
the Faculties of the State.   Now, however, an opportunity of
settling the question seemed to have arrived : and the law of
1875 was the result.   Its discussion in the Assembly began in
December 1874.   By the terms of the original *projet* any
Frenchman was permitted to open an institution for higher
education, and associations might be formed for promoting
the foundation of such.   These *facultés libres* were to have the
right to confer degrees.   The scheme was hotly opposed by
the representatives of the Université, led by Jules Ferry, who
maintained (not unreasonably) that it was the business of the
State to see that a proper standard for degrees should be
maintained, and that for this reason it alone should be em-
powered to confer them.   Eventually a compromise was
effected by which candidates for degrees in the non-State
Universities must appear before *jurys mixtes,* composed
equally of State professors and professors of the *universités
libres,* chosen by the Minister for Education.   With this
change the bill [32] passed into law July 12th, 1875.   The
bishops of central France at once founded a Catholic
University at Paris.   The northern dioceses founded another
at Lille ; while steps in the same direction were taken at
Angers, Lyons and Toulouse.

In addition to all this, the Assembly showed its favour to
the Church in other ways as well.   The *budget des cultes* rose
steadily from $49\frac{1}{2}$ millions in 1871 to $53\frac{3}{4}$ millions in 1876. [33]

[32] Text as passed printed in Debidour, i. 419.
[33] Lecanuet, 225.

A law of 1874 provided *aumôniers* to serve the spiritual needs of the Army. An attempt was even made to provide a day of rest on Sundays for public servants, but without success.

Outside the Assembly the period is signalized by the remarkable work of Comte Albert de Mun, the future great Catholic orator in the French Chamber, in connection with the *Cercles Catholiques d'Ouvriers*. [34] These were designed to combat the growing menace of materialized democracy by organizing the work and leisure of the working-classes on strictly Catholic lines. The first *cercle* organized under de Mun's auspices was founded in Paris in 1871 : and soon, as the result of his enthusiastic propaganda, similar *cercles* were set up all over France, with an elaborate and complicated organization centred in the capital. De Mun's ultimate aim was the restoration of the medieval guild corporations. But after a brilliant start, and despite the noble idealism and self-sacrifice of its promoters, the movement was to prove disappointing. The causes of this failure were various : but chief among them undoubtedly were the frankly aristocratic character of its organization and its devotion to the Syllabus and to the policy of the Extreme Right, which enabled its enemies to represent it as no more than an attempt to bring back the *ancien régime*. In truth Demos had now grown up and intended to settle its affairs for itself.

[34] On de Mun's social activity see, besides Lecanuet (391ff), Nitti, *Catholic Socialism* (Eng. translation, 1908), 270ff.

CHAPTER IX

THE CAMPAIGN AGAINST " CLERICALISM "

1876—1884

THE triumph of the Republicans in the elections of 1876 was of ill omen for the Church. It is true that the Conservatives showed a slight majority in the Senate and were able in this way to hold up for a short time the legislation directed against her. At the Elysée, too, the Monarchist-Clericals still held sway for the time being. But it was clear to all unprejudiced observers that these safeguards were but a " rampart of clay "[1] that must soon be swept away by the rising tide of Republican sentiment in the country. And then the " persecution " would begin.

The only way in which the Church could conceivably have saved itself was to " agree with its adversary quickly " by a frank acceptance of the Republic as the form of government to which France was more and more pledging her adhesion. But such a *ralliement* was not to be thought of at this stage. The clergy still clung to the old alliance between the Altar and the Throne; and for years to come were to be totally incapable of even imagining that any other means of safeguarding the interests of religion was possible. For them the incompatibility between the Church and the Revolution was fundamental and axiomatic. No compromise between them was to be thought of.

The great majority of the influential Catholic laity, wedded as they were to the Royalist cause, shared the same attitude. The eminent Dominican preacher, Père Didon,[2] discovered this to his cost. When in a Lenten course of sermons preached in 1880 at the fashionable church of La Trinité in Paris he dared to urge a reconciliation between the Church and modern society, a section of his audience denounced him

[1] So Broglie himself described the Septennat, Hanotaux, ii. 311.
[2] The life of Didon has been written by Reynaud, *Le Père Didon,* 1904.

to the Superior General of his Order, a narrowly intransigent Spaniard. Didon was sentenced to silence and solitude in the Corsican convent of Corbara for eighteen months, and even when he emerged was only allowed to address occasionally a small community of nuns in Paris. He consoled himself by writing his well known *Life of Christ*. It was not till 1892, when the *ralliement* of Catholics to the Republic was well on its way to becoming an accomplished fact, that he was once more allowed full freedom to exercise his ministry. By that time it was too late. Thus the greatest preacher, perhaps, of his generation, the legitimate successor of Lacordaire, was sacrificed to political prejudice and spite. [3]

If the bulk of Catholics thus believed the Church and the Republic to be incompatible, the most active and influential section of the Republican party was of the same opinion. It shared Proudhon's view: " Christian or Republican—there is the dilemma." [4] A striking feature of the years following 1870 is the great development of Freemasonry—a movement which in continental countries (as is well known) is bitterly and militantly antagonistic to revealed religion, and is, in fact, the chief focus of opposition to the Catholic Church. The membership of the various Masonic lodges rapidly increased, and soon included all the leading figures in the Republican party, from Gambetta and Jules Ferry downwards. [5] Side by side with this went a wide and formidable development of their propaganda. For them the one great obstacle in the way of the triumph of the Revolution was the Catholic Church, the influence of which must therefore be brought to an end by a wholesale and uncompromising destruction of the faith of the masses. Of the ways of bringing this about the most efficacious, it was believed, was education. Hence the three-fold Masonic programme—*l'obligation, la gratuité, la laïcité*. Education must be compulsory for all, must be without charge and, above all, must be entirely divorced from the teachings of religion. With the object of realizing this programme the

---

[3] Lecanuet, *La Vie de l'Église sous Léon XIII.*, 184ff.
[4] Weill, 291.
[5] Lecanuet, *Les dernières années du Pontificat de Pie IX.*, 483.

Ligue de l'Enseignement was brought into existence, in close connection with the Masonic organization. Its founder was Jean Macé, an ardent Freemason and fanatically anti-religious. The doctrines of Freemasonry found firm support in the Radical press, but its most powerful weapon of offence after 1870 was in the multitude of small manuals and *brochures* which were disseminated all over France. The aim of the Masonic cult was quite frankly not merely to destroy Catholicism but to put itself in its place as a kind of "anti-Church." Freemasonry was to become "the Church of the Revolution," with humanity set up as the object of worship in the place of God.

It is worth while to inquire why it was that such doctrines advanced so rapidly in France at this period. To a large extent, of course, they were no new phenomenon. The animus against the Church which found such violent expression during the first French Revolution had never died out. The ideas of Voltaire and Rousseau had commanded a considerable following all through the nineteenth century. It is true that under Napoleon and in the period of the Restoration their expression had been more or less kept in check by the civil authority : and the same policy obtained in the earlier part of the Second Empire. But they lived on, and supplied an important focus of opposition to all three regimes. Moreover, they had entrenched themselves to a considerable extent within the State educational system. Such famous professors of the Université as Michelet and Quinet ranked among the most formidable enemies of the Christian religion : and their influence among the younger generation was great. The extensive vogue of the Positivism of Auguste Comte operated in the same direction.

But from about 1860 onwards the activity of so-called "free thought" betrays a new intensity and aggressiveness—an activity now rather favoured than discouraged by the Government for its own purposes. The causes of this were not confined to France but were common to Western Europe generally. The development of historical criticism on the one hand, and of natural science on the other, was battering breaches in the traditional doctrine of Christendom in all its parts: and the enemies of Christianity laid eager hold on the weapons thus placed in their hands. In this connection the work of Ernest Renan is specially notable—a work the influence of which extended beyond France throughout the civilized world. His famous *Vie de Jésus* has been already mentioned in these pages, and was to be followed up by a series of further works on *The Origins of Christianity* that seemed to be inspired by the principle hurled by John Morley in England at the orthodox believers of his time: "We will not refute you: we will explain you." The charm of Renan's style and the mocking keenness of his wit powerfully reinforced the learning and critical acumen displayed in his writings.

The Catholic world was scandalized by them, but unfortunately was content to answer them by abuse rather than by argument. No real attempt was made to meet the challenge of the new knowledge, still less to effect a synthesis between it and the historic faith of the Church. Dupanloup might resign his seat on the Academy as a protest against the election of Littré:[6] but the more effective protest of a reasoned refutation of the Positivist position was simply beyond his powers. The Catholic apologetic of the period is poor and conventional, even by the admission of Catholics themselves. Père Lecanuet speaks of its "complete sterility" in regard to both philosophy and Biblical exegesis[7]—the two fields in which the traditional doctrine was most seriously challenged. And if this weakness marked the learned and instructed, much more was it to be found in the rank and file of the clergy. The training given in the seminaries may often have been thorough enough on the devotional and pastoral side: but on the intellectual side it was sadly to seek.[8] The teaching was poor and uninspiring, the *professeurs* were ill-equipped, the text-books used in them dull, dry and altogether out of date. Nor did the bishops show any zeal or even interest in their improvement, or desire to encourage the higher studies of their

---

[6] In 1872. Lagrange, iii. 242f.
[7] Lecanuet, *op. cit.,* 316f.
[8] Lecanuet, 292f.

clergy. [9] In consequence the priests turned out by them were
for the most part entirely out of touch with the currents of
ideas that agitated the more thoughtful and educated members of their flocks. A sort of " inferiority-complex " was thus
engendered that led them on the one hand to hold themselves
aloof from the general life and interests of the communities
they served, and on the other to develop an authoritarian and
meddlesome temper in their own special sphere that by no
means conduced to popularity. This latter tendency was increased by the theocratic and intransigent attitude of their
favourite journal, the Univers. [10] " By their haughty tone,
their imperious words," said a clerical critic, " you would
believe them the masters of the world." [11]

However it may have been with his wife and daughters, the
attitude of the ordinary Frenchman towards his religion was
decidedly perfunctory. The church was part of the established order and must normally be treated with respect. But
his interest did not in most cases extend to much church-
going. M. Isoard, later Bishop of Annecy, in a book on
"Preaching" published in 1870, makes it clear that even at that
period men were almost entirely absent from the congregations in the churches. He makes it no less clear that those
who did go received little to help them from the sermons they
heard. [12] It is not surprising that Catholics so lukewarm and
so ill-instructed should have fallen an easy prey to the
propaganda of the enemies of religion. Among the many
directions in which the growing religious indifference manifested itself was in a notable decline in the number of ecclesiastical vocations—a decline which provoked from one of
Dupanloup's vicars-general, the Abbé Bougaud, a resounding
and somewhat exaggerated pamphlet entitled Le grand péril
de l'Église de France. [13] The aristocratic and wealthy
classes had for a long time ceased to give their sons to the

[9] Lecanuet, 311f. The old Cardinal de Bonald is reported to have said
" Des savants, que voulez vous que j'en fasse? " Houtin, La Crise du
clergé, 240.
[10] Ibid., 296. See also Taine, Le régime moderne, ii. bk. v.
[11] Bougaud, Le grand péril de l'Église de France, 56.
[12] Isoard, La Prédication, 1870, ch. i., ii.
[13] Published in 1878.

Church : but now even the ordinary source of recruitment—
the lower-middle and working classes, especially in the
country—seemed to be drying up.

Nor did the press do anything to supply the defence of
religion that was not forthcoming from the pulpit. The most
widely read French newspapers were for the most part anti-
religious in a greater or less degree, or at least anticlerical.
Compared with their circulation, that of a Catholic journal
like the *Univers* was negligible. "*La presse, c'est tout*," said
Crémieux, the Jewish Grand-Master of Freemasonry in
France : "*ayant la presse, nous aurons le reste.*"[14] His
prophecy seemed in a fair way of coming true.

Chief, however, among the causes that led to the triumph
of the Republican anticlericals over the Church was the
identification of the latter with the interests of political and
ecclesiastical reaction, its blind opposition to the "principles
of 1789" and the liberties of the modern world. Whatever
the faults and excesses of the French Revolution may have
been, the average Frenchman was convinced that its general
results had been wholly beneficial, and had no intention of
letting its achievements be swept away in favour of any kind
of restoration of the *ancien régime*. It was not monarchy
that he disliked so much as the whole cycle of ideas with which
in his mind monarchy had come to be associated—the ideas
of the Syllabus, in a word. And he knew that with the eclipse
of Liberal Catholicism those ideas were more than ever
dominant in the Church. Thus it was not difficult for the
Republicans to convince him that only through Republicanism, and that eviction of the Church from all influence in
politics which was the avowed Republican policy, could the
harvest of the Revolution be made secure for future generations. Gambetta showed a sound instinct when he separated
the interests of the clerical order from those of religion and
coined (or rather borrowed)[15] his famous battle-cry, "*Le
cléricalisme, voilà l'ennemi!*" Let the clergy confine them-

---

[14] Quoted in Lecanuet, 334.
[15] The phrase was coined before 1870 by the journalist, Alphonse
Peyrat (Lecanuet, 22 n.).

selves to their spiritual functions and they would not be molested, at least for the time being. It is the attitude thus fostered, more than any hostility to religion itself, that explains the favour—or at least the acquiescence—with which the nation as a whole was to receive the various measures that were soon to be directed against the Church.

I

The policy of Gambetta and his friends was, by their own admission, a policy of " opportunism." [16] It might be summed up in the homely saying that " Half a loaf is better than no bread." The whole loaf, they believed, would be theirs in due course : but meanwhile they must be content with what they could get and not strive after the impossible. We have seen how Gambetta had already put this policy into practice after the fall of the Duc de Broglie in 1874. He might have worked to end the Assembly altogether : but he preferred to use it for his own ends, so far as the circumstances permitted their realization. The same policy was to govern the action of the Republicans after their success in the elections of 1876. Great though that success had been, it was not sufficient as yet to place the anticlericals in a position to realize their designs against the Church. Not only was the new Senate opposed to them, but the Conservative MacMahon was still President, and by the terms of the Septennat was to remain so for another five years. Nor was the new Premier, M. Dufaure, likely to lend himself to an attack on the Church. A member of the Right Centre, he had been appointed in the place of M. Buffet, who had been defeated in two constituencies and resigned as soon as Parliament assembled. Yet something must be done to throw a sop to the anticlerical ardour of the Republican majority in the Chamber. This had already displayed itself in connection with the *vérification des pouvoirs* of the newly-elected deputies at the beginning of the session, when the election of the Comte de Mun at Pontivy was declared invalid on the ground of undue clerical influence

[16] See Hanotaux, ii. 696.

—though his constituency promptly re-elected him—and Chesnelong was similarly disqualified.

Pressure was therefore brought to bear on Dufaure to induce him to consent to a modification of the law on higher education of the previous year. Dufaure was forced to yield : and the measure was introduced into the Chamber on March 24th, 1876. While maintaining the rest of the law intact, it deprived the new Catholic Universities of the right to confer degrees and abolished the *jurys mixtes*. The importance of this lay in the fact that such degrees were a vital qualification for entering the learned professions and that Catholic Faculties compelled to submit their students to examination by their State rivals in order to secure them would inevitably be prejudiced in the public eye. The Bill, championed by Jules Ferry, passed the Lower House on June 7th by 357 votes to 128 and was then sent up to the Senate. In the course of a speech in support of the measure, Challemel-Lacour made malicious capital out of a letter sent to Dupanloup the previous year by Pius IX., in which the pontiff, while complimenting him on his " skilful and opportune " defence of the law of 1875, at the same time condemned in principle " the attempt to put truth and falsehood on the same level and to accord equal rights to both." [17] Dupanloup felt the thrust deeply : but he none the less affirmed in his reply the devotion of Catholics to " modern liberties " and attacked the Bill as an unworthy concession to political rancour. It was, however, a speech of Broglie, urging the duty of the Senate to oppose a barrier to hasty legislation, that really turned the scale in favour of the Catholics. The Bill was rejected by a small majority—144 votes to 139.

Beaten on this issue, the Republicans had to content themselves with voting a reduction of the *budget des cultes* by over two million francs. Here, again, the Senate resisted at first : but it was compelled to submit. By this time Dufaure, who had done his best to oppose the reductions, had been forced to resign and give place to Jules Simon.

The year 1877 saw a revival of the Roman Question. In

[17] Lecanuet, 506.

an Encyclical Pius IX. denounced the Mancini Bill recently passed by the Italian Chamber, imposing severe penalties on ecclesiastics who should dare to attack its anti-Church legislation, and called upon bishops to use their influence with their Governments in support of his protests. The bishops obeyed, and one of them, the Bishop of Nevers, was unwise enough to write not only to the President but also to the *maires* of his diocese. The matter was raised in the Chamber and gave rise to a debate in the course of which Gambetta first raised his slogan, " *Le cléricalisme, voilà l'ennemi!* "[18] A division was taken on the following motion : " The Chamber, considering that the Ultramontane manifestations, the renewal of which might well compromise the internal and external security of the country, constitute a flagrant violation of the laws of the State, invites the Government, in order to repress this anti-patriotic agitation, to use the legal means at its disposal."[19] The Prime Minister accepted the motion and it was carried by 348 votes to 114 (May 4th).

Twelve days later MacMahon retorted by the *Coup* known as the *Seize Mai*. On May 16th, 1877, he dismissed Simon and appointed Broglie in his place. On the following June 22nd, at the President's request, the Senate decreed the dissolution of the Chamber.

During the elections that ensued the President undertook a personal campaign in the country in support of his handiwork. Gambetta, on his side, led the van in opposition to what he called " the Government of the *curés*."[20] It was not difficult to persuade the people that the *Seize Mai* was nothing but a final and desperate attempt to bring back the monarchy and with it the domination of the Church. In consequence, the result of the election, in Veuillot's phrase, " would discourage hope itself."[21] The Republicans were indeed returned with a reduced majority, but they still outnumbered their opponents by 100 votes : and when that majority had been considerably increased by the disqualification of deputies on the other side,

[18] Lecanuet, 533.
[19] Debidour, i. 172.
[20] Debidour, i. 175.
[21] Lecanuet, 549.

Gambetta could boast that he had achieved his prophecy:
"We go out 363 and shall return 400." [22]

Broglie, after some hesitation, decided to confront the new
Chamber, but was immediately forced to resign. In his stead
MacMahon again appointed Dufaure at the head of a ministry
of moderate Republicans. Its moderation was reflected by
Gambetta himself, who counselled his followers to hold their
hand until the senatorial elections of 1879 should (as he
correctly forecast) secure for the Republicans a majority in
both Houses.

The next year, 1878, was thus got through without striking
incident. The only ruffling of its calm was provided by a
decision of the Radical Municipal Council of Paris to associate itself officially with a great celebration in the
capital of the centenary of Voltaire's death in 1778 that was
being planned by the Freemasons as a demonstration against
the Church. The bishops at once raised the alarm.
Dupanloup, now a dying man, buckled on his armour for the
last time to write his *Ten Letters to the Conseil Municipal of
Paris*—characterized by Cardinal Guibert of Paris as "*le
Rosbach de Voltaire.*" [23] The effect was so great that the
Government censured the municipal council for its action and
forbade any part of the celebration to be held out of doors.

On the following October 11th Dupanloup died at Hyères.
The Cardinal's hat which his friends (and presumably himself
too) so ardently desired for him had never come his way,
despite the strenuous efforts of successive Governments since
1871 to wring it from the inflexible rancour of Pius IX. But
whatever the mistakes and failings of the great Bishop of
Orléans may have been, no prelate of his time had deserved
it better : and had he lived longer, without doubt Leo XIII.
would have made the *amende honorable* to him as he did to
Newman.

Meanwhile, outside the Chamber, Gambetta was sowing
the seeds of the coming victory. In September he undertook
a tour in Lyonnais and Dauphiné in which he declared war

[22] Debidour, i. 174.
[23] Lagrange, iii. 455.

against the Church more loudly than ever. His programme for crippling its influence was concentrated on three points. The congregations must be dispersed, education must be laicized and the Church in general must be imprisoned within a rigid application of the existing laws—especially in regard to the compulsion of seminarists to serve in the army. [24]

The senatorial elections of 1879 fulfilled the hopes of Gambetta and brought the Republicans at last within striking distance of " the enemy." Of eighty-two vacant seats, sixty-six were captured by Republicans. MacMahon could not ignore the portent, and began to talk of resigning. At this juncture Cardinal Bonnechose, of Rouen, the principal prop of the Bonapartist cause in the episcopate, sought an interview with the Marshal-President and urged him to lend himself to a *coup d'État* in the interest of the Prince Imperial, only son of Napoleon III., who had died in England six years before.[25] But the " modern Bayard " was too much a gentleman and a man of honour to support such a scheme, which in any case could have had small chance of success. On January 30th, 1879, MacMahon resigned and was succeeded by M. Grévy, President of the Chamber of Deputies, a cautious, rather cold-blooded specimen of the second-rate type of moderate Republican politician.

II

Even in this hour of victory Gambetta did not abandon his " opportunism." The Radicals would have liked to abolish the Concordat altogether and so bring about the "separation" of Church and State without delay. But they only counted some eighty votes. The bulk of the Republican party was composed of the *Union Républicaine* under Gambetta and the *Gauche Républicaine* under Jules Ferry : and neither of these leaders regarded " separation " as a practicable proposition at present. Their aim for the moment was confined to the realization of the programme outlined by Gambetta in his campaign the previous September. The religious congrega-

[24] Lecanuet, *Les premières années du Pontificat de Léon XIII.*, 15.
[25] *Ibid.*, 16.

tions—the chief focus of Ultramontane influence in France—must be attacked and rendered powerless for harm. The national educational system must be reformed in accordance with the formula " *l'obligation, la gratuité, la laicité.*" It was the achievement of these two objects—and in that order—that was to form the target of Republican effort for the next four years.

Even so, the path was not without its difficulties. The Senate might be now Republican, but its Republicanism was of a rather pale hue. Its leading spirit was Jules Simon, who, though not a Catholic, was also not in any sense an enemy of religion. Further, there was the strong dislike and distrust of the new President for Gambetta. This was shown at once when Grévy appointed as Premier, not the organizer of the Republican victory, but the very moderate M. Waddington, a Protestant of English family who had been educated at Rugby under Arnold. Waddington had been responsible for the measure abolishing the *jurys mixtes* rejected by the Senate in 1876 : and to this extent at least he might be regarded as committed to change in the existing educational system as established by law.

The measure in question was now to be revived. The new Minister of Public Instruction was Jules Ferry, who at once prepared two *projets* to restrain the privileges of the Church in the sphere of education. The first of these once again remodelled the *Conseil Supérieur de l'Instruction Publique,* as also the local *Conseils Académiques.* In the case of the former the representatives of the Church and of the other *grands corps sociaux* were once more eliminated : and in their place were substituted representatives of the three grades of State education—higher, secondary, and primary, together with four representatives of *l'enseignement libre.* The Council thus became a purely professional body. The clergy were similarly excluded from the *Conseils Académiques,* which henceforth were to be composed entirely of *professeurs.*

The second of the *projets Ferry* related to higher education and largely repealed the law of 1875. Articles 1 and 5 respectively suppressed the *jurys mixtes* and restored to the

State Faculties the sole right of conferring degrees. The fourth Article forbade non-State institutions for higher education to take the name of " University " : while the eighth forbade any such institution to be recognized as " of public utility " save in virtue of a law. It was, however, in the famous " Article 7 " that the worst sting of Ferry's measure lay. This ran as follows : " No one is allowed to assume direction of any public or private educational institution of any kind whatever, or to give any instruction in it, if he belongs to an unauthorized congregation." [26] Such a provision was obviously quite outside the main scope of the measure and could be dictated by but one object—to blast the whole educational activity of such congregations and in particular that of the Jesuits, whose schools were mainly responsible for the education of the upper classes.

The publication of the *Lois Ferry* filled the Catholics with dismay. The bishops and clergy at once protested : and petitions were organized all over the country. But Ferry stuck to his guns. On May 20th he proposed in addition the suppression of the " letters of obedience " granted to members of teaching congregations by their superiors and permitted by the *Loi Falloux* to take the place of other qualifications.

The second of Ferry's measures was the first to come up for consideration by the Chamber. The commission appointed to consider it reported in its favour : and on June 16th the debate began. The first articles were carried without difficulty : but Article 7 gave rise to a two days' battle, in the course of which the fanatical and atheist anticlerical Paul Bert [27] made its true objective clear by a venomous attack on the Jesuits. On July 9th the article was carried by 347 votes to 143. The debate on the law concerning the *Conseil Supérieur* followed immediately and it was carried on July 19th.

The *Lois Ferry* were now sent up to the Senate. Jules Simon was appointed *rapporteur* of the committee charged to

---

[26] Debidour, i. 209.
[27] A specimen of Bert's polemical style is printed by Debidour (i. 425ff) in the form of a résumé of his book, *La morale des Jésuites*.

examine that containing Article 7–a significant choice. During the parliamentary recess that followed, Article 7 was the exclusive topic of conversation all over France. It was condemned not only by the Catholics, but by eminent Republicans like Littré and Vacherot as well. Ferry and Paul Bert, on the other hand, toured the country in its defence. A toast proposed by the latter (August 24th) at Auxerre in the midst of the vine-growing country became notorious : " I drink to the destruction of the phylloxera—the phylloxera that hides itself under the vine, and the phylloxera *que l'on cache sous les feuilles de vigne.* For the first we have sulphur carbonate : for the other Article 7 " ! [28] The division in the Republican ranks was reflected in the Government. On December 21st Waddington resigned, and was succeeded by the sinuous and accomplished M. de Freycinet. In the new ministry, however, Ferry retained his post as Minister of Public Instruction.

Meanwhile, on December 8th, Simon had presented his report in the Senate. It was unfavourable to Ferry's *projet.* Before the debate began, the Chamber, by way of showing that it was in earnest, passed other measures unfavourable to the Church. The clergy were excluded from the *bureaux de bienfaisance* for the administration of public relief; the salaries of the bishops were reduced; and the military *aumôniers* suppressed. But none of these measures, of course, could become effective until approved by the Senate.

The debate on the *Lois Ferry* in the Senate began on January 23rd, 1880. The law relating to the *Conseil Supérieur* was taken first and carried on February 23rd. The discussion of the other measure began the same day. The first six articles were voted on March 2nd : and the senators then proceeded to consider Article 7. A battle royal ensued in which Simon attacked, while Ferry and Freycinet defended, it. The scale was turned by a speech of Dufaure denouncing it as " an act of war," " the offspring of the sectarian spirit." [29] The article was rejected on March 9th by 148 votes to 129 : and on March 15th the Senate passed the Bill without it. In

[28] Lecanuet, *op. cit.*, 34.
[29] *Ibid.*, 44.

this form it was accepted by the Chamber next day. The Bill thus became law minus Article 7. [30]

The position of disadvantage thus created for the young Catholic Universities, uncompensated as it was to be by a sufficient enthusiasm in the Catholic laity to make them ready to face its material consequences, effectively destroyed whatever chance there had been of their taking a serious place in the national life. In 1900 the students in the Catholic Institutes totalled only 1,207 as against 27,000 in the State Universities. [31]

III

The Premier had already informed the Senate that if Article 7 were rejected the Government would be compelled to " apply the existing laws." [32] This threat was immediately made good by the publication of the " decrees of March 29th." [33] By the first of these the Jesuits, as an unauthorized congregation, were to dissolve and vacate their houses within three (or in the case of schools six) months. The other laid it down that all other unauthorized congregations must apply for authorization within three months. " In the case of male congregations," it went on, " the authorization shall be effected by a law, in the case of female congregations by a law or by a decree of the Council of State."

The Pope at once protested. The bishops, laying aside the distrust with which they were not infrequently inclined to regard the independent activity of the congregations, made their cause their own and denounced the " Masonic plot." The clergy and the laity followed suit : and meetings of protest were held all over the country. The Freemasons retorted by a counter-agitation.

On May 3rd M. Lamy, a Catholic deputy, raised the matter in the Chamber. He called in question the legality of the decrees, and protested against the Government's reported intention to proceed by administrative methods and ignore

[30] Text as passed printed in Debidour, i. 435.
[31] Baunard, *Un siècle de l'Église de France,* 130.
[32] Debidour, i. 238.
[33] Complete text, *ibid.,* i. 436ff.

the courts of law. The Chamber, of course, backed the Government. But the opposition was supported by a large section of the legal profession and of the magistrates, many of whom had been appointed under the Conservative regime. An eminent advocate, M. Rousse, gave counsel's opinion that the decrees were illegal, as also the Government's proposed method of procedure. His opinion received more than 2,000 adhesions.

The Government paid no heed. On June 24th it ordered the administration to carry the decrees into effect. At the same time it enjoined that if an appeal were made to a civil court, it must declare the court incompetent : and that if the court maintained its competence, it must appeal to the *tribunal des conflits,* which was presided over by the Garde des Sceaux and would support the Government. In consequence, before the end of the year nearly 400 magistrates and officials honoured their convictions—and incidentally, no doubt, gratified the Government—by resigning their posts.

Meanwhile, what had been the line taken by the congregations themselves? The question was debated at a meeting held at the Paris Oratory on April 27th and attended by the superiors or delegates of forty-eight unauthorized congregations. It was unanimously resolved to make common cause with the Jesuits and refuse to ask for authorization. A memorandum was circulated explaining the reasons prompting this decision, and the Pope approved of the action taken. On June 29th, the day on which the three months' grace expired, the Government put into execution the decrees against the Jesuits. In Paris and in the provinces alike the Fathers were forcibly expelled from their houses in the presence of sympathizing crowds of Catholic bystanders. The action of the Government created a bad impression abroad. The *Times* stigmatized the expulsion as an " act of despotism." [34]

The Government was becoming more and more uncomfortable. President Grévy made no secret of his hostility to the decrees. Freycinet himself disliked them and was anxious for a compromise. In this he was at one with the Pope, who

[34] July 1st, 1880.

now for the first time intervened actively and personally in the affairs of the French Church.

Pius IX. had by this time been dead over two years. So long as he lived it had been useless to expect that Rome would depart from her attitude of blind, cantankerous opposition to the new order of things in Europe. But the death of the aged pontiff on February 7th, 1878 (a month after that of his despoiler, Victor Emmanuel) held out at least the possibility of better things. The choice of the Cardinals was thus a matter of vital concern both to the Church and to the European governments. It fell, fortunately for the interests of Catholicism, on Cardinal Pecci, who assumed the name of Leo XIII. Pecci had never been a favourite of his predecessor, who had kept him as long as he could at a safe distance in his see of Perugia. " Yes," he would say to Pecci's admirers, " he is an excellent bishop : let him keep to his job." [35] When he could no longer refuse his request to be allowed to return to Rome he appointed him Chamberlain of the Holy See—Roman gossip said because it was a tradition that the Chamberlain was never elected Pope! In this case, however, the tradition was falsified. The new Pope showed without delay that a change of policy was at hand. He did not indeed abandon his predecessor's rôle of " prisoner of the Vatican." Nor indeed did he seriously diverge from him as regards the *theory* of the relations between the spiritual and civil powers. He fully accepted the doctrine of the " thesis " and the " hypothesis," to which, in fact, in his Encyclical *Immortale Dei* of 1885, he gave its classic formulation. But this identity of theory and ideal was compatible with a far greater elasticity in the matter of practical application. The limits of the " hypothesis " were much less tightly drawn. Leo was as much a diplomat and a *politique* as his predecessor was the reverse—in him, indeed, diplomacy was raised to the rank of a fine art. He was fond of saying that " There is no one from whom one cannot obtain something if one can make him hear the language of reason." [36] This attitude

[35] Lecanuet, 5.
[36] *Ibid.*, 8.

found an echo in Gambetta, who, on hearing of his election, wrote: "If he does not die too soon we may hope for *un mariage de raison*" of the Republic "with the Church." [37]

The March decrees gave Leo an opportunity of putting his theories to the test. In the secret negotiation [38] with the French Government on which he now embarked, his intermediary was Mgr. Lavigerie, Archbishop of Algiers [39]—destined, now that Dupanloup was dead, to be the most striking figure in the French Church of his time. He is most celebrated for his work as the Apostle of North Africa, which will be touched on later. But his diocesan and missionary efforts were never incompatible with much activity elsewhere. He was a man of immense vision, initiative and driving power—essentially a realist and a man of affairs. His political opinions after 1870 were Legitimist: and the anticlerical historian, Debidour, retails with zest a letter written by him to the Comte de Chambord in August 1874, urging the Prince to come and take his kingdom by force with the help of the heads of the Army. "There will be," he wrote, "a street-fight in some towns: but it will serve your cause and last but a day." [40] Legitimism, however, was by now a lost cause. The Republic had arrived, and it was necessary to make terms with it. Prompted by his aged friend Maret, Lavigerie proposed to the Pope a plan for easing the situation created by the March decrees. Leo approved, and bade him set to work.

Accordingly, in June, Lavigerie sought an interview with Freycinet. The Premier was accommodating: and agreed that if the congregations would make it clear that their refusal to ask for authorization was not prompted by political motives, the execution of the decrees might be at least deferred. With this object Lavigerie drew up a declaration to be signed by them, in which they were made to repudiate "all solidarity with political passions" and to express their "submission and respect" to the Govern-

[37] *Ibid.*, 9.
[38] The authoritative account of this is in Tournier, *Le Cardinal Lavigerie et son action politique,* 1913, 52ff.
[39] On Lavigerie see Baunard, *Le Cardinal Lavigerie,* 2 vols., 1896.
[40] Debidour, i. 126.

ment." [41]   Freycinet approved the declaration :   and it was
sent to the congregations for signature.   But all, acting on the
advice of Cardinal Guibert, declined to sign.

Lavigerie refused to be discouraged and appealed again to
Rome.   The Pope wrote to Cardinal Bonnechose intimating
his desire that a declaration similar to Lavigerie's should be
signed.   Guibert thereupon joined with Bonnechose in
addressing a letter to the bishops, indicating the form of
declaration and authorizing the congregations to sign it.   Most
of the congregations then yielded, albeit most unwillingly :
but a few persisted in their refusal.

The declaration was intended to be kept a profound secret.
But on August 30th it was maliciously published in *La
Guyenne,* a Legitimist journal of Bordeaux which had
somehow come into possession of its text. [42]   The anticlericals were furious, many of the Clericals hardly less so.
Freycinet was forced to resign, and Ferry became Premier in
his place.   At once the Minister of Religions wrote to inform
the congregations that the second decree must be carried out.
This was done both in Paris and in the provinces during
October and November, to the rage and grief of the Catholics,
though the country in general remained indifferent for the
most part. [43]   When the congregations appealed to the courts,
the great majority of the latter decided that they were competent to try the issue.   But the Government appealed in its
turn to the *tribunal des conflits,* which gave judgment in its
favour all along the line. [44]

Even so the vengeance of the anticlericals remained unslaked.   Not content with dissolving the unauthorized congregations, they now took steps to doom the authorized to
slow extinction.   With this object, proposals were introduced
to impose upon them new and heavy taxation, and were duly
passed by the Chamber. [45]

[41] Full text in Tournier, 66.   See also Lecanuet, 66f.
[42] On the alleged responsibility for this of a French Royalist-Ultra-
montane bishop see *ibid.,* 75 n.   Text in *ibid.,* 69.
[43] Debidour, i. 248.
[44] Two of the chief of these decisions are printed in Debidour i., 440ff.
[45] For details see Lecanuet, 95ff ; Debidour, i. 260ff.   See also below,
ch. xi., p. 237.

IV

The problem of the congregations had been dealt with. It remained to tackle the educational question. Ferry had already been responsible for introducing more than one proposal on this subject. It now fell to him as Premier to secure their passage into law. He was not an extremist in politics generally : but, as Hanotaux says, " he held the anticlerical faith. He was a convinced, reasoned, practising free-thinker : he was the man of a doctrine, the Positivist doctrine, not by *entraînement* and hearsay but by meditated adhesion. More than anyone else he was concerned with the problem of souls." [46] His vehemence and energy dragged the " Left-Centre Republic " along, and obtained its support for the measures against the Church in which his anticlerical ardour found expression.

For the first educational law to be carried through Parliament he was not personally responsible, though, of course, he supported it. The provision of State *lycées* for girls of the better class was eagerly desired by the anticlericals as a means of breaking the virtual monopoly of secondary education for girls hitherto enjoyed by the congregations. We have already seen the first steps in this direction made by Duruy under the Second Empire. The Republican triumph made it possible to carry the work to a more successful issue. In October 1878, Camille Sée, a Jewish Freemason, introduced a measure with the object of providing such *lycées*. In the original form of the *projet* nothing was done to secure either religious or moral instruction in them. But the report on the Bill (May 1879) introduced an amendment by which moral instruction was to be given to all and religious instruction to boarders—the latter by ministers of the different denominations. Nothing was said about religious instruction for day-girls, who would form the great majority of the pupils. In this form the *Loi Camille Sée* was passed by the Chamber on June 20th, 1880, and by the Senate the following December.

It was next the turn of Ferry's own *projets*. These were concerned with primary education and had their origin in a

[46] Hanotaux, iv. 582.

measure proposed by M. Barodet in December 1877, involving a complete reform of primary education in all its aspects. The measure was submitted to a committee under the presidency of Paul Bert, who reported in its favour just a year later. Ferry, however, deemed the *projet Paul Bert* to be too elaborate and comprehensive as it stood, and decided to distribute its main provisions among a number of measures which should be introduced *seriatim*.

The first of these has been already mentioned. It decreed the suppression of the " letters of obedience " held by members of teaching congregations. Proposed by Ferry in 1879, it came up for discussion in the Chamber on May 24th, 1880, and was passed by a large majority. Its consideration by the Senate was delayed till a year later, when Ferry had been Premier for some months. Here, too, it was successful and passed into law. Its effect, however, hardly answered all the expectations of its promoters. The holders of " letters of obedience " passed the examinations now required of them without difficulty, with the result that the efficiency of the congregational schools was improved rather than impaired.

The second of the *lois scolaires* was designed to provide primary education free of charge—*la gratuité*. This was justly held to be a necessary preliminary towards making it universal and compulsory. The law declared that henceforth no payment should be exacted in the State primary schools or in the *Écoles Normales* for the training of teachers. The discussion of the measure began in the Chamber on July 15th, 1880. It was vehemently opposed by Mgr. Freppel, the fiery and ambitious Bishop of Angers, who had taken Dupanloup's place as the episcopal mouthpiece in the legislature.[47] But it was carried on November 29th by a large majority. The Senate adopted it in May of the following year.

The third of Ferry's *lois* made provision for realizing the

[47] Freppel's life has been written by Cornut, Charpentier and others. Père Lecanuet (*Les dernières années du Pontificat de Pie IX.*, 49 n.) gives some details about him which these biographers have not thought well to mention. They do not present the prelate's character in a very favourable light. A strong Gallican-Liberal before his promotion to the episcopate in 1869, he appears as an Ultramontane of the Pie school immediately after. Leo XIII. did not wish to see him in Parliament.

two other members of the Masonic trinity—*l'obligation* and *la laïcité*. Ferry himself would have desired to separate the two and defer the latter to a subsequent period. But the Freemasons insisted, and he was compelled to combine them. The first two articles dealt with the religious question and ran as follows :

1. " Religious instruction shall no longer be given in public primary schools of various kinds. A regulation of the administration of Public Instruction will decide the hours which must remain free so that the children, if their parents desire it, may receive religious instruction outside the school buildings from ministers of different denominations."

2. " The provisions of the law of 1850 are repealed in so far as they give to ministers of religion a right of inspection, supervision and direction in public and private schools." [48]

The remaining articles made primary education compulsory and determined its legal sanctions.

The debate on this measure began in the Chamber on December 4th, 1880. In a reply to Freppel, Ferry disclaimed any hostility to religion in itself. It was merely the teaching of it on denominational lines that the Bill was designed to exclude. The measure passed the Chamber on December 24th by 351 votes to 151.

The debate in the Senate did not begin till the following year. Broglie proposed to substitute "moral and religious instruction " for the " moral and civic instruction " laid down by the Bill : but his proposal was negatived. Another amendment by Jules Simon proposing that the children should be taught their duty " towards God and *la patrie* " was, however, carried, and the Bill was passed without other serious modifications. But the Chamber vetoed Simon's amendment (July 25th), and the fate of the Bill thus remained undecided.

Almost immediately afterwards the existence of the Chamber came to an end : and France gave itself up to the business of electing its successor. In the electoral campaign Gambetta, as usual, took the lead. In a speech at Belleville he declared that the resistance of the Senate on the schools

[48] Lecanuet, 117f.

question must be broken and the power of " Clericalism " annihilated for ever. The result of the elections seemed to show that the country as a whole was on his side. The Republicans obtained a crushing victory and returned 457 strong, as against but 100 of their opponents.

In the face of a triumph so overwhelming Grévy could only bow to the inevitable and invite Gambetta to become Premier. The bias of the new ministry was clearly shown by the inclusion of Paul Bert as Minister of Public Instruction and Religions ! But its existence was short-lived. On January 26th, 1882, it was defeated on a motion involving a revision of the Constitution in the Republican interest, and Gambetta resigned. The egregious Paul Bert disappeared from his ministry, leaving nothing behind but a collection of *projets* intended further to humiliate and weaken the Church. [49] Some of these were to be heard of again later.

In Gambetta's place Grévy again appointed Freycinet, and Ferry resumed his old post as Minister of Public Instruction. The third *loi scolaire* came up for reconsideration in the Senate on March 11th, 1882. Jules Simon again pleaded for some recognition of God in national education, but this time without success. The law was voted on March 23rd by 179 votes to 108. [50]

The " school without God " had thus become an accomplished legal fact. Catholic opinion was divided as to how the menace should be met. Some declared for open resistance, such as the Belgian Catholics had offered to a similar measure three years before. The *Univers* advised parents to refuse to send their children to the communal schools and face the consequences. But the Pope and the bishops were opposed to such extreme measures. They confined themselves to making two recommendations : first, that a careful watch should be kept on the State schools to see that the provisions of the law were not exceeded by anti-religious fanatics; secondly, that as many Catholic schools as possible should be founded in opposition to those of the State. The latter

---

[49] For details of these see Debidour, i. 296ff.
[50] Text printed in Debidour, i. 445ff.

recommendation was carried out with such enthusiasm that in a short time new Catholic schools had been set up all over the country, and were often more successful than their rivals.

The Government, too, showed no anxiety to press things to extremes. Here again the principle of " opportunism " governed its action. Its motto was " slow but sure." Ferry again declared his respect for religion. The Council of Public Instruction laid stress on the duty of teachers to observe a strict neutrality on the religious question. Among the numerous manuals of " moral and civil instruction" that now appeared many made no scruple about introducing the name of God. Others, however (among them one by Paul Bert), were frankly anti-religious. In consequence, four of these were placed on the Index. The Government forbade the clergy to publish this condemnation from the pulpit : but many refused to obey, and five bishops and 2,000 priests were punished by the suspension of their salaries. When the Council of State was appealed to, it supported the action of the Government.

Meanwhile the movement in support of " separation " seemed to be gathering weight. In the elections of 1881, 227 candidates had pronounced for it conditionally and 143 unconditionally.[51] This attitude was reflected in the new Chamber. Two proposals were made by deputies—the one demanding the abrogation of the Concordat, the other not this only but a complete secularization of ecclesiastical property as well. One of Paul Bert's *projets* was also disinterred which, while leaving the Concordat untouched, insisted that it should be applied with all possible rigour and that severe penalties should be inflicted for any encroachments on its terms by the clergy. The Chamber submitted all these plans to a committee. The committee rejected the more radical proposals, but largely adopted that of Paul Bert.

These developments gravely alarmed the Pope. At all costs a rupture with the Government must be averted. His first Nuncio at Paris, Mgr. Czacki (appointed in 1879) had gallantly seconded his pacific aims. Determined to " turn

[51] Lecanuet, 163.

Catholic sentimentalism into Catholic policy," Czacki had lost no time in showing the Legitimists that the Holy See regarded their cause as lost. He asked the Comte de Chambord's intimate counsellor, the Marquis de Dreux-Brézé, to face the fact that a restoration was now impossible and to concentrate the efforts of his friends on the defence of the Church. When Chambord heard of this, he remarked bitterly, " I thought that the Church forbade suicide." The following year Czacki wrote a letter to Gambetta indicating the terms on which the French clergy might adhere to the Republic : but Gambetta thought the price too high. [52] Czacki, however, was recalled to Rome in August 1882. His successor, Mgr. de Rende, was of inferior calibre. Faced with the threat to the Concordat, Leo XIII. determined to intervene again personally. On May 12th, 1883, he wrote a letter to President Grévy,[53] asking him to use his influence to restore peace between Church and State. Grévy returned a courteous reply.

It was indeed high time that something was done. The uncompromising Royalism of the Catholic leaders, both clerical and lay, was a perpetual provocation to the Republicans to attack the Church. Here and there a warning voice was raised. Even before Pius IX. was dead Mgr. Guilbert, Bishop of Gap, had written two letters[54] urging that the clergy should steer clear of politics and seek a reconciliation with the Republic. These sentiments found an echo in a work published by Maret in 1882 (just before his death), called *La vérité catholique et la paix religieuse.* The author bade the clergy recognize that the " principal strength " of their foes was the conviction that they were " irrevocably hostile to modern institutions."[55] But such a protest was *vox in deserto.* When the Comte de Chambord died in August 1883 the hopes of the Monarchists were transferred to the Comte de Paris, though the ultra-Legitimists and the *Univers* looked gravely askance at his liberal tendencies and would gladly have supported

[52] See Soderini, *Leone XIII.*, ii. 278ff. ; Lecanuet, 170f.
[53] Analysed in Lecanuet, 175f.
[54] Analysed in Lecanuet, *Les dernières années du Pontificat de Pie IX.*, 517f.
[55] Lecanuet, *Les premières années du Pontificat de Léon XIII.*, 182f.

someone else. In August 1884, the Senate and the Chamber met in joint session at Versailles to consider a partial revision of the Constitution. When it was decided to declare the Republic henceforth " definitive," Freppel made passionate protestation of his devotion to the " House of France " and his hopes of its return. His speech drew from Cardinal Guibert the caustic remark : " There are too many bishops in the Chamber." [56]

Such challenges had the inevitable result of increasing the determination of the anticlericals to break the power of the Church by every possible means. The appearance of the papal Encyclical *Humanum genus,* denouncing Free-masonry [57] (April 20th, 1884), operated in the same direction. Proposal after proposal directed against the Church was introduced in the legislature : and a number of these were passed by the Chamber, though in most cases they had to wait awhile for ratification by the Senate. The Upper House, however, was not backward in serving the campaign against the Church. At the instance of M. Waldeck-Rousseau, Minister of the Interior, it rejected a Bill (originally proposed by Dufaure in 1879 and later sponsored by Simon) for according to all associations, political or religious, the same freedom (March 1883). The Municipal Law of April 5th, 1884, [58] seriously impaired the parish priest's control over his own church, as well as his and its claims upon the communes. A Bill to legalize divorce that had been passed by the Chamber in June 1882 was accepted by the Senate on July 24th, 1884. [59] The *budget des cultes* for 1885 was down by five million francs. Meanwhile the municipality of Paris was busy driving the Sisters and chaplains out of the hospitals, despite the protests of both patients and doctors.

The Pope refused to be discouraged. On February 8th, 1884, he addressed a special Encyclical to the French bishops with the flattering title of *Nobilissima Gallorum gens.* [60] In

[56] *Ibid.,* 189.
[57] Debidour, i. 342f.
[58] *Ibid.,* 450 (extracts).
[59] Text in Debidour, i. 451.
[60] Analysed *ibid.,* 216f.

this he urged them to defend the Church in such a way as not to incur the charge of hostility to the Republic, and exhorted the Catholics to unity among themselves. The bishops received his admonitions with deference. But the *Univers* refused to listen and even suggested that the Pope's words had been mis-translated. Far from seeking to heal the dissensions among Catholics, it was at this very moment inflaming them further by opening its columns to a series of articles in which a certain Abbé Maynard assailed the memory of Dupanloup by way of a venomous criticism of Lagrange's recent *Life* of that prelate. The Pope ordered the articles to cease: but Maynard republished them at once in a book which the *Univers* described as *une œuvre doctrinale*. Thus doubly defied, Leo XIII., through the Nuncio, addressed to it a sharp rebuke (November 4th)[61]: and Maynard's book was put on the Index.

The Pope's efforts were not in vain. From 1884 onwards, though the legislature remained hostile, a certain slackening of tension is visible between the Government and the Church. Even Ferry was not unaffected by it. His antagonism to "separation" grew more pronounced: and he did not interfere when the congregations returned to the houses from which they had been driven.

[61] Text in Tournier, *Le Cardinal Lavigerie et son action politique*, 198f.

CHAPTER X

THE more pacific attitude exhibited by successive Governments towards the Church after 1883 is not solely to be explained by the skilful and conciliatory policy of Leo XIII. No doubt it was much that the Head of the Church should be averse from pushing the issue between Church and State to extremes. But for the time being he had hardly any serious support among the Catholics of France. Bishops, clergy and enthusiastic laity alike were still bitterly opposed to the Republic as such, and saw no hope for religion save in its overthrow and the return of monarchy. As time went on, the papal policy, backed by the stern lessons of experience, was to acquire a steadily increasing volume of support. But the process was slow and, at the period we have reached, had hardly even begun. Faced by an apparently irreconcilable Right, the Republican leaders would have hardly found it worth while to conciliate Catholic opinion if, besides the Pope's attitude, there had not been other reasons to urge them in the same direction.

Such reasons, however, existed.[1] In the first place, the Republican leaders were profoundly divided among themselves. Between the Opportunists and the Radicals there was not only conflict of political attitude but intense personal rivalry as well. And as time went on this division was to increase rather than diminish. In particular, Ferry and his friends were more and more convinced that at the present stage the separation of Church and State would create far greater difficulties than it would solve—might even result in civil war. It was not that they objected to Separation in itself—indeed, they regarded it as the final goal of Republican policy. But that goal could not be achieved at

[1] Debidour, i. 316ff.

present. While determined to maintain at all costs the anti-Catholic legislation of the last few years, they feared for the moment seriously to add to it or even to apply it too rigorously. The Radicals, on the other hand, were bent on securing Separation at once. But their violent and unscrupulous attacks on the Opportunists made the latter only more resolute to abstain from extreme and provocative measures against the Church. Nor were its dissensions the only or the worst source of weakness in the Republican party. The whole political world of the Left was deeply honeycombed with corruption— a corruption so shocking that its exposure in the scandals of 1887 and 1892 shook the Republican regime to its base.

These considerations drawn from the internal political situation in the country were powerfully reinforced by others affecting its external policy. The situation of France in Europe was one of almost complete isolation. Not only had the Triple Alliance of 1882 banded together Germany, Austria and Italy against her, but neither England nor Russia was at this time well-disposed. From the former she had been estranged by the Egyptian question, while the attitude of her rulers towards religion was little calculated to please the Tsar. It was, therefore, the more necessary to conciliate the Holy See, which under the accomplished pilotage of Leo XIII. was becoming more and more a force to be reckoned with in European affairs, and had no cause to serve the interests of Italy or Germany more than it could help. Further, the new colonial policy of France could not afford to despise the assistance of the Church. The protagonist of this policy was Ferry, who had conceived the idea that, if the Triple Alliance cut France off from the hope of avenging the wrong of 1871 in Europe, she might still find some solace for her humiliations in Asia and Africa. In the pursuit of such expansion no agent was more important than the French Catholic missions. In the East, France enjoyed a traditional protectorate of Christian interests of which the anticlericals of the Republic were by no means prepared to forgo the advantage. In Africa the wonderful missionary work of Lavigerie and his *Pères Blancs* not only civilized and consolidated Algeria and Tunis but supplied the spear-head for the expansion of French interests and domination in the Sahara and Central Africa and on the west coast. The colonial designs of France were jealously watched by the other Powers, all of whom at this period were occupied in similar fashion. Thus it was vitally important to keep on good terms with the Pope and his spiritual children, in France or elsewhere. The favour which the Republic denied to the Church at home could not be withheld from it abroad, where the interests of the two were largely identical. Anticlericalism might be a useful policy in France : but, in Gambetta's celebrated phrase, it was " not an article for exportation." And even at home it must be used with caution.

I

The year 1885 was to furnish Leo XIII. with fresh opportunities for dissociating himself from the line taken by the extreme Monarchist-Clericals. In the first half of the year a curious incident enabled him to strike a resounding blow at the partisans of blind reaction within the Vatican itself—the *Zelanti* who, faithful to the uncompromising tradition of Pius IX., strongly disliked the moderation of his successor. A French journalist in Rome called Des Houx, who, as editor of the *Journal de Rome,* had made himself notorious by his intransigent views, was reproved by the Pope. Thereupon a Dutch Ultramontane journalist named Brouwers asked Cardinal Pitra, Vice-dean of the Sacred College and a leader of the *Zelanti,* for his views on the matter. The Cardinal, in his reply, expressed himself in Des Houx's favour and went on to make an unpardonable attack on the Pope, whose reign he likened to that of Antichrist![2] Des Houx printed the letter, together with another from Freppel very complimentary to himself. The Pope was deeply incensed at the Cardinal's attack and expressed to him his " displeasure and disgust." But Pitra declined to withdraw anything. An *impasse* seemed to have been reached when Lavigerie persuaded Cardinal Guibert of Paris to write a letter of sympathy to the Pope. The latter replied by a letter severely rebuking

[2] Lecanuet, 289.

those Catholics who, " not content with the submission which is their rôle in the Church, aspire to take a part in its government." [3] The day after the publication of this letter (June 19th) Pitra wrote a letter to the Pope couched in terms of abject humility, though actually he made no retractation of what he had said. Des Houx was asked to leave Rome and returned to France, where he continued his campaign against the papal views. The Pope, for his part, received letters of sympathy from the bishops all over Christendom, including a large majority of the French episcopate.

Meanwhile, important events had been happening in France. In view of the approach of the General Election of October 1885, the Conservatives were anxious to direct a slashing blow at the existing regime. The opportunity was a favourable one : for the war in Annam in pursuit of Ferry's colonial projects was far from commanding general approval in France, and the Premier was at this moment the most unpopular man in the country. The Radicals hated Ferry no less than the Conservatives (though for different reasons), and on the arrival of news of an alleged military disaster (which turned out later to be greatly exaggerated) the two parties of the opposition combined to overthrow the minister. His successor, Brisson, albeit a Radical, made no serious departure from the religious policy of his predecessor, apart from the secularization of the Panthéon as a preliminary to the imposing national funeral accorded to Victor Hugo (May 26th). The Pope, reciprocating the attitude of the Government and anxious to conjure the peril in which Clerical intransigence might involve the Church in the coming election, would have liked to suggest to the clergy an acceptance of the Republic. But in the end he had to be satisfied with a carefully guarded hint to that effect in a letter [4] written by Lavigerie at his request (August 15th).

The progress of the election appeared at first to promise well for the Conservatives. At the first voting 176 Conservatives were elected as against only 127 Republicans. But, alarmed

[3] Lecanuet, 291.
[4] Text in *ibid.*, 299.

by the danger, the Republicans closed their ranks, and in the
ballot a fortnight later they were returned with a majority of
383 to 201.

Once again, then, the Monarchist-Clericals had been
defeated at the polls. What was to be done? Already, before
the elections took place, de Mun had adumbrated, in a letter
to Admiral Gicquel des Touches, the union of all Catholics,
irrespective of their political complexion, into a *parti
catholique* with a programme designed not only to vindicate
the rights of the Church but also to champion the cause of
social reform. The proposal was at first not ill-received : but
soon opposition began to appear. Accusations of " socialism "
were levelled against its author : and a leading Royalist asked
where was the need of it. " A Catholic party exists already,"
he wrote in a party newspaper : " it is the Royalist party." [5]
Fearing to see confusion worse confounded, Rome intimated
its disapproval. De Mun at once withdrew his scheme.

The formation of a *parti catholique* was indeed not what
Leo XIII. wanted. Such a solution would only be a means of
evading the step which, he rightly believed, alone offered any
hope of healing the feud between the Republic and the Church
—*le ralliement,* the frank and loyal acceptance by Catholics
of the Republican regime as the unalterable expression of the
people's will. It was with the object of assisting such a con-
summation that he issued immediately (November 19th, 1885),
the Encyclical *Immortale Dei,* [6] designed to give authoritative direction on the question which had so long divided
Catholic opinion—the question as to how far the Church
could accept the liberties on which modern society rested.
Such liberties, he laid it down, could not be regarded as a
counsel of perfection. The ideal principles governing the
social structure had been divinely revealed : and in a society
constituted as it should be, these principles would be accepted
universally and without question. The Pope, therefore, was
careful to lay down the " thesis " in unmistakable terms. But
at the same time he gave a much wider application to the

[5] Lecanuet, 309. The writer was M. Cazenove de Pradines.
[6] Analysed in Lecanuet, 313ff.

" hypothesis " than his predecessor had been prepared to do. " The greater or less participation of the people in the government has nothing blameable in itself : and at certain periods and under the sway of certain laws this participation may be not only an advantage but a duty for citizens." Again, the Church does not condemn the toleration of religions other than the true " in view of a benefit to be achieved or an evil to be avoided " : nor is it in any way opposed to the work of scientific discovery, if directed to the welfare of the human race. The Pope, in conclusion, exhorts Catholics to use the existing institutions of their country " for the profit of truth and justice " and warns them against attacking each other on questions concerning which freedom of opinion is permitted.

The language of the Encyclical was guarded enough, and might seem to a critical eye neither very clear nor very logical. But at least it was a far cry from it to the Syllabus. The intransigents professed outward deference, but were secretly by no means pleased, especially as the surviving " Liberal Catholics " claimed that it gave the papal *imprimatur* to the doctrine of Montalembert and Dupanloup. For saying this Mgr. Thomas, Archbishop of Rouen, was publicly censured by Freppel, who also denounced him to the Holy See. The Pope, while admitting that the Archbishop had " engaged the Sovereign Pontiff more than the Encyclical warranted," [7] declined to regard Freppel's denunciation as justified and inflicted upon him a severe rebuke. Thomas on his side took the first opportunity of toning down the offending utterance : and the Pope was satisfied.

At the beginning of 1886 Brisson gave place to Freycinet, who became Premier for the third time. His Cabinet contained a considerable Radical element, to which he found it necessary to give some satisfaction. Not content with denouncing the clergy for their intervention in the recent elections, he allowed his Radical Minister of Education and Religions, Goblet, to recall a Bill for the laicization of the personnel of State primary schools from the slumber in which it had re-

[7] In an interview with Mgr. Perraud of Autun, December 31st, 1885. Lecanuet, 321.

posed since its adoption by the Deputies in 1884, and to bring
it before the Senate.   By its terms the members of Catholic
teaching orders still employed in such schools were to give
place to lay instructors—the men within five years, the
women as vacancies should occur.   A further article compelled the male members of these orders to serve in the army.
The debate began on January 28th: and despite the denunciations of the Conservatives and an eloquent speech from
Jules Simon, the bill was carried on March 30th by 171 votes
to 100. Re-passed by the Deputies, it became law on October
30th.   The effect of it, however, was largely mitigated by the
enthusiasm of the Catholics, who founded thousands of *écoles
libres* all over the country and filled them with children.
Between 1886 and 1897 the number of children in Catholic
schools rose from 907,246 to 1,477,310. [8]

Having flung this sop to the Radicals, Freycinet allowed
the religious question to lie dormant.   He permitted a parliamentary committee to play with the idea of Separation, but
declared that the time was not yet ripe for it.   For the next
three years no serious action was taken against the Church.
But the indignation of the Catholics was not mollified, and
was increased by two events that happened in 1886.   The one
was the law of June 22nd compelling the heads of the rival
monarchical houses, the Orléans and the Bonapartes, with
their eldest sons, to leave France.   The other was the appearance (in the previous April) of Édouard Drumont's *La France
Juive*. [9]   This book—a fantastic compilation, full of false-
hoods and exaggerations—was an exposure of the alleged
control of the public affairs of France and Europe by the
Jews " in virtue of the most appalling financial exploitation
that the world has ever seen."   Further, Judaism and Freemasonry were depicted as the same thing under different
aspects.   The Masonic organization and all who did its work
were inspired, paid and controlled by Jews, who in this way
gratified their agelong hate against the Church and its Divine
Master.   The book created an immense sensation and excited

[8] Baunard, *Un siècle de l'Église de France*, 326.
[9] Lecanuet, 337.

particular enthusiasm among the clergy. Undoubtedly it did much to foster the growth of that antisemitism which found such hateful expression in the Dreyfus affair, and in the long run was to bear so bitter a harvest for the Church.

The gulf between the Catholics and the Republic seemed to widen rather than diminish. Yet it was at this moment that the first real advance towards *ralliement* was made. An ex-Bonapartist deputy of the Right, M. Raoul Duval, in a notable speech [10] delivered on November 6th, 1886, exhorted the Catholics to abandon their policy of vain and senseless obstruction, and to " accept a form of government which they had not chosen, but which left them complete freedom to pursue the triumph of their cause by loyal discussion, by perseverance, by legal and incessant struggle." " The Republic," he exclaimed, " belongs to no one : it belongs to all, to me, to you : it is yours if you will only take your place in it." But the appeal evoked no response for the time being.

The closing months of the following year (1887) were a time of grave trouble and scandal for France. The exposures of the " Wilson affair " proved that the son-in-law of the President had been guilty of grave political corruption, and compromised by implication President Grévy himself. Grévy at first refused to resign : but on December 2nd public opinion compelled him to do so. Of the candidates for his succession Ferry was the strongest : but the Radicals would have none of him, and the choice fell upon M. Sadi Carnot (grandson of the " organizer of victory " of 1792), an honourable, level-headed man of moderate views, who was to serve well the Pope's ministry of reconciliation.

A further step in pursuance of that ministry was taken in 1888, when Leo XIII. in connection with his sacerdotal jubilee issued another Encyclical, *Libertas præstantissimum bonum* [11] (June 20th). This Encyclical, defining the nature and limits of human freedom, was a kind of appendix to that of 1885. It explained in what sense " modern liberties " might be recognized by the Church, and admitted once again the principle

---

[10] Reproduced *verbatim* in Dabry, *Les Catholiques Républicains,* 54ff.
[11] Printed in part in Debidour, i. 454ff.

of toleration. "Not only may liberty be accorded to non-Catholics, but there are cases where it ought to be." The charge that the Church would suppress such liberty if it had the power was denied. The Encyclical was greeted by Catholics with respect and sympathy, but was variously interpreted according to the views of the commentator.

How little the Royalists had really made the papal policy their own was revealed by the unscrupulous alliance concluded by them with the would-be Dictator, General Boulanger, in 1888-9. This unprincipled soldier of fortune had been closely associated with Clémenceau and other Radicals, and had distinguished himself by his anticlerical vehemence. He was specially eager for the conscription of seminarists—"*les curés sac à dos!*" The pressure of his Radical friends secured for him the post of Minister of War in the Goblet ministry of 1886. By posing as the embodiment of the policy of *revanche* against Germany he sought to curry popular favour, and soon became the idol of the Paris mob. The substitution of Freycinet for Goblet as Premier in 1887 involved (fortunately for France) his supersession at the War Office, and he was given a command in the provinces. But political intrigue was more to his taste. The Wilson scandals and the consequent demoralization of the political world excited in him the ambition of becoming master of the destinies of France on the ruins of the Republican regime. He presented himself as a candidate in several constituencies at once with the programme: "Dissolution of the Chambers and Revision of the Constitution," and was elected by enormous majorities. "Boulangism," said the *Univers,* "is ceasing to be a farce and is becoming a force." [12]

Such a chance of overthrowing the Republic was too good to be missed. The parties of the Right entered into league with Boulanger; the Comte de Paris accepted his programme; the Duchesse d'Uzés poured three million francs into his war-chest. In vain the more prudent or scrupulous Monarchists urged caution, and the Pope refused all en-

[12] Lecanuet, 359.

couragement. De Mun openly espoused the General's cause[13] and carried the Catholics with him. The *Univers*, which a little before had scoffed at the "vulgar adventurer," now backed him with might and main.[14] Boulanger on his side forgot his anticlerical past and declared at Tours on March 17th, 1889, that "the Republic must repudiate the Jacobin heritage of the present Republic : it must bring to the country religious pacification by an absolute respect for all beliefs and all opinions."[15]

But already the bubble was on the point of bursting. The ineffective Government of M. Floquet had given place on February 21st to a ministry headed by M. Tirard, which was explicitly a ministry of "Republican resistance." The new Minister of the Interior, M. Constans, was a strong man and determined to crush the menace at all costs. Faced with a trial for high treason, Boulanger fled to Brussels on April 1st. Immediately his popularity was at an end, and the Catholics were left to face the consequences of their disastrous move. A new blow was levelled without delay at the Church in the law of July 18th,[16] compelling seminarists to serve in the army; though by grace of the Senate their term of service was limited to one year, and in the case of mobilization their duties were to be confined to tending the sick.

The General Election of 1889 followed soon after. The Monarchists continued their alliance with Boulangism in the desperate hope that something might still come of it. The Pope urged the bishops not to compromise the Church further : but the majority paid no heed. Their hopes were rudely shattered. Only forty Boulangists were elected, and the total of the Opposition parties in the new Chamber was but 210 seats, as against a phalanx of 366 Republicans.

II

It might have been anticipated that the collapse of their Boulangist escapade would have brought upon the Catholics a

---

[13] Lecanuet, 361.
[14] *Ibid.*, 360, 361.
[15] *Ibid.*, 363.
[16] Relevant clauses printed in Debidour, i. 466.

terrible vengeance at the hands of the victorious Republicans, and that the gulf between Church and State would yawn wider than ever. Actually the reverse was the case. The years following 1889 were a time of steady *rapprochement* between the Republicans and the Catholics.

The reasons for this must now be examined. First on the side of the Republicans.[17] The Boulangist movement had given their nerves a bad shaking: and this fear persisted even after victory was secured. The Catholics had helped to put the Republic in imminent peril. What they had done once they might do again. To prevent this it was necessary at the same time to conciliate and to control them. For both purposes no better weapon could exist than a skilful use of the Concordat, which in consequence came to appear to the Opportunists as an " ark of salvation." Gambetta had once said : " Separation would be the end of the world."[18] The moderate Republicans were more and more of that opinion. The Concordat gave them at least some hold upon the Church—a hold that Separation would destroy for ever. Even the Radicals, for all their theoretic hatred of the Concordat, showed themselves very shy of tampering with it when political power was actually in their hands. But, secondly, the danger to the Republic at this time came not only from the Right : it also came from the Left. Socialism was a growing power in the country : and to conjure the peril that thus threatened the whole existing social order the Moderates might well be glad of so powerful a conservative force as the Church. A third cause was the influence upon Ministers of the State administration. At this period the great public services, despite the " purge " of 1883, still displayed a strong Conservative tinge. The Army, in particular, officered by men largely educated under Jesuit influence, was very well disposed to the Church —the Navy even more so. The same thing was true of the Académie Française. For statesmen who coveted nothing more than the fauteuil of an Immortal it was important to do nothing that would prejudice them in its eyes. Finally, the

[17] Debidour, ii. 2ff.
[18] Quoted Anatole France, *L'Église et la République,* 25.

interests of France abroad, not less than the interest of the Republic at home, counselled a respectful attitude to the Pope and the Catholic body. Both in China and the Ottoman Empire, as we have seen, the French protectorate was an invaluable weapon of national expansion : and Leo XIII. was a good enough diplomat to make the maximum use of his opportunity; now (in the case of China) threatening to take it away, now confirming it. In the same way, as the alliance between France and Russia seemed to French statesmen to become at once more covetable and more and more a practical possibility, they became increasingly desirous to avoid anything that might seem to identify their country with the spirit of revolution and hostility to religion.

On the Catholic side, too, the logic of facts was beginning to do its work. Once again the Monarchist-Clericals had challenged public opinion at the polls, only to sustain another crushing defeat. Even the *Univers* was compelled to admit that " this country desires the Republic." [19]   Again, if the Pope had not yet ventured to pronounce openly in favour of *ralliement,* he had at least made it clear that overt hostility to the Republican regime was not to his liking. The example of the Head of the Church was bound to have an increasing effect on Catholic opinion. It is true that the majority of Catholics in 1890 were still far from seconding his views. Those (and they were many) who were Monarchists first and Catholics afterwards, who regarded the Church chiefly as a pawn in playing the Royalist game, were little likely to favour a step that would make their objective more remote than ever. And even those Catholics who, like de Mun, were *catholiques avant tout* were slow to make a sacrifice of their political creed that had not yet been proved to them to be necessary or desirable. Among these were most of the bishops. The majority of the French episcopate were men of rather inferior calibre—the administration that had the choosing of them saw to that—deficient therefore in the power of taking comprehensive and independent views. It was not easy for them to forget the blows inflicted by the Republic on the Church.

[19] *Univers,* February 7th, 1890.

In addition, they were very dependent upon the Royalists. In taking an independent line in politics they were well aware that they ran the risk of cutting themselves off from the chief source of their diocesan funds. This consideration weighed no less heavily with the bulk of the lower clergy : and the influence of their favourite journals, such as the *Univers,* led them in the same direction. [20]

In this quarter, however, a new current of opinion was beginning to show itself which was powerfully to reinforce the papal policy. Here, as in the case of Ultramontanism earlier in the century, the lower clergy were to give the higher a lead. The French priesthood at this period included a group of young and enthusiastic abbés who had the courage and vision to take a line of their own. [21] It is possible that their motives were not entirely disinterested. For the most part they were of the clerical publicist type—fond of being in the public eye and more at home on the platform and in the newspaper-office than in the routine of parochial work. Nor perhaps was it without some satisfaction that they, humble abbés sprung from the ranks, set themselves in opposition to the aristocracy and their imperious Fathers in God. Yet it would be difficult to quarrel with the main motive that inspired them. They at least had the courage to face the fact that the Church in France had almost entirely lost grip of the people— and most of all in the cities and towns. The women might still feel some attachment for it : but the men were hostile or at best completely indifferent. The reason for this alienation, they believed, was obvious. The Church had identified itself with the rich and had been heedless of the legitimate grievances and aspirations of the poor. The chief parties of the State—the Right and the Left alike—dominated as they were by *laissez-faire* doctrines of political economy, had shown themselves no less indifferent. Thus the working

---

[20] Debidour, ii. 20.
[21] The story of the *abbés démocrates* has been well told by one of their number, Pierre Dabry, in *Les Catholiques Républicains,* 1905. Dabry was to leave the Church in despair under Pius X. See also Lecanuet, *La Vie de l'Église sous Léon XIII.,* 609ff.

classes were fast turning to Socialism, which alone seemed to promise them the social justice of their dreams.

It is true that the Catholic de Mun had made a gallant attempt to solve the urgent social problems of the time by means of his *Cercles*, designed to unite employers and employed in an organization that should honestly pursue the interests of both under the ægis of the Church and (ultimately) to bring about a revival of the trade-corporations of the Middle Ages. In the north of France, too, an association of Catholic employers was formed that conscientiously sought to secure the welfare of their workmen. But such schemes were in fact too undemocratic to meet the urge of the time. What the workers wanted was not to be paternally controlled for their own good, but to settle their problems for themselves. When, during the debate on the law of 1884 legalizing *syndicats professionnels*[22]—" Trades Unions," as we should call them—de Mun strove to secure special privileges for his favourite *syndicats mixtes*, embracing employers and employed, he was unsuccessful : and indeed the workers wanted that kind of *syndicat* even less than the legislature. Furthermore, if the working class remained obstinately indifferent to de Mun's efforts on their behalf, the Catholic leaders, clerical and lay, were not less so—though for an opposite reason. His theories were regarded as dangerously akin to Socialism : and his increasing inclination towards State intervention in industrial matters hardened the suspicion. So much so that in 1890 a *Société catholique d'économie politique et sociale* was founded, including the leading Catholic laity, and with Freppel as President, to combat the " dangerous tendencies " of de Mun and his friends.[23]

None the less his efforts had been by no means without fruit. It was a great gain that even a small number of Catholics were willing to study economic problems in a serious and constructive way. Side by side with the practical activities of the *Œuvre des Cercles* there went, from 1878 onwards, the " research work " of a sister organization, the

---

[22] Lecanuet, *Les premières années du Pontificat de Léon XIII.*, 428.
[23] *Ibid.*, 442.

Conseil des Études, under the direction of the Marquis de la Tour du Pin,[24] the scientific leader of the Catholic Social movement, as de Mun was its orator and organizer. The fruits of its examination of social problems and theories were embodied in a series of valuable *Avis,*[25] and gradually took shape as a considered corpus of social doctrine.

The interest of Catholics in such matters was not confined to France alone : similar movements were at work in all the leading Catholic countries.[26] With the object therefore of co-ordinating their efforts with those of his own group and of evolving a common programme, La Tour du Pin conceived the idea of an international conference. The first of these was held at Fribourg in 1884 : and similar meetings took place every year till 1891. The deliberations of this *Union de Fribourg* were watched with close attention and sympathy by Leo XIII., who instructed Cardinal Mermillod of Geneva to keep him posted as to their debates and conclusions.

In the later 'eighties interest in the social problem was further kindled by the growth of the American " Knights of Labour "[27]—an organization founded to champion the rights of the workers and including many Catholics. The position of Catholics in the United States was a source of particular interest to the more progressively minded of their co-religionists in France and elsewhere, as serving to prove the compatibility of democratic institutions with a virile and expanding Catholicism. The United States episcopate, headed by Cardinal Gibbons of Baltimore, was well disposed generally to the " Knights." But in the more conservative American Catholics the rather militant attitude of the organization excited serious misgivings : and the Canadian bishops denounced it to Rome. After the great strikes organized by it in 1885, Leo XIII. excommunicated the order. Cardinal Gibbons, however, wrote a memorandum in its defence : and his brother, Cardinal Manning of Westminster, also pleaded

[24] On La Tour du Pin, see Nitti, *Catholic Socialism,* 281f.
[25] The first volume was published in 1883.
[26] These movements are described in Nitti, *op. cit.*
[27] On these see Nitti, 333ff.

its cause. After prolonged consideration the Pope decided that it might be tolerated for the present (1888).

The sympathetic attitude of the Sovereign Pontiff towards the working class was further displayed in the warm welcome accorded by him to a great pilgrimage of 10,000 workmen that visited Rome in the autumn of 1889 under the leadership of Cardinal Langénieux of Reims. Some eighteen months later the Pope issued his Encyclical *Novarum rerum*[28] (May 15th, 1891), in which he defined the attitude of the Church towards the social evils of the modern world and claimed that it alone possessed the remedy for them. The exploitation of labour by capital was denounced as a deadly sin: and the right of the workers to just and equitable treatment was recognized even to the extent of recommending a minimum wage. The principle of State intervention was conceded, though only in exceptional circumstances and in default of other remedies. The right of association was also stressed, and the Encyclical recommended a return to the old guilds—guilds of workmen only, if guilds combining employers and employed were not possible.

The august approval of Rome thus largely given to their projects was a great encouragement to de Mun and his friends: and in 1892 a *Ligue de propagande catholique et sociale* was formed to give them wider extension. In the meantime, however, a dual trend of opinion had begun to reveal itself within the *Œuvre des Cercles*. While La Tour du Pin and de Mun remained faithful to their guilds project, a more advanced section, recognizing that the combination of employers and employed in a single organization was not feasible, strove to develop the movement on more democratic lines. The leader of this section was the admirable M. Léon Harmel, who in his works at Val-au-bois had created the classic example of a " Christian factory "[29] and had permitted his workmen to organize themselves separately. Harmel laid special stress on the duty of workmen to study economic questions for them-

---

[28] Text of French translation in Debidour, ii. 500ff. Analysis in Lecanuet, 453ff.
[29] On this see Nitti, 293f. Also Dabry, 190f.

selves : and under his direction study circles were formed in many parts of France and held their first joint Congress at Reims in 1893. About the same time a number of kindred organizations were founded on similar lines : and a powerful movement towards " Christian democracy " began to define itself.

In this movement the group of *abbés démocrates,* already mentioned, played a leading part–notably the Abbés Garnier, Naudet, Dabry (the historian of the movement) and Lemire, who was to secure election as deputy for Hazebrouck in 1893. Their avowed aim was to jolt the Church out of the rut of a narrow ecclesiasticism and to substitute for the *petites dévotions* that had become the staple of Catholic piety—the " tithing of mint, anise and cummin "—a zeal for the " weightier matters " of the Christian law : for justice between man and man and the refashioning of society in accordance with the spirit of Christ. In this way, they believed, the people might be won back to the Church and the pernicious spread of materialistic Socialism be checked. With the object of spreading their ideas they multiplied organizations and journals all over France : nor is it easy to say what the effects of the " new apostolate " [30] might have been if the calamitous events of the last years of the century had not arrested it in mid-flight.

The Catholic democrats were naturally well disposed to the Republic. Unlike the Catholic Conservatives, they had no fear of the people : and the Republic was for them the expression of the people's will. Theologically they were Ultramontanes, but of the newer sort—not the brand of Pius IX., but the later brand of Leo XIII. On their lips indeed the ideas of the latter were not only echoed but exaggerated. Yet the Pope regarded them with a tolerant eye—and not less so because they were useful auxiliaries to his policy of *ralliement.*

Another contemporary movement assisted in the same direction, sponsored in this case, not by seculars, but by

[30] The phrase is Dabry's and provides the title of one of the most interesting chapters (ch. vi.) of his book.

religious—the members of the Assumptionist Order. This
Order, founded by Père d'Alzon in 1850, had grown rapidly
in wealth and importance. A daily newspaper, the *Croix,*
first published in 1883, served as the organ of its views.[31]
The editor, Père Bailly, united a flair for popular journalism
with remarkable business capacity: and under his direction the
Croix not only grew rapidly in circulation and influence but
a network of *comités de la Croix* was created all over France
to second its design of Christianizing the masses. In addition
to the Paris *Croix* a number of local *Croix* were brought into
existence: and the headquarters of the movement, the
Maison de la Bonne Presse, poured forth a stream of tracts
and other popular literature. Passionately Ultramontane and
partisans of a policy *catholique avant tout,* the Assumptionists
had more and more inclined to the recognition of the Republic
with the object of refashioning it in the interests of the
Church. Later on a deterioration of their aims and methods
was to give a fatal twist to Catholic action in France. But at
the present period they undoubtedly did useful work in helping to close the gulf between the Republic and the Church.[32]

III

We have reviewed the factors that in the years 1890-4
favoured the papal policy of *ralliement.* It remains to
describe the process by which *ralliement* was gradually
brought about. The early days of the new Parliament witnessed an important first step in the desired direction. The
appeal of M. Raoul Duval had been unsuccessful for the
moment: but it was now to bear fruit. A deputy of the
Right, M. Piou, had initiated a new party, the *Droite Con-
stitutionnelle,* which was to accept frankly the principle of the
Republic, while seeking at the same time to obtain the repeal
of such of its legislation as was obnoxious to Catholics. The
Pope watched his efforts with approval: and soon, encouraged by the pacific attitude of the Government, he
determined to give a public, if indirect, lead to Catholic

[31] Lecanuet, *La Vie de l'Eglise sous Léon XIII.,* 220ff.
[32] Dabry, 84f., 220f.

opinion. Anxious to avoid the risk of appearing to dictate in political matters, he decided to employ a French mouthpiece for the time being. The dangerous honour of serving as such was accepted by Lavigerie, though it might well alienate Royalist support from his missionary work. The visit of a French naval squadron to Algiers provided him with an occasion. In the absence of the Governor-General Lavigerie gave a banquet in the visitors' honour : and it was then that he proposed the famous " Toast of Algiers " (November 12th, 1890).[33] The crucial part of his speech ran as follows : " When the will of a people has clearly affirmed itself and when the form of a Government contains nothing contrary (as Leo XIII. recently proclaimed) to the principles that can alone secure the existence of Christian and civilized nations : when there is required in order to rescue one's country from the gulfs that threaten it an adhesion *sans arrière-pensée* to that form of government, the moment comes to declare the issue finally settled *(l'épreuve faite)*, and, with the object of putting a term to our dissensions, to sacrifice what honour or conscience allows each one of us to sacrifice for the saving of our country." " In speaking thus," the Cardinal added, " I am certain of not being disavowed by any authorized voice."

The sensation produced by so clear-cut a pronouncement may be imagined. The moderate Republicans did not conceal their satisfaction, but the Monarchist-Clericals were infuriated. The journals of the latter heaped abuse and insults on Lavigerie. Of the bishops, only two gave public approval to the toast, while two others publicly repudiated it. One of these, Freppel, went so far as to make a virulent attack on Lavigerie's speech in a journal controlled by him, *L'Anjou*. The article was unsigned : but everyone knew who had written it.[34]

Meanwhile a number of the bishops had appealed to Rome for guidance. For the moment Leo, alarmed by the outcry, shrank from committing himself too much

[33] Lavigerie's speech is printed in full in Debidour, ii. 499f.
[34] Lecanuet, 398.

personally. But, in a reply to one of the bishops, the
Cardinal Secretary of State, Rampolla, gave what amounted
to a vague endorsement of Lavigerie's advice. At the beginning of the following year, too, the Pope, in an interview with
M. Piou, not content with expressing his entire approval of
the toast, charged his interlocutor to go and see the Archbishop of Reims, Cardinal Langénieux, and request him to
make a declaration similar to his brother Cardinal's.   The
receipt of the papal message put Langénieux in a quandary :
for not only was he a Royalist by conviction, but his friend
and adviser, Mgr. d'Hulst, had been urging him to make a
declaration that should minimize the effect of Lavigerie's. He
therefore did nothing.   Meanwhile, the Royalists had been
active on the other side.   In February Freppel even paid a
visit to Rome in the hope of inducing the Pope to disavow the
toast. But the bishop got no satisfaction.   Leo, in fact, had
already made up his mind to come into the open. On February
9th, 1891, he addressed to Lavigerie a flattering letter containing these words : " All that your Eminence has done
answers entirely to the needs of the time, to our expectation,
and to the other marks of particular devotion that we have
received from you." [35]   This letter its recipient hastened to
communicate to his flock.

The secret was out. Lavigerie's policy was that of the Pope.
But in what sense was it to be interpreted ? Here, in the case
of the majority of Catholics, the wish was father to the
thought. What the Pope really wanted, they chose to believe,
was not an acceptance of the Republic in principle, but only
that Catholics should abstain from attacking the constitution
and abandon their divisions, uniting on the basis of the defence
of their religion. This was the line taken by Cardinal Richard
of Paris in a printed *Reply to certain eminent Catholics* [36] who
had consulted him. It was the *parti catholique* over again.

The Royalists breathed more freely : and sixty-two bishops
intimated their approval of the recommendation.   At once
steps were taken to give it practical expression. At the twentieth

[35] Lecanuet, 407.
[36] Analysed in *ibid.*, 409. See also ch. xviii. of Clément, *Vie du
Cardinal Richard,* 1924—a typical specimen of " edifying " biography.

Catholic Congress held in Paris in April it was decided to form a *Union Chrétienne de la France*. The programme of this, issued on June 19th, declared for political *neutrality*.

Such a policy was an evasion, not a fulfilment, of the Pope's wishes. Acceptance was one thing, " neutrality " quite another. The *Union* indeed was no more than the old Royalist party in a thin disguise. Its President was Chesnelong : and its other leading members, like him, were Royalists without exception. Of the real attitude of the Monarchists towards *ralliement* Lavigerie had cruel experience when he visited Paris in June. He was received with icy coldness by the aristocratic faubourg, which closed to him its purse as well as its heart. Stricken to death, he left Paris and died the following year.

The moderate Republicans, on the other hand, while under no illusions as to the real significance of the *Union,* maintained their policy of *apaisement,* in the hope that better things might come in time. The Pope, too, refused to be discouraged. Finding that the Nuncio at Paris, Rotelli, was indifferently disposed to his designs, he put in his place Mgr. Ferrata, who, he knew, would second them with heart and soul.

Such was the uneasy situation when a totally unexpected incident precipitated an explosion. Encouraged by the Encyclical *Novarum rerum* of the preceding April, the promoters of the workmen's pilgrimage of 1889, Cardinal Langénieux and Léon Harmel, had devised a more imposing demonstration still. In September more than 20,000 workers made their way to the Eternal City and were soon joined by members of the *Association de la Jeunesse Française,* an upper-class organization controlled by the Jesuits. One of the latter section, visiting the Pantheon (where Victor Emmanuel was buried) on October 2nd, wrote in the visitors' book the words " *Vive le pape!* " Unfortunately, the revolutionary element in Rome was on the watch and seized on the incident as a pretext for violent demonstrations against the pilgrims and even against the French Embassy. The Pope at once suspended the pilgrimage and arranged for the pilgrims to leave Italian soil immediately. But, not content with this, the Minister of Religions, M. Fallières, sent on October 4th a rather curt com-

munication to the French bishops [37] asking them to "abstain
from all participation in such pilgrimages for the present," on
the ground that "all the authorities of the country must avoid
being compromised by manifestations which may easily lose
their religious character."

The bishops for the most part received the monition with
chilly silence: but fifteen or sixteen protested, and one, Mgr.
Gouthe-Soulard, Archbishop of Aix, addressed to the Minister
a letter [38] of unpardonable insolence, accusing him of being
the tool of Freemasonry. Fallières was at first for ignoring the
letter; then, yielding to Radical pressure, decided to summon
the Archbishop before the Court of Appeal for *outrage* to his
office. The bishops at once rose in protest: and the Royalists
were enchanted. At his trial (November 24th) the defendant
made a fierce attack on the anti-Church legislation of the
Republic and declared, "We desire *apaisement*: but such
apaisement as is offered us would be a degradation." [39]   He
was found guilty and fined 3,000 francs, and on leaving the
court despatched a braggart telegram to Rome. But the Pope
vouchsafed no reply.

The Radicals, of course, made the most of this unfortunate
incident: but the Government refused to allow its policy to be
deflected. The bishops, too, having made their demonstration,
were not disinclined to some slight modification in their attitude
—a modification which Freppel (who died on December 23rd,
1891) was no longer there to resist. This was shown in a
Declaration signed by five of the six French Cardinals (it was
not even sent to Lavigerie) which was published January 20th,
1892 and obtained the prompt adhesion of seventy-five other
bishops. The Declaration began with a vehement denunciation of the sins of the Republic against the Church, but went
on to exhort Catholics to "frank and loyal acceptance of
political institutions," while bidding them offer "a firm resistance to the encroachments of the secular power upon the
spiritual domain." [40]   Even this was not quite what the Pope
wanted: but it was at least a step in the right direction.

---

[37] Printed in Lecanuet, 477.   [39] Lecanuet, 484.
[38] Complete text in Debidour, ii. 62 n.   [40] Lecanuet, 494f.; Debidour, ii. 71.

It was, however, the first part of the Declaration and the defiant part of the second on which the Radicals laid hold. Compelled to do something to pacify them, Freycinet permitted the introduction into the Chamber of a law on associations granting full freedom to all associations save those of a religious character, which were largely put at the mercy of the Government. Not content with this, the Radicals demanded that it should be proceeded with immediately on the ground of " urgency." Freycinet replied that if to concede this was to be regarded as tantamount to a declaration in favour of separation, he would refuse. After an implacable speech from Clémenceau, who maintained that the Church and the Republic were " mutually exclusive terms," the bill was put to the vote : and the Government, beaten by another infamous coalition of Radicals and Monarchists, was forced to resign (February 18th).

Once again, then, the fanatics of the Right had resorted to what was called *la politique de l'abîme* (or, alternatively, *de l'excés du mal*)—the desperate resolve to precipitate a situation that might explode all hope of reconciliation for good and all. So flagrant and unscrupulous a disregard of his known wishes could not be passed over by the Pope. For some time he had had in preparation an Encyclical giving formal and reasoned expression to his policy. The publication of this could no longer be delayed : and it appeared on February 20th (it was dated February 16th). In the Encyclical [41] (which by way of exceptional compliment was in French) the Pope, having laid it down that Catholics are bound to accept the established form of government whatever it may be—" for the civil power is of God and always of God "—draws the conclusion that it is not merely permissible but obligatory for French Catholics to accept the Republic. The difficulty raised by the Republican laws against the Church is countered by a distinction between " constituted authority " and " legislation." The Catholics have the right and the duty to work for the abrogation of such laws, but only by " honest and legal means." The Encyclical concludes by

[41] Text printed in full in Debidour, ii. 524ff.

exhorting Catholics not to attack the Concordat and protesting against the theory of separation.

As might have been expected, the Royalists were furious against the Encyclical and soon proceeded to attack it. Some declared the Pope " ill-informed," others denied his right to interfere in secular politics. " We are Catholics at Rome and Frenchmen in France." [42] A large number hedged for the moment, hoping still to find some middle course. The bishops for the most part published the Encyclical but maintained a non-committal attitude. The *Univers* and the *Croix,* on the other hand, faithful to their principle of obedience to Rome, loyally submitted. The obedience, however, of the former (edited since 1883 by Louis Veuillot's brother Eugène) was at the cost of a schism in its staff. Two of Louis Veuillot's dearest disciples, MM. Loth and Roussel, broke away and founded *La Vérité Française,* which received the enthusiastic support of the *réfractaires* and was to be the focus of the opposition to the papal policy. A stinging rebuke from Rome was without effect.

A fresh dispute between the Government and the Church gave the Pope an opportunity of proving the sincerity of his desire for peace. A number of bishops had added to their diocesan catechisms a supplementary portion dealing with the duty of Catholics in regard to the exercise of the vote, the education of children, etc. The Government demanded the withdrawal of these. The bishops were inclined to resist, but the Pope persuaded them to submit. He had already, in a letter (dated May 3rd) addressed to the French Cardinals, re-affirmed the instructions of the Encyclical. [43] In consequence of this, the *Union de la France Chrétienne* was dissolved.

Numerous adhesions to the papal policy followed at once. Some of the Royalist leaders kept silence : others retired from public life, unwilling to sacrifice the creed of a lifetime. But d'Hulst, Mackau (a former leader of the Right), and, above all, de Mun, felt it their duty to obey the Pope, and sorrowfully submitted. A number of Royalists, however, (including d'Haussonville) remained obdurate.

[42] Lecanuet, 517.   [43] *Ibid.,* 539.

The hatred of these last for the Republic and their eager desire to scuttle the new Catholic policy found their opportunity in the scandals of the "Panama affair," which broke out at the end of 1892. It was the revelations of Royalist journals (particularly Drumont's organ, *La Libre Parole*) that first brought these scandals to the public attention: and as the appalling story of fraud and corruption slowly unwound itself the *réfractaires* were almost beside themselves with joy. Many of the leading Republican politicians, both moderates and Radicals, were involved, including Freycinet (who was forced to retire into private life) and Clémenceau. The *ralliés*, however, maintained on the whole a wise reserve: and the Pope took the same attitude.

Meanwhile the Catholic *ralliés* were taking steps to organize themselves politically on the platform provided by the Encyclical. Three leaders, Piou, de Mun and Etienne Lamy, put themselves at the head of the movement. Unfortunately, instead of taking action in common, they preferred to operate separately, and this undoubtedly weakened the position of all three. All, however, accepted more or less the *mot d'ordre* of Rome: "The minimum programme is the ideal programme." [44] The Republican moderates, still reeling under the Panama disclosures, alarmed, too, at the Anarchist outrages that were terrorizing Paris, were only too willing to meet them half way. During the campaign preceding the General Election of August 1893, they abounded in promises of religious pacification.

The result of the election showed the disastrous effects of Catholic disunion. The *ralliés* won but 35 seats, the Royalists barely 60: while the Republican moderates came back 311 strong. But if the Catholics had lost cohesion, the Republican *Bloc* had disintegrated too. Moderates and Radicals were wider apart than ever: and before the growing menace of Socialism and Anarchism the former swung more and more in a Conservative direction. Immediately after the new Chamber met M. Casimir Périer became Premier, with

[44] *Moniteur de Rome,* January 13th, 1893. Article quoted textually in Dabry, *Les Catholiques Républicain,* 279f.

M. Spuller as his Minister of Education and Worship. Both were strongly in favour of religious peace. For a moment fresh trouble threatened to break out in connection with a law of January 26th, 1892, compelling Catholic places of worship to submit their accounts annually to Government inspection in the same way as other " public establishments." But the Pope intervened, and the conflict came to an end.

So intent was the Government on conciliating Catholic opinion that it did not wait for this question to be settled before making a gesture that seemed to promise the opening of a new era. On March 3rd, 1894, Spuller was questioned in the Chamber respecting the action of a Socialist Paris *maire,* who had forbidden the exhibition of Catholic emblems as a funeral passed through the streets to the cemetery. [45] Did he regard this, he was asked, as consistent with religious freedom? In replying, Spuller began by declaring the prohibition " inadmissible in law and in fact," and from that went on to declare his desire for " an enlightened and superior toleration which has its principle not only in freedom of mind but in the warmth of charity." " It is time," he said, " to fight against *all* fanaticisms and *all* sectaries." The Government, while maintaining the independence of the civil power, would evince " a new spirit, the spirit that tends to reconcile all Frenchmen round the ideas of good sense, justice and charity." The old Radical, Brisson, demanded that the Minister should explain this " new spirit " further. Spuller did so. The times, he said, had changed : and the Republican policy should change too. To the " petty and vexatious war " against the Church in the past must succeed " a lofty and broad toleration, an intellectual and moral renewal." Brisson retorted by proposing a motion affirming the fidelity of the Chamber to " the anticlerical principles which have always inspired Republican policy." This brought the Premier to his feet with a speech on similar lines to his colleague's. The Radical motion was put to the vote and lost, and a vote of confidence in the Government carried instead.

[45] There is a vivid account of this debate in Dabry, 289ff.

CHAPTER XI

THE " NEW SPIRIT " AND THE DREYFUS AFFAIR
1894—1899

I

L'esprit nouveau! The phrase had been launched: it only remained for the thing to follow. Certainly in the latter part of 1894 the prospects were rosy. The Government was sincere in its desire for religious peace: and the election to the presidency of Casimir Périer in the place of Carnot, assassinated on June 24th, seemed to set the seal on the new order of things. The Catholics were still divided: but the papal policy had made great way and to a large extent *ralliement* was an accomplished fact. The reconciliation, of course, was still far from complete. The Radicals on the one hand, the Royalists on the other, were still obdurate. Yet, such as it was, it secured for the Church five years at least of comparative peace. And in the new atmosphere the Church flourished abundantly. The years between 1892 and 1900 show a notable development of Catholic activity in all directions.

Casimir Périer's presidency was of short duration. The Radicals and Socialists did their best to make his life a burden. His temperament was sensitive, and he was not personally popular. After six months he resigned. His successor was Félix Faure, who, though a Freemason, was well disposed to the Church.

Immediately after his election Faure appointed M. Ribot as Premier. Ribot at once declared himself in favour of *apaisement:* and no doubt his professions were sincere. At the same time he was not prepared to let the Church have everything its own way. In particular he was concerned to secure a more faithful discharge by the religious orders of their financial obligations. It had long been a grievance against them that their corporate character enabled them largely to elude the charges which in the case of an individual citizen

were payable to the State on the transfer of property by death.
The authorized congregations indeed paid a mortmain tax :
but the unauthorized paid nothing at all.   To meet this difficulty a law of 1880 (confirmed in 1884) had subjected them
to a *taxe d'accroissement*, by which, on the death of a member
of a congregation, each of the houses belonging to that congregation must pay a percentage on the deceased's share of
the common property.   The congregations, however, had
shown a brilliant and progressive ingenuity in evading it.
The tax which in 1890 brought in over 1½ million francs had
in 1893 sunk to 350,000 francs.[1]   Ribot proposed to substitute a *taxe d'abonnement*, consisting of a small percentage
levied annually on the capital value of the property of each
congregation.   The law speedily passed both the Chamber
and the Senate.

The Catholic press, led by the *Croix*, at once made an
outcry and exhorted the congregations to passive resistance.
The bishops, too, were for the most part in favour of resistance : but first they wanted to know what Rome thought.
Cardinals Langénieux and Richard consulted the Pope, who
replied that, while regretting the law, he could not himself
counsel resistance to it.   He would neither approve nor condemn :   the bishops and the superiors must decide for
themselves.[2]

Meanwhile a letter[3] had been published addressed by
Fuzet, Bishop of Beauvais, to the superior of a female congregation, advising submission.   Fuzet was a Gallican of the
old-fashioned authoritarian type, whose one idea was to
maintain the Concordat at almost any cost—" *grand politicien
devant l'Éternel,*" Loisy calls him.[4]   Langénieux promptly
rebuked his suffragan, who was bitterly attacked by the
Catholic press.   However, he did not stand alone.   Cardinal
Meignan of Tours, a Liberal of the Dupanloup school, wrote
to the Pope hinting a hope that he would counsel submission :
but the Pope declined to change his attitude.   Rampolla, in a

[1] Lecanuet, *Les signes avant-coureurs de la Séparation*, 24.
[2] Much of this letter is quoted *verbatim* in Lecanuet, *op. cit.*, 36.
[3] Printed *ibid.*, 38.
[4] *Mémoires*, iii. 195.

letter to Meignan (May 3rd),[5] again left the question to the
bishops and superiors, but urged them to avoid "risky and
premature decisions." This rather Delphic utterance was
variously interpreted. Langénieux for his part set himself to
organize resistance.

On the same day on which Rampolla wrote his letter the
superiors had met in Paris to discuss their line of action. The
majority were in favour of resistance, and formed a committee
to implement it. But five of the leading authorized congregations (including the Sulpicians and Lazarists) asked the opinion
of an eminent jurist, M. Louchet. He replied in favour of
submission. The Pope approved of his memorandum; but
repeated that the superiors enjoyed full liberty to decide.
"The question of conscience," wrote Rampolla, "is in no
wise involved."[6] The Croix, on the other hand, violently
attacked Louchet's memorandum. Throughout the controversy it had made as much fuss as if it concerned not a
comparatively trivial money-payment but an article of the
Creed. Cardinal Bourret of Toulouse (a prelate considerably
in the confidence of the Pope), because he asked his communities to obey the law, was told that he was paying the
price for his archbishopric and purple.[7] When the tax fell
due (October 16th) some two-thirds of the congregations refused to meet it. The rest paid up, and in the event did not
seem much the worse.

The same month of October saw the fall of the Ribot
ministry. Its Radical successor under M. Bourgeois (with
M. Combes as its Minister of Religions) was strongly anticlerical : and if it had lasted longer the *esprit nouveau* would
have been seriously compromised. But the following April
the opposition of the Senate forced it to resign.

II

The new Premier, M. Méline, was an extreme moderate
and very anxious to work in harmony with the Pope for re-

[5] Printed in Lecanuet, 52f.
[6] *Ibid.*, 61.
[7] Article in *La Libre Parole*, October 25th, 1895, *ibid.*, 67.

ligious peace. His ministry, which lasted for two years, was the golden age of the *ralliement* period. No new legislation was initiated against the Church, which was left free to do its work in its own way. The Catholics continued to squabble among themselves : but even this was powerless to prevent a striking expansion of Catholic activity, especially in the direction of bringing the Church into closer touch with the masses. The movement of " Christian democracy " made remarkable progress. Side by side with its lay leaders, headed by the venerable Léon Harmel and his three brilliant young henchmen, Henri Lorin, Paul Lapeyre and Georges Goyau, the *abbés démocrates* made gallant and untiring effort on its behalf. The Catholic *Cercles d'Ouvriers* received a wide extension, and became the centre of multiple activities for the amelioration of the lot of their members and their education in self-help. At a Congress held at Reims in 1896 these *Cercles* were formed into a single federation for the whole of France with a comprehensive programme of social reform.

A further impetus was given to the movement by the *Association Catholique de la Jeunesse Française.*[8] This had been founded in 1886 at de Mun's suggestion by a small group of young Paris students. It proclaimed as its aim the " reconstitution of a Christian social order," and adopted "Prayer, Study and Action " as its motto. The association soon made rapid progress, and at a Congress held at Paris in 1893 it was definitely constituted as a federation of " groups " covering the whole of France. The local " groups " were organized in a hierarchy of " unions "—diocesan, regional and general— the last with a *Conseil General* and a smaller *Comité General* charged with the oversight of the whole. Each group had its *aumônier* appointed by the bishop of the diocese : and the *aumônier général* was always a Jesuit. The basis of the association was in principle non-political and in its earlier years it shared the " aristocratic " tendencies of de Mun's own *Cercles.*[9] But before long it began to evolve in a de--

---

[8] On this see Lecanuet, *La Vie de l'Église sous Léon XIII.,* 66off.
[9] It may be recalled that a member of it was responsible for the so-called *guet-apens du Panthéon* in 1891. (*v. supra,* p. 231.)

finitely democratic direction—always however in strict dependence on the Holy See and on the lines of the Encyclical *Novarum rerum*.

To these same years, too, belong the beginnings of the movement known as *Le Sillon*, [10] though its apogee was not reached until the opening years of the next decade. It was founded in 1894 by a young student preparing for an army career at the Collège Stanislas, Marc Sangnier, who obtained permission to hold a weekly meeting for mingled devotion and discussion in a room at the college called the " Crypt." When he and his friends entered the École Polytechnique (the French Woolwich) they continued to meet in the Crypt, which became a centre of active Catholic influence among their fellow *polytechniciens*. After a year as sub-lieutenant at Toul, Sangnier returned to Paris in 1898. By this time the Crypt had become too small for its frequenters : and it was decided to inaugurate a definite movement on a wider basis. The aim of its members was first to " Christianize themselves " and after that to " Christianize democracy." The bond uniting them was to be one of the closest brotherhood— *l'amitié du Sillon*. Though at first disclaiming any political aim, they made no secret of their devotion to the Republican and democratic idea. The object of the movement was to form an intellectual and moral *élite* of all classes which was to be the salt of a new and Christian social order. Study-circles were formed in Paris and the provinces, which grew quickly in numbers and were grouped together for the purpose of holding *Congrès régionaux* and *Congrès nationaux*. Side by side with these *Cercles d'Études* were *Instituts populaires* for the higher education of the masses. Sangnier's moving eloquence and the radiant fascination of his personality rapidly won for the movement an amazing success. He was hailed as Montalembert *redivivus*. The working class responded as they had never responded to any previous effort to win them for the Church. The bishops praised the *Sillon* with enthusiasm : and Leo XIII. and (at first) Pius X. gave it their heartfelt benediction. The intransigents, on the other hand,

[10] See again Lecanuet, *op. cit.*, 677ff.

watched it with malignant eyes, and were to bring it down in the end. But that story lies outside the range of this work.

Apart from the *abbés démocrates,* the clergy at first held aloof from the Christian democratic movement. But it was obviously necessary to enlist their help if it was to be really successful. An important part of the work of the *abbés démocrates* was directed to this end. In 1893 the Pope had said to the Bishop of Coutances (Germain): "Advise your clergy not to shut themselves up within the walls of their churches or presbyteries but to go to the people." [11] For this " new apostolate," as the abbé Dabry calls it, new pastoral methods seemed to be necessary: and the *abbés démocrates* made it their business to point the way. Numerous public discussions were held in which spokesmen of the Christian faith met its opponents, both of the educated and the working class, on their own ground. A great Ecclesiastical Congress was planned to be held at Reims in 1896, [12] as one of a whole series of congresses representing various aspects of the national life and forming part of the celebration of the 1400th anniversary of the conversion of Clovis. A programme was drawn up and invitations were sent to the clergy all over France. The Congress was a great success, and over 700 priests assembled. For several days they pooled their experience, stated their problems and discussed the methods of solving them. The bishops did not regard these developments with a wholly favourable eye, [13] distrusting any initiative not their own, and fearing that their subalterns might become too independent. They disliked, too, the democratic sentiments of the promoters. When in 1900 another Congress was held at Bourges under the presidency of Mgr. Servonnet, the Archbishop, two bishops, Turinaz of Nancy (always a " diehard ") and Isoard of Annecy, vehemently assailed the line that had been taken: [14] and there was much talk of " presbyterianism." But Leo XIII. stood by his servants, even though he could not always go the whole of the way with them.

[11] Dabry, *Les Catholique Républicains,* 429.
[12] For an enthusiastic account of this and its inception see *ibid.,* 450ff.
[13] See Richard's letter to Leo XIII. (1897) in Clément, *op. cit.,* 391.
[14] Dabry, 68off. Lecanuet, *Vie de l'Église sous Léon XIII.,* 642.

Whatever their faults and exaggerations may have been, at least the Church was being shaken out of its rut and brought nearer to the masses.

A similar result followed from the encouragement given by the Pope to the Third Order of St. Francis, which from the early days of his pontificate he had sought to raise from the state to which it had fallen of being a mere pious confraternity into a real social force on the lines of its founder's intentions —a Catholic counterpart, even, of the vast Masonic organization. [15] The new orientation was little to the taste of one of the two great branches of the Franciscan family, the Capuchins, who were largely dominated by reactionary influences and believed (despite St. Francis) in keeping the poor in their place. But the other branch, the Franciscans proper, supported it with enthusiasm : and under their auspices and the zealous leadership (in particular) of Père Ferdinand a series of successful Franciscan congresses was held in different parts of France.

To the Royalists and *réfractaires,* whose one idea was to put back the clock, all these new-fangled ideas and methods were naturally anathema. They hated the policy of *ralliement* : they hated still more the " Christian democracy " to which it had opened the door and which seemed likely now to secure its triumph all along the line. The Pope, of course, was at the bottom of it all. As they dared not attack him personally, they fell tooth and nail on those who were trying to carry out his wishes. The *abbés démocrates* in particular were the target of their venomous hate. When, on the death of Mgr. Hulst in 1896, one of their number, Gayraud, was put forward by the *ralliés* as parliamentary candidate for Brest, the Monarchists not only ran a rival against him but their press organs made scandalous and quite unfounded charges against his character. [16] This, however, did not prevent him from being elected. Unfortunately, too, the Assumptionist organization and newspaper, the *Croix,* intoxi-

---

[15] See Dabry, 495ff.
[16] Dabry, 537ff. Lecanuet, *Les signes avant-coureurs de la Séparation,* 100f.

cated by success, took the bit between its teeth and by its
fanaticism gravely compromised the papal policy with which
it was nominally identified. A disastrous impression (which
the anticlericals, of course, exploited to the full) was created
by an outrageous discourse delivered by the Jesuit, Père
Ollivier, at the solemn requiem at Notre Dame for the victims
of the appalling fire at a Catholic charity bazaar in 1897,
when the victims included the Duchesse d'Alençon, a princess
of the House of France, and several ladies of the high *noblesse*.
As a tribute of sympathy, the President of the Republic—for
the first time for twenty years—was present in person, only to
hear the fanatical Jesuit declare that the victims were a
"holocaust" accepted by "the God of our fathers" in expiation of the " crimes " committed against Him by the nation. [17]

The blind malevolence of the *réfractaires* was not confined
to the sphere of politics only. Let their hated opponents but
sponsor any movement whatever and it was sure at once not
only to incur their condemnation but to bring down the full
weight of their hate and spite upon its promoters. The story
of Sœur Marie du Sacré Cœur was a tragic illustration of
this. [18] A member of a teaching order, she had become convinced of the need of improving the teaching of the convent
schools for girls that catered for the children of the better class.
The State *lycées des filles* had grown greatly in number and
were admirably efficient. But the aristocracy and bourgeoisie
for the most part still preferred to send their daughters to the
convent schools. Such schools were regarded as providing at
once a superior social *cachet* and a better training in character.
On the other hand, their intellectual standard was decidedly
open to criticism. The education given in them was mostly of
the primary type, and the professional qualifications of the
good nuns were seldom of a high order. Sœur Marie, therefore, initiated about 1894 a campaign to secure the establishment of a Catholic *École Normale supérieure* to which the
female teaching orders might send the more promising of their

[17] Lecanuet, *La Vie de l'Église sous Léon XIII.*, 195. The good
Father well asks: " *Qui donc avait revélé a l'orateur les secrets
divins?* " Debidour, ii. 160.
[18] See Lecanuet, *op. cit.*, 286ff.

younger members, with a view to their receiving a training not inferior to that given in the State training colleges. Rebuffed by her own diocesan, she went to Paris, where she obtained influential support. When, however, the Bishop of Versailles gave permission for the foundation of her *École Normale* in his own diocese, Cardinal Richard of Paris interposed his veto. Sœur Marie then wrote two books setting forth the defects she desired to see remedied and her plan for mending them. These books received considerable support in the episcopate. Unfortunately for the writer, they were also greeted with enthusiasm by the *abbés démocrates* and the progressive Catholic journals. This was quite enough for the *réfractaires*. The *Croix,* the *Libre Parole* and other journals of the same sort assailed them and their author with fury. The incorrigible Mgr. Gouthe-Soulard informed Sœur Marie in a public letter that her book was "not only a lie but a disgrace," and told her that she was "a false sister." A number of bishops appealed to public opinion in her defence, together with some of the most distinguished of the Catholic laity. The saintly but narrow Richard, however, was inflexible, and the attacks of the intransigents became fiercer than ever. Gradually her friends fell away; while her enemies appealed to Rome. Leo XIII. had at first encouraged her : but now he felt compelled to sacrifice her in the interests of religious peace. On March 17th, 1899, her book was censured. The Pope, however, gave her a kindly reception soon afterwards.

If so great a storm could be raised about a comparatively small question of educational reform, it is not surprising that the *réfractaires* should have been excited to frenzy by a movement which, to their malevolent eyes, appeared to involve a denial of the Church's doctrinal tradition. [19] This movement,

---

[19] On "Americanism" see Lecanuet, *op. cit.,* Ch. XII. 544ff. Houtin, *L'Américanisme,* 1903, is valuable for the documents it gives, but should be used with great caution in other respects on account of its author's intense animus against the Church and his greed for any tittle-tattle that may reflect upon the sincerity of its leaders. In *Une vie de prêtre* (Eng. tr. 187 n.) he goes further still and maintains upon "the most reliable information" that Ireland and Spalding were "pure rationalists." But poor Houtin became more and more the prey of his complex as time went on.

nicknamed " Americanism," has been described by Loisy as a
" phantom heresy of which it has never been possible to find,
in the New World or in the Old, a single authentic representative." [20] In actual fact, it was at worst no more than a
new conception of the action of the Church in the modern
world.

It has been already observed that the Catholic Church in
America was a subject of deep interest to the more liberally-
minded French Catholics. This interest was greatly stimulated
by a visit to Paris of the eloquent Archbishop of S. Paul, Mgr.
Ireland, in 1892. In the presence of an audience including
many distinguished French Catholics, the archbishop delivered
a speech in the course of which he said : " The Church in
America is the Church of the people. Our priests, our bishops,
are all devoted to the people : they live among the people
which recognizes them as its protectors and friends. We give
much time to the sanctuary and the sacristy, but we give
much, too, to public life. . . . The American people likes to
see the clergy occupying themselves with all the interests of the
country. They feel that they are necessarily a social force."
He went on : " Our hearts beat always for the Republic of
the United States. In the past it was said that the Catholic
Church could not reconcile itself with the Republic and that
the free air of America would be fatal to it. The Catholic
Church has breathed the air of the Republic and thrives very
well on it." [21] The speech was rapturously received : and it
undoubtedly gave a great encouragement to *ralliement*.

A year later further interest was excited by the " Parliament of Religions " held in September 1893 in connection
with the Universal Exhibition at Chicago. The Roman
Church sent its representatives to mingle with those not only
of the various Christian bodies but of the non-Christian religions as well. Cardinal Gibbons was present, clad in his
scarlet robes. The exponents of each religious creed set forth
their convictions : and a spirit of tolerance and goodwill
reigned throughout. Following this lead, a project was

[20] Loisy, *Choses Passées,* 1913, 264.
[21] Quoted in Dabry, 263f.

immediately set on foot to hold a similar Parliament in connection with the Paris Exhibition of 1900. The idea received considerable support among French Catholics, and a campaign was inaugurated to bring it to fruition. But the intransigents were furious; while the scheme was compromised by the indiscretion of some of its promoters, notably the Abbé Charbonnel, who was later to leave the Church. The bishops pronounced against it: and Cardinal Richard roundly declared that as long as he was Archbishop of Paris a Parliament of Religions would never be held there. The Pope, too, was consulted and advised the Catholics to hold their congress apart. The scheme was therefore abandoned.

It was not, however, till 1897 that the storm really broke—in connection with the publication of a French translation of the *Life of Father Hecker,* founder of the Paulist Order in U.S.A. Hecker, a Protestant baker turned Catholic priest, had had a marvellous success in the United States as an apostle of the people. His success was largely due to his sympathetic allowance for the American character. He had specially stressed two points: the importance of the *active* virtues, not as opposed to, but as equally valuable with, the passive, and the direct action of the Holy Spirit on the individual soul. The translation of his biography was preceded by an enthusiastic preface from the pen of a well known Paris priest, the Abbé Félix Klein. "In the last half-century," wrote the Abbé, "the world evolves, humanity transforms itself and demands a new apostolate. The apostle has come. In Father Hecker it has found the ideal priest for the new future of the Church." He went on to expound Hecker's spiritual teaching and concluded: "The time is coming when the Church, having strengthened what was attacked in its hierarchy and become free to give its whole strength to its essential work, will direct its effort more and more towards the practice of the inner life and its attention towards the intelligible side of the mysteries of the faith." [22]

The book enjoyed a great success: and at first nobody seemed to find anything wrong in it. But at the Catholic

[22] Quoted Lecanuet, *op. cit.*, 569.

Scientific Congress at Fribourg in September Mgr. Turinaz
sounded the alarm.   At once the old guard of reaction rushed
to man the breach, including the half-insane Canon Delassus,
most refractory of *réfractaires*,[23] and the Abbé Periès, who,
having been deprived of his post at the Catholic University of
Washington, had a score to pay off against the American
episcopate.   The Jesuits, too, joined in the mêlée.   They also
had a grudge against the Church in America for founding the
Washington University in their despite.[24]   " Americanism,"
it was alleged, was a monstrous portent—the hideous offspring
of the old Liberal Catholicism mated with young Modernism.
Its aim was to set up a non-miraculous Christianity, which
would become in the end a mere Religion of Humanity.   One
writer even saw in it the twin-sister of Satanism.[25]   To these
attacks the moderate Catholics made indignant reply.

Meanwhile, the controversy was under consideration at
Rome.   The Jesuits found a backer in Cardinal Satolli, a
former Apostolic Delegate to the United States who had
crossed swords there with the bishops and had come back with
more money than popularity.   The American bishops, on their
side, defended themselves : and Cardinal Gibbons wrote to the
Pope.   Leo hesitated long.   He was unwilling to inflict any
censure on zealous servants of the Church : yet the incrimin-
ated book seemed to him dangerous.   On January 22nd, 1899,
he wrote a reply to Gibbons[26] in which he declared his disapproval of " certain opinions as to the manner of living the
Christian life . . . designated by some under the name of
Americanism."   He was careful to distinguish between two
meanings of the word " Americanism."   If it meant merely
the American spirit and institutions, it was blameless.   But in
the sense of the doctrines condemned he was sure that the
American bishops would be the first to repudiate it.   The
bishops eagerly seized on the loophole offered and declared

[23] His book, *L'Américanisme et la conjuration anti-chrétienne* (1899), is
fittingly described by Dabry as " *le roman d'un malade.*"   Dabry gives
some amazing excerpts, *op. cit.*, 643ff.
[24] Lecanuet, 576.
[25] *Ibid.*, 576f.
[26] Printed in substance, *ibid.*, 586f.

that such opinions had never entered their heads. But the French defenders of the book felt that a grievous blow had been struck at their ideal of a progressive Catholicism : and many persons hovering on the verge of the Church were alienated for good. [27]

The divisions of French Catholicism seemed indeed to be past healing. In the sphere of political action it had just been proved that in the face of imminent peril from the Church's enemies even the *ralliés* could not really act together. [28] As the General Election of 1898 approached, the Radicals and Free-masons had initiated a vigorous campaign against the Méline ministry. The Pope was anxious to maintain it ; and recommended that as the Catholics were not strong enough to stand by themselves, they should not only close their own ranks but should make an alliance with the Republicans against the Radicals and Socialists. He asked M. Lamy to bring this alliance about. Lamy accepted the task, but soon found that it would be very difficult. Not only were the Royalists as refractory as ever, but the group of the *Croix* was hardly less so. Its promoters had formed an electoral organization called *Justice-Égalité* which, backed by their ample resources, had spread all over France and hoped to play a leading part in the election.

Lamy did his best, and succeeded in forming a Federation of all the non-Royalist Catholic groups on the basis of acceptance of the Republic, reform of anti-Catholic legislation and union with all who desired " a regime of peace in liberty and justice." Its policy was to put forward Catholic candidates only where they had a good chance of being elected ; otherwise to support the moderate Republicans. But the latter shrank from a definite pact : and the union of the *ralliés* was a union only in name. The *Justice-Égalité* organization declined to hand over its war-chest to the common fund and pursued a very independent line of action. In consequence the result of the elections was far from satisfactory. Only

[27] It was this pronouncement in particular which finally alienated the *néo-chrétiens* from the Church (*v. infra*, p. 291f.). Lecanuet, 592.
[28] Lecanuet, *Les signes avant-coureurs de la Séparation*, 129.

seventy-four *ralliés* were returned : and the Government majority was weakened rather than otherwise.

The Pope was very disappointed. At the end of June a letter from him was read to the Federation Committee, re-affirming his policy, but at the same time maintaining " the autonomy of its several groups in their own sphere." [29] Lamy, regarding this as a disavowal of his policy, resigned : and the Federation came to an end.

III

Hitherto we have looked at the years 1894-8 from a purely ecclesiastical point of view. But the Church life of the time was set against a lurid background of national excite-ment. It was during these years that France was kept at fever heat by the first and most thrilling stages in the drama of the " Dreyfus affair." [30]

The tortuous and complicated story cannot be told at length in these pages. It must suffice to indicate very sum-marily its most salient events, with special reference to their repercussion on Catholic opinion and, in particular, the alleged complicity of the Church in the hideous business.

In September 1894, a *bordereau* or memorandum fell into the hands of the Intelligence Department of the French War Office which had evidently accompanied the transmission to the German Embassy in Paris of a number of secret docu-ments. The handwriting was not unlike that of a Jewish officer on the General Staff, Alfred Dreyfus. The strong anti-semitic prejudice of the discoverer of the *bordereau,* Colonel

[29] Text in Lecanuet, 130.
[30] The most famous and imposing history of the Dreyfus affair is Joseph Reinach, *Histoire de l'affaire Dreyfus,* 6 vols., 1901—8. Reinach is worthy of all praise for his share in righting a foul wrong. But his book was written under the influence of the passions of the time, and its tone is very partisan. Debidour's attitude is similar. The other side is well presented in Lecanuet, *Les signes avant-coureurs de la Séparation,* Ch. iv. and v. It is a very sober and balanced account, and makes no attempt to dissimulate the faults of the Catholics. Père Lecanuet tells us frankly (p. 140) that, before examining the subject with a view to writing on it, he had believed Dreyfus guilty ; but that his studies had entirely convinced him of his innocence.

Henry, and his colleague, du Paty de Clam, leaped on its opportunity—though the former at least was perfectly aware who the real traitor was. Dreyfus was arrested, despite his passionate protests of innocence. His trial by court-martial began on December 19th and was held *in camera*. As the *bordereau* by itself was hardly enough to convict him, Henry, with the connivance of the Minister of War, General Mercier, had concocted a "secret *dossier*" consisting of documents which had nothing to do with Dreyfus. This *dossier* was communicated to the court, but neither Dreyfus nor his counsel was allowed to see it. Dreyfus was found guilty and sentenced to public degradation and imprisonment for life. He was sent to the Ile du Diable on the fever-stricken coast of French Guiana.

Such was the first act of the drama. It is a terrible story enough : but one cannot see how, up to the present at least, any direct responsibility attaches to the Church. The legend of a "Jesuit plot" is mere moonshine. Neither Henry nor Mercier was a Catholic : both were free-thinkers. On the other hand, it is impossible to exonerate the Church from the charge of helping to manure the soil in which the foul seeds of injustice and falsehood were to attain such monstrous growth. The rage of antisemitism that actuated both Henry and his fellow-criminals and inflamed the army and public opinion alike against Dreyfus from the start was chiefly the work of Catholics. It is true that Drumont and his precious *Libre Parole* were working in the interest of Royalism rather than of the Church : but the Catholics had lent a willing ear to his insane denunciations of the Jews and did their best to propagate them. When Mercier after Dreyfus' arrest hesitated to bring the prisoner to trial, it was the denunciations of the *Libre Parole* (to which Henry had communicated the alleged treason) that forced his hand and probably made him an accomplice in the fabrication of the *dossier*. Nor can it be denied that a large number of the officers of the army had been educated at Jesuit hands. It was scarcely in that quarter that they were likely to learn immunity from religious and professional prejudices, even if we gladly admit that their instructors would never have taught them to resort to lying and forgery in the service of these.

The second act of the drama begins some fifteen months later. In May 1896, Colonel Picquart, now head of the Intelligence Department, lighted on a *petit-bleu* or express-letter addressed to Commandant Esterhazy, a French officer of by no means savoury reputation. The circumstances of its discovery arousing his suspicions, he secured specimens of Esterhazy's handwriting and was at once struck by its identity with that of the *bordereau*. He communicated his discovery to the heads of the General Staff, through whom Henry became aware of this new development. At once the latter took steps to prevent it going further. He secured the publication in the *Matin* of September 10th of an article which, by way of reinforcing Dreyfus' guilt, divulged for the first time the use of the secret *dossier* at the trial. Immediately Mme. Dreyfus presented a petition for the revision of her husband's condemnation on the ground of illegality. A Royalist deputy, on the other hand, proposed to interpellate the Government in the Chamber concerning its excessive lenience to the traitor. The Minister of War, now General Billot, attempted to meet both these developments by declaring in the Chamber that the case was " *chose jugée* " and that it was impossible to go back on it (November 17th). A week earlier he had published a facsimile of the *bordereau* in the *Matin*. Mathieu Dreyfus promptly declared that the writing was not his brother's. Meanwhile Picquart, to get him out of the way, had been sent on a mission to Tunis, where he was kept for more than a year. In his place Billot appointed Henry. The latter had already crowned his infamy by forging a new document, which, unlike the earlier ones in the *dossier,* mentioned Dreyfus by name.

The publication of the *bordereau* having given Mathieu Dreyfus something to go on, he redoubled his efforts on his brother's behalf and secured an important ally in M. Scheurer-Kestner, Vice-President of the Senate. In June 1897, Picquart paid a flying visit to Paris and confided his secret to his lawyer. The lawyer soon communicated it to Scheurer-

Kestner. On November 15th Mathieu Dreyfus formally denounced Esterhazy to Billot as the writer of the *bordereau*. The General Staff made frantic attempts to hush the matter up, and declared that there were elements in the case which if disclosed must bring about immediate war with Germany. At its instigation Esterhazy demanded to be tried by court-martial. He was unanimously acquitted and received a wild ovation on leaving the court (January 11th, 1898). Picquart was put under arrest.

A few weeks before (December 4th), the Premier, Méline, had declared in the Chamber: " *Il n'y a pas d'affaire Dreyfus.*" Esterhazy's acquittal seemed to prove that he was right. But two days after it took place Émile Zola published his famous open letter " *J'accuse,*" denouncing the War Office and stating the facts. He was prosecuted at once and sentenced to a year's imprisonment and 3,000 francs fine (February 21st).

The General Election of May 1898 followed. The new Chamber soon forced Méline to resign: and a Radical ministry under Brisson came into power. The new Minister of War, Cavaignac, declared his determination to " liquidate " the Dreyfus affair. His solution was simple: Dreyfus and Esterhazy were *both* guilty. This conviction he expressed in the Chamber on July 7th. But a month later a sudden *coup de théâtre* changed the whole situation. On August 13th an officer at the War Office discovered that the crucial document incriminating Dreyfus by name was a palpable forgery. Henry was summoned before Cavaignac. At first he denied his guilt, then abjectly confessed it. He was sent to the prison of Mont Valérien and next morning was found dead with his throat cut (August 31st). Immediately afterwards Esterhazy fled to England.

The recital of the facts makes it clear once again that the primary responsibility rests with the War Office, and the War Office alone. Even there the original fastening of the charge on Dreyfus and the fabrication of false evidence to support it were the work of a small group of malefactors. The judges at Dreyfus' trial acted illegally, yet in good faith. But a reputation for infallibility is nowhere more prized than in military circles: and when once a mistake had been made, it became a matter of professional prestige to avoid at all costs admitting it. " The honour of the army " is always a potent weapon with which to work on public opinion, especially in France: and in this case it was used to the utmost. Nor indeed did public opinion need much persuading. Not only the anti-semitic press but the press as a whole clamoured for justice on the traitor. Fear always makes men cruel and unjust: and the German menace was ever at the gates. The honour-able disclaimer by the German authorities of any knowledge of Dreyfus increased suspicion rather than allayed it. It was only gradually that the small *élite* of free-thinking intellectuals to which Zola belonged formed the suspicion that the whole truth had not been told: and for them at first there was nothing but rage and contempt.

If, then, the Catholics were against Dreyfus, so was nearly everybody else. Their responsibility was no greater than that of the nation as a whole. It is to be noted, too, that throughout the whole business the episcopate and the main body of the clergy maintained a non-committal attitude in public. No doubt, like the rest of their fellow-countrymen, they believed Dreyfus guilty—it was hard for them to believe otherwise: but they refused for the most part to take sides openly. The Pope followed the same attitude. On the other hand, it is not to be denied that, when the first indications of the truth began to appear, an opportunity was given to certain leading Catholics to assist in its further elucidation. The Pope indeed can hardly be blamed if, when Mme. Dreyfus appealed to him after the revelation of the existence of the secret *dossier,* he declined to take action. [31] He might fairly claim that the business was none of his: and his intervention, it is certain, would have been passionately resented in France. But there were others whose responsibility could not be so easily dis-claimed. Before approaching Scheurer-Kestner and Zola, Mathieu Dreyfus invited de Mun to interest himself in his brother's case: but de Mun declined even to discuss the

[31] Debidour, ii. 174; with a reference to Reinach, ii. 378.

subject.[32] So, too, when Cardinal Richard was similarly approached some months later he replied : "It is not for the Church to intervene: the matter concerns the French tribunals."[33] It was the attitude of Gamaliel—"wait and see" —to which a hierarchy is always prone. And no doubt those who assumed it had no difficulty in justifying it to their conscience—especially in view of the prejudices which made it so hard for them to be impartial in such a matter. Yet there are times when a duty is laid on men to find out the truth for themselves : and such times constitute a κρίσις on which the fate of great institutions may hinge. The Catholics had their chance. They refused it and left it to their enemies. And their failure was to help to bring a fearful punishment on the Church.

The responsibility of the hierarchy and secular clergy is, however, slight in comparison with that of the press and certain religious orders. Of the Royalist papers we have already spoken. The culpability of the *Libre Parole* is only second to that of the War Office. Unfortunately the *Croix* was hardly less to blame : and its action implicated the Church itself. Ostensibly an organ of *ralliement,* it could not resist the temptation to use the *Affaire* as a stick for beating the Republic, and lent itself with enthusiasm to serve the designs of the War Office camarilla. It would show the world whether Catholics were patriotic or not. The rôle of the Jesuits is less palpable than that of the Assumptionists : but it is not without its sinister features. It is asserted that after Picquart's discovery of the *petit-bleu* his chief Boisdeffre consulted his confessor, the well known Paris Jesuit, Père du Lac, and was told that his conscience need not be troubled if he left things as they were.[34] Whether this be true or not, the Jesuits were certainly more than unwise in allowing the appearance, at a time when passions were at their height just before Zola's trial, of an article in their Roman organ, the *Civiltà Cattolica,*[35] declaring that "the Jew has been created

[32] Lecanuet, 175.
[33] *Ibid.,* 184.
[34] So Debidour, ii. 172, after Reinach. But see Lecanuet, 182 and n.
[35] Printed in Lecanuet, 180.

by God to serve as a spy" and demanding the withdrawal of French nationality from all of his race. More atrocious still was an utterance of the celebrated Dominican, Père Didon, publicly denouncing " governments which mask their criminal weakness behind the plea of an insufficient legality and let the sword rust in the scabbard " [36] (July 1898).

Such sentiments cannot be defended on any grounds. Yet it may be conceded that up to August 1898 the opponents of revision might fairly claim that a case for revision had not been fully made out. The suicide of Henry and the flight of Esterhazy created a very different situation. At first the demand for revision was wellnigh universal. But the War Office continued to struggle fiercely against the inevitable. Cavaignac, while admitting Henry's forgery, maintained that the other documents in the *dossier* retained their validity: and, when the Premier declared for revision, resigned. His short-lived successors, Zuerlinden and Chanoine, took the same attitude. The latter even put Picquart in prison again ; and resigned rather than hand over the *dossier* to the Cour de Cassation, to which the Government had referred the matter. The attitude of the War Office restored the confidence of the opposition : and France was now rent in twain by the passionate conflict of revisionists and anti-revisionists. The former had already (February 1898) formed a *Ligue des Droits de l'Homme* which, composed mainly of Radicals and Socialists, rapidly assumed an attitude of extreme hostility to the Church. The anti-revisionists retorted by forming (January 1899) a *Ligue de la Patrie Française*. This contained a large number of Royalists and Catholics side by side with many who, while indifferent to the religious claims of the Church, shared the militaristic nationalism with which its unofficial spokesmen had so dangerously identified it. These nationalists even went to the length of exalting the forger-suicide as a hero and martyr. A prime mover of the *Ligue,* Charles Maurras (later notorious as the leader of the *Action*

[36] Lecanuet, 182. It is only fair to add that later Didon repented bitterly of this. Reynaud, *Le Père Didon,* 379. That the disciple of Lacordaire should have erred thus is a proof of the distorting effects on men's minds of the passions of the time.

Française) declared that "it is only our bad half-Protestant education that makes us incapable of appreciating such intellectual and moral nobility."[37]   The *Libre Parole* raised a fund of 130,000 francs in support of a suit by Henry's widow against Joseph Reinach for "defaming" her husband's "character," and to present a "sword of honour" to his children.   Among the subscribers was, alas!, de Mun: and the *Croix* blessed the project and helped to raise the money.[38]

Despite all this the revisionist cause made steady headway. On October 29th, 1898, the Cour de Cassation decided that there was a case for revision.   In the ordinary course the issue would have been tried by the *Chambre Criminelle*.   But the anti-revisionists questioned its impartiality with such vehemence that the new Premier, Dupuy, introduced a Bill into the legislature to substitute the Cour de Cassation, sitting in full assembly, in the belief that it would find Dreyfus guilty. The Chamber passed the Bill on February 10th, 1899: the Senate on March 1st.   In the interval the anti-revisionist President, Faure, had died suddenly.   His successor, Loubet, was a revisionist.   The public opinion of Europe had long been in favour of revision and could not understand why it had not been carried out long ago.   The Pope, too, broke silence at last.   In an interview with a representative of the Paris *Figaro* in March he expressed his amazement at the delay and said of Dreyfus: "Happy is the victim whom God judges righteous enough to assimilate his sacrifice to that of His Son!"[39]   He thus definitely ranged himself on the side of the small group of Liberal Catholics which had been for some time working on Dreyfus' behalf under a *Comité catholique pour la défense du droit,* presided over by a noted jurist, M. Paul Viollet.   The most distinguished of them was the eminent Catholic thinker Anatole Leroy-Beaulieu, who had long been tireless in denouncing antisemitism along with all the other *doctrines de haine.*[40]   But despite the Pope the

[37] *Gazette de France,* September 6th, 1898.   Quoted Lecanuet, 168.
[38] Lecanuet, 170 and n.; Debidour, 212 n. supplies a curious collection of the outrageous insults with which the "patriots" accompanied their subscriptions.
[39] *Figaro,* March 15th, 1899.   Quoted Lecanuet, 188f.

bulk of the Catholics, like the majority of the nation, remained obstinately opposed to revision.

The case came before the Cour de Cassation in June. Dupuy's hope proved vain. The Court annulled the sentence of 1894 and ordered a retrial. Immediately afterwards the Chamber forced Dupuy to resign : and Waldeck-Rousseau became head of a ministry of " Republican Defence." Himself an opportunist, he allied himself with the Radicals and even the Socialists, and made it clear that he intended not only to secure justice for Dreyfus, but also to put the Church in its place. On August 7th Dreyfus was brought for his second trial before a court-martial at Rennes. The *milieu* was very unfriendly : for Brittany was a hotbed of Royalist and Catholic fanaticism. In addition, the nationalist press, before and during the trial, assumed a most menacing tone, declaring that the court must choose between Dreyfus and the army and denying the necessity of " proofs." [41] Thus worked on, the court again found Dreyfus guilty, with the amazing qualification " with extenuating circumstances " ! (September 9th). He was sentenced to ten years' detention. But the verdict was so grotesque that the President gave him a free pardon immediately. Dreyfus, in accepting it, said that he would never rest till his innocence was established. For this he had to wait for nearly seven more years : and even then a vast number of Catholics were not convinced. Many of them believe in his guilt to this day.

[40] Weill, *Histoire du catholicisme libéral*, 226.
Lecanuet, 194.

CHAPTER XII

1899—1905

I

IF Waldeck-Rousseau had not been entirely successful in his first objective—the rehabilitation of Dreyfus—he was to have better luck with his second—the curbing of the Church. His ministry marks the beginning of the final counter-attack of the Republic on the Church which, having swept away both the congregations and by far the greater part of the Catholic educational system in its course, was not to come to rest till it had destroyed the Concordat.

For these consequences he was not personally responsible: they were the work of more fanatical hands than his. He himself did not desire Separation: and if he viewed the congregations with no favourable eye, his idea was to control, not to destroy them. But the march of events was stronger than he. The part played by Catholic fanaticism in connection with the Dreyfus affair had given the Freemasons and the anticlericals their opportunity. The recurrent scandals of the Third Republic had sorely damaged its moral prestige in the past: but now the anticlericals felt themselves able to retort the charge of unrighteousness upon the Catholics. The charge was wildly exaggerated. We have seen that there is no reason to believe that the Church had any responsibility at all for the condemnation of Dreyfus in 1894, nor any but a purely secondary responsibility for the long delay in righting the wrong. If the Catholics believed Dreyfus to be guilty, the whole nation for a long time believed the same. But when the madness was past and the nation began to come to its senses it was necessary to find a scapegoat. It is always easy to rouse a scare in France on the subject of the Jesuits: and now the national conscience was to be salved at their expense.

As a matter of fact their share in the business was probably slight at the most. But their fellow congregation, the Assumptionists, had undoubtedly compromised the Church badly. It was therefore not difficult to represent the congregations as at the bottom of the whole affair. They had never been popular with the mass of the nation, which was only too pleased now to transfer its responsibility to their shoulders. This largely explains the indifference with which popular opinion watched the campaign against them that was now to begin.

The sin of the Assumptionists against the Republic had been greatly aggravated by their close association with the Nationalists. About the desire of the latter to overthrow the existing regime there could be no doubt. On two occasions in 1899—on the day of the funeral of President Faure (February 23rd) and again in August, just as Dreyfus' second trial began—they had made an abortive attempt to effect a *coup d'État*. For their complicity in the second of these conspiracies the nationalist leader, Paul Déroulède, the antisemite Orléanist, Jules Guérin, and twelve others stood their trial before the Senate (November—February), and three of them were sentenced to banishment or imprisonment.

It was amid the impression produced by these events that Waldeck-Rousseau presented to the Chamber on November 14th two Bills designed to cripple the influence of the congregations on the national life. The first—called *projet sur le stage scolaire*—demanded of all candidates for public employment a certificate proving that they had been educated in a State school for a certain period. As, however, this would have placed persons educated entirely in Catholic schools at a serious and lifelong disadvantage by their parents' action, not their own, the committee to which the *projet* was referred decided against it, and it was abandoned.

The second *projet* was to have a very different fate. It was the famous Law of Associations which, first refashioned almost beyond recognition by the anticlerical majority in the Chamber and then used by Waldeck-Rousseau's successor, Combes, in a way totally opposed to its author's intention, was to sweep the unauthorized congregations out of existence altogether.

Waldeck-Rousseau's original *projet* [1] made no specific mention of the religious congregations at all. It was in form a general measure designed to determine the conditions under which Frenchmen might associate themselves for a common object. The tradition of the Revolution had always frowned on such associations. Hitherto any association of more than twenty persons for any purpose whatever—even an anglers' club or a village choral society—had to receive the formal authorization of the State, which might at any moment dissolve it. The *projet* put an end to this by giving permission to any association to exist that did not offend against public order or morality and respected the liberty of the individual, including his right to leave the association at will. On the other hand, if an association desired the status of a civil personality distinct from that of its members and, as such, to enjoy a corporate possession of its property, it must receive the authorization of the State : nor must it attempt to elude the obligation by any kind of private pact between its members. It was also enacted that a special authorization by decree of the Council of State was required for any association that combined Frenchmen and persons of foreign nationality, or was directed from abroad. The manner of liquidating the property of a dissolved association was laid down : and anyone reviving it was to be punishable by fine or imprisonment.

Meanwhile, by way of showing that he really meant business, Waldeck-Rousseau, immediately after the introduction of his *projets,* had struck a preliminary blow at the Assumptionists. The Paris office of the *Croix* was ransacked, and twelve members of the order were summoned on the charge of participating in an " association of more than twenty persons unauthorized by the Government." The *procés des Douze,* as it was called, began on January 22nd, 1900. The accused were fined, and their association was declared dissolved. At once sixty bishops protested, and Cardinal Richard paid an official visit of sympathy to the Paris house of the

[1] Complete text in Debidour, ii. 534ff.

order. The Government retorted by formally censuring him, and also suppressed the salary of five other bishops. It further denounced the agitation to Rome: and the Pope expressed his disapproval of it. Soon after (March) he ordered the Assumptionists to give up the direction of the *Croix*. They obeyed, but the journal was purchased by a layman, M. Féron-Vrau, who intimated that " La Croix *sera toujours* La Croix."

An examination of the provisions of Waldeck-Rousseau's *projet des associations* suffices to show that if the congregations were not mentioned by name, it was against them that the Bill was really directed. Its effect was briefly this—to liberate secular associations from State control, but in the case of the religious congregations to make that control far more stringent than it had been before. Even so, however, it did not go far enough in the eyes of the strongly anticlerical parliamentary committee which was appointed to give it preliminary consideration. This committee proceeded to stiffen its provisions in various ways. [2]   In particular, they added to the two categories of associations requiring special authorization a third—viz. all associations of which the members lived in common : and decreed that in the case of these last, and of associations directed from abroad, such authorization must be not by decree of the Council of State but by a *law* passed by both Chambers.

The consideration of the Bill as thus emended was held up for a long time owing, first, to the delay in passing a law of amnesty for those implicated in the Dreyfus affair, and secondly to the preoccupation of the Government with the Boxer rebellion in China in 1900. It was not until January 15th, 1901, that the debate on it began in the Chamber. In the form in which it was finally presented it had undergone further changes : and the concluding section (the third) was devoted to the religious congregations by name.

The Bill was attacked in the name of liberty not only by the Clerical leaders, but also by Ribot and other Republican moderates. It was also denounced as a violation of the Concordat : to which the Government replied that the Concordat

[2] Text as amended in Debidour, ii. 537ff.

made no mention of the congregations at all and had only guaranteed the rights of the secular clergy. A number of amendments were rejected : and having voted the "urgency" of the Bill, the Chamber on January 31st passed to the discussion of its clauses. The opposition fought these step by step in the case of the concluding section concerning the congregations, and produced numerous amendments. But their efforts were vain. The Bill as a whole was passed on March 29th by 303 votes to 224. The debate in the Senate began on June 11th. The senatorial committee had voted in its favour : and the clauses were all carried without any amendment, except one giving a pension to members of dissolved congregations who had no other means of support. It was voted June 22nd : and the Chamber voted it as amended on June 29th. [3] On July 2nd, 1901, it was officially promulgated—" the most decisive act of anticlerical policy," says Debidour, " since 1870." [4]

Its main provisions respecting the congregations may be briefly summarized thus : (1) No religious congregation may be formed without an authorization given by a legislative act *(loi)*. It may found no branch-house *(établissement)* except in virtue of a decree of the Council of State. The dissolution of a congregation or the closing of an *établissement* may be pronounced by decree of the Council of Ministers (Art. 13). (2) No one may direct or teach in an educational establishment of any kind if he belongs to an unauthorized religious congregation (Art. 14). (3) Every congregation must draw up annually a balance sheet and an inventory of its property, moveable and immoveable. These must be delivered to the prefect on request (Art. 15). (4) Any congregation formed without authorization shall be declared illegal and its members punished (Art. 16). (5) All arrangements designed to elude these requirements shall be null and void (Art. 17). (6) Congregations hitherto unauthorized must comply with the requirements of the present law within three

[3] For complete text of *Loi des Associations* as passed see Debidour, ii. 540ff.
[4] ii. 314.

months. If they do not they shall be considered as dissolved, as also congregations to which authorization is refused. The liquidation of the property of such shall be effected by a liquidator appointed by the courts. The private property of members shall be restored to them, and gifts and legacies (apart from those specially assigned to some charitable purpose) may be claimed by the donors or their heirs. After six months the liquidator shall sell all surplus real property, the proceeds to be deposited with the *Caisse des Dépôts*. The net surplus remaining shall be divided among those who have a legal right to it (including the members of the congregation). Provision shall be made, either by a capital sum or by a pension, for those ex-members who have no other means of support (Art. 18).

The consternation of the Catholic world may be imagined. The Pope protested against the law in Consistory, and also in a letter from Rampolla to the Government. [5] Waldeck-Rousseau replied that he would apply it with the greatest moderation. In regard to the practical question whether the congregations should apply for authorization or not, Leo XIII. declined to give any direction. Once again he would neither command nor forbid. Each congregation must decide for itself, with the proviso that the rights of the Holy See must be duly safeguarded in the case of those exempted from episcopal control. [6] Actually, the Pope would appear to have been in favour of authorization being sought : but he would not say so.

Left thus to their own devices, the congregations were divided. By far the majority—615 in all—decided to apply for authorization. But 84 male congregations and 150 female refused to do so—including the Jesuits (who well knew that in their case the step would be futile), the Benedictines and the Carmelites. (The Assumptionists had been gone a year.) In some places the populace regretted their departure—especially

---

[5] Dated July 6th, 1901. Printed in full in Lecanuet, *Les signes avant-coureurs de la Séparation*, 289.
[6] These instructions were given in a circular issued by Cardinal Gotti, Prefect of the Congregation of Bishops and Regulars, dated July 10th. Text in Lecanuet, *op. cit.*, 291.

when its material interests were affected. But generally speaking their fate was regarded with indifference. [7]

By this time another General Election was approaching. The issue lay between the Radical *Bloc*—the Governmental party of Radicals and Socialists—on the one hand, the Progressists or Moderates, the Nationalist-Royalists and the Catholics on the other. The collapse of the Federation of 1898 had left the last completely disorganized : but Piou and de Mun had made a gallant attempt to remedy the defect by forming a parliamentary group called the *Action Libérale*. The policy of this, as defined by Piou, combined " a strenuous resistance to the enemies of the Church with a cordial understanding with every section of the opposition." [8] The Pope encouraged Piou, and Cardinal Richard promised his help. The elections (April 1902) however, were again a disappointment to the Catholics. The Government came back with a majority of 87—339 deputies filled with a passionate hatred of the Church.

Waldeck-Rousseau trembled at the prospect before him. If the last Parliament had dragged him further than he meant to go, the new one was likely to drag him much farther. His health, too, was in a very shaky state. On June 3rd he put his resignation in the hands of the President. In a fatal moment he suggested Combes as his successor, and four days later the new Cabinet was constituted—a Cabinet of Freemasons.

II

The enemies of the Church could hardly have desired a better instrument of their designs than the new Premier. To a natural obstinacy of temper and narrowness of mind he added the passion of the renegade. In his youth he had studied and taught in a seminary, and had been noted for the fervour of his Ultramontanism. [9] Leaving the Church he had turned doctor and then gone into politics. But the fierce dogmatism

[7] Lecanuet, 302. Quotation given from an article by M. de Vogué in the *Gaulois*, October 9th, 1901. " *La masse du pays ne s'est pas émue.*"
[8] Lecanuet, 316.
[9] *Ibid.*, 325.

of his clerical days had not disappeared : it had merely taken another direction. As Loisy says, " *les fanatiques de tout bord se ressemblent.*" [10] His ministerial declaration (June 11th) left no doubt as to his intentions. " The Law of Associations," he said, " has entered on the period of its application. The Government will see that none of its provisions is stricken with impotence. We propose at the same time to repeal the law of 1850." [11] In Combes' mind the two parts of this programme were intimately connected. Throughout his war on the congregations it was their educational work he had specially in view, as the stoutest bulwark of the social and political influence of the Church.

His policy proclaimed, *le petit père* (such was Combes' nickname among those of his own kidney) lost no time in getting to work. [12] As the congregations required a law for their authorization, it was impossible to touch them until the legislative machinery had begun to function. But the unauthorized *établissements* at least were within the range of the executive's fire. To these, therefore, Combes first directed his attention.

Some of these *établissements* belonged to authorized congregations, some to unauthorized. Combes dealt with the former (mostly schools) first. The majority of them had applied for authorization, but the rest had not, believing it to be unnecessary. These fell into two categories : those that had existed before the promulgation of the law, and those founded since. The former, Waldeck-Rousseau, by declaring that the law would not be retrospective, had undertaken to leave untouched. The others he had threatened to close, but without effect. They were in truth a deliberate evasion of the law by the teaching congregations, which had established their schools in houses belonging to private individuals, hoping in this way to secure immunity for them on the ground that they were not really *écoles congréganistes.*

Combes attacked these *établissements* first. The schools

[10] *Mémoires,* ii. 33.
[11] Lecanuet, 327.
[12] On what follows see Debidour, ii. 341ff. Lecanuet, 329ff.

(125 in number) were closed and the teachers put into the street. He then attacked the schools of the first category. When Waldeck-Rousseau reminded him of his promise, Combes said he knew nothing about it—in any case, the old Government could not bind the new. Some 2,700 of them closed voluntarily, in order to avert action against the congregations to which they belonged. The rest were closed by force. Some 3,000 schools in this way ceased to exist. The people remained unmoved except for some demonstrations in the most Catholic parts of Brittany. [13]

There remained the *établissements*—about 11,000 of them —that had applied for authorization but had not yet received it. Some of these were hospitals: but the great majority were schools. To the latter Combes intended to refuse authorization *en bloc*. In order to avoid delay in dealing with them, he secured from the Council of State a decree declaring that the Government need not transmit to it the *dossier* of any *établissements* that it did not intend to authorize (September 4th). The Chamber and Senate approved of his action, and passed a law decreeing penalties against anyone who reopened a closed school. On December 23rd following, Combes informed the congregations concerned that their applications for authorization were all refused and that the schools must be closed, except in certain cases where it was for the time being impossible to replace them. In this way some 9,000 more Catholic schools came to an end.

Against such proceedings the bishops were in duty bound to protest, and they had done so. The Organic Articles forbade concerted action on their part, and Combes was not the man to hesitate to apply them. The organization of the protest—which was to take the form of a petition to both Houses of the Legislature—had thus to be effected in secret. [14] The initiative was taken by three bishops—Fulbert-Petit of Besançon, Chapon of Nice and Bardel of Séez. Each made himself responsible for a section of the episcopate: and in their correspondence the gathering of signatures assumed the disguise of

[13] Lecanuet, 346.
[14] Lecanuet, 364ff.

a " collection of photographs " of cathedrals! To such undignified shifts does anticlericalism compel its victims to
resort. The petition was to be presented at the reassembling
of Parliament on October 15th : but six days before that date
it was divulged by the *Gaulois,* and this considerably damaged
its effect. When it was presented it was seen that seventy-four
bishops (including all the Cardinals) had signed and five only
abstained. The Government at once summoned the signatories
before the Council of State. None appeared, and all were
found guilty of *abus.* The three organizers, with Touchet of
Orléans, [15] had their salaries suppressed. The Pope, on the
other hand, warmly approved the bishops' action.

By this time the assault on the unauthorized congregations
was fairly under way. Sixty-three male congregations and
some 400 female had applied for authorization. Combes
decided to deal with the former first. His original idea was to
follow the procedure contemplated by the Law—to have a
separate *projet* for each congregation and to have each *projet*
considered by both Houses. But the committee of the
Chamber appointed on October 30th to give preliminary
consideration to the *projets* was of a different mind. It consisted of thirty-three fanatical anticlericals and was determined to doom the congregations to extinction without
delay. After consultation with Combes it decided to apply to
the Council of State for a change in its *réglement* of the
previous year, laying down the manner of putting the law into
execution. The Council was once again obliging, and decreed
(November 27th) that, instead of the Government having to
submit all the *projets* to both Houses it might submit them to
either. If a *projet* were accepted by one House it would have
to be considered by the other as well : but if one House rejected a *projet,* it became unnecessary to refer it to the other
at all.

The Premier's next business, then, was to settle which congregations should have their *projets* submitted to the Senate

---

[15] Touchet had signed the petition but had had nothing to do with
organizing it. The Government penalized him by mistake instead of
Chapon, who then pointed out the error and shared the fate of his
brethren.

and which to the Chamber. Knowing that the Senate was more moderate in its sentiments than the Chamber, he decided to entrust to it those congregations that he was willing to see authorized, together with the Salesians, whose petition he knew that even the Senate would reject. [16] The remaining fifty-four, which he wished to suppress, were handed over to the tender mercies of the Chamber. Them he divided into three classes : (1) teaching (25); (2) preaching (28); (3) " trading " —so he contemptuously described the Carthusians because of their liqueur-making.

The case of the fifty-four congregations referred to the Chamber was thus hopeless. Late in January its committee decided to refuse authorization to all. In the senatorial committee Waldeck-Rousseau pleaded in vain for a return to the original procedure. The debate in the Chamber began on March 12th. The petitions of the congregations submitted were grouped into three *projets* following Combes' classification. Each group was considered in turn and the petitions rejected. The fifty-four congregations were thus suppressed *en bloc*.

The sentence was speedily followed by execution. On April 1st the congregations were informed that they were dissolved and that their *établissements* must be closed. The preaching orders must disperse within a fortnight, the teaching at the end of a period varying according to circumstances. The Oratorians obeyed at once, the Dominicans after an abortive attempt to negotiate. The rest declared that they would only yield to force. The Government therefore proceeded to expel them, and by the end of May practically all had dispersed.

A large number of their ex-members immediately turned themselves into secular priests with the approval of the bishops. Combes countered this by two circulars (dated April 9th and 11th respectively) addressed to the latter : the one ordering them to close all the congregational chapels in their dioceses,

[16] As being mainly composed of foreigners, and as also (according to Combes) " nothing but an exploitation of childhood and of public credulity, while at the same time it constitutes a danger for trade and industry." Lecanuet, 394.

the other forbidding them to allow ex-religious to serve as
" special preachers." But all but ten declined to obey. The
attitude of the episcopate had been throughout disappointing
to the Government. It was well known that the bishops
generally (like Cardinal Manning in England) resented the
independence and popularity of the religious orders : and the
enemies of these had hoped that the episcopate would leave
them to their fate. But it preferred to make their cause its
own. Combes retorted by closing as many chapels as he
could : but he dared not touch such great basilicas as Montmartre and Lourdes, especially as in the case of the latter the
railway companies, hotel proprietors and vendors of " objects
of piety " made vociferous protest. The silencing of ex-
religious preachers was undertaken by members of the newly-
formed *Association des Libres-Penseurs,* who made noisy
demonstrations in the churches. But when the Catholics
organized themselves to meet violence by violence these
brawlers thought better of it.

It was, however, specially in the sphere of education that
Combes meant to prevent the ex-religious from carrying on
their work in secular guise. With this object he propounded
to the Chamber an additional article to the law of 1901,
forbidding them to teach in the communes where they had
taught before. The *projet* [17]—called the *Loi Massé* after its
rapporteur—was voted on June 23rd. But four days later
Waldeck-Rousseau made a speech in the Senate, vehemently
denouncing Combes' policy and accusing him of having
" falsified " the law of 1901 and of having " transformed a
law of control into a law of persecution, applying it not with
moderation *mais à coups de pieds et à coups de poing.*" [18]
The speech made such an impression that Combes consigned
the *Loi Massé* to oblivion.

Meanwhile the Chamber had proceeded at once to settle
the fate of 81 female congregations, described (not always
accurately) as " teaching," whose demands for authorization
had been submitted to them by the Government. Two days

[17] Text in Lecanuet, 461.
[18] *Ibid.,* 468f.

(June 25th—26th) sufficed for the purpose. Their petitions were rejected *en bloc*. A week later (July 2nd—4th) the Senate in its turn fulfilled the task assigned to it of rejecting the petition of the Salesians and doing its part in authorizing the five other male congregations whose fate lay in its hands.

By this time Leo XIII., now in his ninety-fourth year, lay on his death-bed. The last months of his pontificate had been clouded, not only by grief at the fate of the congregations but by a fresh dispute with the French Government regarding the nomination of bishops. Seven years earlier Combes, as Minister of Worship in Bourgeois' Radical Government, had raised difficulties on this score: and he had not grown less difficult in the interval. The conflict raged round two points. In the first place, Combes objected to the phrase " *nobis nominavit* " in the bulls of institution to bishops, alleging that it implied that the Government merely presented its candidate for the Pope's consideration. Further, he rejected the so-called *entente préalable* by which, since 1871, before a candidate for the episcopate was actually nominated, the Nuncio was allowed to make enquiries as to his suitability. He therefore formally demanded from the Holy See on December 21st, 1902 the suppression of the word " *nobis,*" and two days later informed the Nuncio that he proposed to nominate to three vacant sees without previous consultation with him. Rampolla took up both challenges. On January 9th he informed the Government that its nominations were rejected. Two months after (March 9th) he declared that the Holy See declined to give up the disputed formula. Combes was furious, and on March 21st, apropos of a motion in the Senate for the denunciation of the Concordat, said that if the clergy wanted Separation they could have it—" *nous y sommes résignes.*" [19] The dispute was still unsettled when on July 20th, 1903, the great pontiff breathed his last.

III

Who was the new Pope to be? To no nation was this question quite so momentous as to the French. Leo XIII. had

[19] *Ibid.*, 481.

always been the friend of France—to such a degree indeed as to give grave umbrage to her enemies of the Triple Alliance. For this reason the Governments of the latter were anxious above all to avert the election of Rampolla, who would continue his old master's policy. It was no less the interest of France to secure it. The French Foreign Minister, Delcassé, therefore asked the French Cardinals to vote for him. Rampolla seemed likely to be elected when at the third scrutiny the Cardinal of Cracow, in the name of the Austrian Emperor, pronounced the *veto*. The election of Rampolla was thus rendered impossible : and in the succeeding scrutinies the voting steadily mounted in favour of Cardinal Sarto, Patriarch of Venice. The Cardinals of the Triple Alliance, unable to secure the election of a candidate of their own, had already supported him as one interested in piety rather than politics and therefore unlikely to take a strong line either for or against their nations. This same quality also recommended him to Rampolla's supporters, when it was clear that their own candidate could not succeed. On August 4th Sarto was elected and assumed the name of Pius X.

The new Pope was as different as possible from his predecessor. Leo had been an aristocrat, a scholar and a diplomat. Pius was none of these things. His mentality and outlook were always those of the simple parish priest that he had been for many years. His sanctity of character and sincerity of motive cannot be questioned. Unfortunately, much more than this was required in one who was to have to steer the bark of the Church amid the shoals and storms of a peculiarly difficult time.

At the outset of his pontificate the Pope hardly seemed to know himself what his policy was to be. His first Encyclical (dated October 4th) dealt with spiritual matters only, and defined his aim as "*instaurare omnia in Christo.*"[20] But his appointment of the youthful Merry del Val (half Englishman and mentally much more than half Spaniard) as Cardinal Secretary of State excited misgivings in liberal circles. Merry

[20] Extracts in Lecanuet, 508. The phrase, however, was closely associated with Cardinal Pie. See *ibid.*, 509 n.

del Val was to be the evil genius of his reign–an Ultramontane theocrat of the most positive sort. It was also observed that, if the Pope was gracious to Piou, he was even more gracious to the veteran Royalist Keller. The *abbés démocrates* had welcomed his election : but they were soon to find that their day was done. Merry del Val might declare that " nothing is changed " [21] at the Vatican : but already there were signs that things were going to be different, even though the new Pope was willing to concede to the French Government the suppression of " *nobis*," while remaining firm as to the nominations themselves.

The effect on Combes' obstinacy of Waldeck-Rousseau's attack had been transient, and he soon set to work again. The female congregations suppressed by the Chamber were ordered to disperse. Their schools were closed and the Sisters turned out into the world to fend for themselves as best they might. But this was not enough. The authorized teaching congregations still remained to be dealt with. Had not Combes undertaken to make the *Loi Falloux* a dead letter? [22] In the course of a tour of the south and west he declared that he would never rest till congregational education had been entirely wiped out.

Further measures followed against the Church. The nuns were expelled from naval hospitals (November). A decree of the Minister of Justice (April 1st, 1904) ordered the removal of the crucifix from courts of law. The Government even imposed restrictions on collections for the poor in churches, and forbade soldiers to attend Catholic social clubs.

Combes' campaign against the Catholic schools had been hitherto mainly in the sphere of primary education. But already the anticlerical fire was levelled against the secondary schools—the more so because it was here that Catholic competition with the State had been specially successful. In 1900 there were 91,140 male pupils in Catholic secondary schools as against 81,321 in those of the State. [23] In October 1902, the

[21] *Ibid.*, 513.
[22] *Vide supra*, 266.
[23] Baunard, *Un siècle de l'Église de France*, 126, quoting a parliamentary report.

Minister of Education, M. Chaumié, had presented to the
Senate a Bill[24] allowing anyone to open a " free " secondary
school by making a declaration to the local representative of
the education department, so long as he could show academ-
ical qualifications of a high order. The Bill came before the
senatorial education committee just a year later. It was
unfavourably received : and the *rapporteur*, M. Thézard, produced another measure substituting for a mere declaration
a definite authorization by a *loi*. The two rival Bills came
before the Senate on November 5th, 1903. The *projet
Thézard* was rejected on November 19th, but an amendment
to the *projet Chaumié* was voted, requiring from all directors
of secondary schools a declaration that they did not belong
to any congregation, authorized or unauthorized. With this
amendment the law was passed on February 23rd, 1904. But
it never came before the Chamber, to which Combes, by this
time more the servant than the master of his majority, had
already (December 1904) propounded a measure far more
stringent still.

This Bill sought nothing less than the extinction of
congregational education altogether. It (1) forbade teaching
of any kind to congregations, (2) suppressed all teaching
congregations within five years and forbade them to take any
more members, (3) closed all congregational schools within
five years, (4) ordered the property of the congregations to be
liquidated. The debate began on February 29th, 1904 : and
on March 7th the Chamber voted the " urgency " of the law.
In the discussion of its several clauses which followed, an
amendment was successful allowing the continuance of
novitiates for service abroad. The period of grace, too, was
extended to ten years. In place of the last eight clauses the
Chamber voted a single clause empowering the Government
to make a regulation on the matters with which it dealt and
allotting the surplus after liquidation to State schools ! In
this form the law was voted on March 28th. The Senate
passed it on July 5th : and it was promulgated on July 7th.[25]
The new law was at once put into force.

[24] Lecanuet, 538f.   [25] Text in Debidour, ii. 545f.

All that remained now was to complete the liquidation of the assets of the suppressed congregations, authorized and unauthorized. In recommending their designs to national opinion the enemies of the congregations had made much of the *milliard* (i.e. 1,000 million francs) which, they asserted, would accrue to the public funds from their extinction. The amount was in any case grossly exaggerated : and even the real amount was to shrink to very meagre proportions as the process of liquidation went on. The legal expenses were enormous : for those whom the Associations Law permitted to make claims on the property of suppressed congregations were often compelled to vindicate those claims in the law courts. In addition, the taint of corruption that had been the curse of the Third Republic all along now again reasserted itself. The liquidators indulged in malversation and corrupt sales to their hearts' content, until the truth could no longer be concealed and was admitted in the report of a senatorial committee. In March 1910, the shameful business was denounced in the Chamber by the Socialist Jaurès, who declared that " dishonesty in this country is organized in gangs." One of the chief liquidators was sent to penal servitude and another was lucky to escape a similar fate. [26]

IV

Only one more step remained to be taken and the Masonic programme was accomplished—the abolition of the Concordat. For all his threats Combes was not really in favour of this. But he was now at the mercy of his supporters. The time was propitious : for the feeling of the nation had recently been stirred to its depths by what Debidour has described as " the act of Pius X. which certainly most contributed to the separation " of Church and State. [27]

A visit of President Loubet to the King of Italy had been proposed for the spring of 1904. Leo XIII. had heard of it before his death, and had informed the Government that if the visit were paid he would not be able to receive the

[26] See Lecanuet, 58off.
[27] Debidour, ii. 394.

President at the Vatican. It is likely, however, that if he had lived no overt protest would have been made. But Pius X. was less prudent. Refusing to consider the fact that owing to the immobilization of Russia through her war with Japan it was urgent for France to cultivate good relations with Italy, he chose the very moment when the President was in Rome (April 28th) to instruct Merry del Val to hand a written protest [28] to Nisard, the French Ambassador to the Vatican, in which the visit was described as " an offence to the Holy See "—an offence all the greater in view of the " proofs of a particular goodwill " that it had bestowed on France. Not content with this, he ordered the note to be communicated to all the Governments with which the Holy See had diplomatic relations. Inevitably its text leaked out and it was published in France by Jaurés in his newspaper, *L'Humanité*.[29] The Government's retort was to tell Nisard to quit Rome, leaving a *Chargé d'Affaires* in his place. The subject was raised in the Chamber : and even the Moderates raised their voice to reprobate the Pope's action. Combes used the opportunity to bid the Chambers see in the Ambassador's departure a proof of the Government's determination " to have done once for all with the superannuated fiction of a Temporal Power that had been gone for thirty years." [30]

The Holy See refused to be warned. It quickly gave further offence to the Government by its action in regard to two bishops, Geay of Laval, and Le Nordez of Dijon, who had been denounced to it as unworthy of their office. [31] Geay's alleged offence was a suspicious " friendship " with a nun : Le Nordez' that he was a Freemason ! Whatever the truth about them may have been (in the case of Le Nordez the real offence was probably that his overbearing and tactless

[28] Text in Debidour, ii. 547.

[29] Jaurés had got it from the Prince of Monaco, who was on ill terms with the Holy See. See *ibid.*, 402 n. It was he who tried to get Loisy made a bishop. See below p. 310.

[30] Debidour, ii. 404.

[31] *Ibid.*, 405ff. See also Houtin, *Une Vie de prêtre* (Eng. tr.) 194ff. The present writer offers no opinion as to their guilt or innocence—the question is too complicated by alien considerations for him to form a judgment. But certainly Le Nordez was not a Freemason. He was by all accounts, however, not a very attractive clerical type.

demeanour had given umbrage to the Royalists of his diocese), the fact that both were well-disposed to the Republic [32] was not likely to commend them to the new regime at the Vatican. Both were ordered to come to Rome for an inquiry (July). The Government not only forbade them to leave France, but further informed Merry del Val on July 23rd that the action of the Holy See was an infringement of the Concordat. Merry del Val refused to yield. On July 30th, therefore, Nisard informed the Pope that the Government had decided to put an end to the " official relations which, by the will of the Holy See, are without object." [33] Next day the whole Embassy staff left Rome.

These events greatly strengthened the current of opinion in France favourable to Separation. The parliamentary committee which had been appointed on June 11th, 1903 to consider four private members' Bills [34] for bringing it about quickened the pace of its deliberations. In the commission the lead had come to be taken more and more by the Socialist Aristide Briand, an orator of singular eloquence and a most accomplished parliamentarian. The principle of Separation was accepted, though by a very small majority : and the commission proceeded to elaborate a *projet* for putting it into execution. This *projet* [35] it was anxious to submit to the Chamber when it reassembled on October 17th. Combes, however, now that he was expected to come to the point, showed signs of drawing back—the more so because the majority of his colleagues were indisposed to Separation. In addition, his position at the moment was very difficult in consequence of an exposure of the system of delation (nicknamed " *les fiches* ") that had been for some time practised in the army by Freemasons at the expense of their Catholic fellow-officers, with the connivance of the Minister of War, General André, and of Combes himself. The scandal was ventilated in the

[32] They had both been among the five bishops who had refused to sign the episcopal petition to Parliament in October 1902. *V. supra* 268.
[33] Debidour, ii. 411.
[34] *Projets Dejeante, Ernest Roche, Pressensé* and *Hubbard*. These with two later ones, *projets Grosjean et Berthoulat* and *Senac* are analysed in Debidour, ii. 548ff.
[35] Called *projet Briand*. Text in Debidour, ii. 552ff.

Chamber : and not only the Right, but deputies of all parties denounced it. Combes was thus forced back on the extreme Left to save himself from resignation. For this he had to pay the price. On November 10th he presented a Separation Bill [36] in the name of the Government.

It is unnecessary to give an account either of this *projet* or of that of the commission, as neither was destined to pass into law. That of Combes was indeed less a Separation Bill than a Bill to tighten the grip of the civil power upon the Church. Thus the commission, when it attempted to reconcile them, found its task very difficult and made slow progress. Meanwhile Combes had thrown the compromising André overboard (November 15th), but without much effect in propitiating his critics. The *Bloc*, too, was getting tired of supporting him. The section of it called *Union Démocratique* even broke off rather than defend him any longer. On January 19th, 1905, the stubborn old man saw that the game was up and resigned.

In his place President Loubet, who had never cared for Combes' policy and cared even less for Separation, set the old Opportunist Rouvier in the hope that he might thus avert, or at least postpone, the latter. But the *Bloc*, despite the recent secession, was still strong enough to compel Rouvier to its will : and in his ministerial declaration he was forced to include Separation among the " urgent reforms " that he was pledged to effect. But he did not say which of these would be dealt with first.

The *Bloc*, however, was not to be put off. Before its steady pressure the Premier had to give way : and on February 9th he laid a new Separation Bill [37] before the Chamber. As this was much more like its own than Combes' had been, the commission found its task comparatively easy. It was anxious too to get the matter settled. On March 4th Briand as *rapporteur* introduced into the Chamber a *projet définitif* [38]

[36] *Projet Combes.* Text in Debidour, ii. 559ff.
[37] Called *projet Bienvenu-Martin.* Text in Debidour, ii. 564ff.
[38] Text in Debidour, ii. 570ff. Briand's *rapport* accompanying the presentation of the law was published in book form as Briand, *La Séparation des Eglises et de l'Etat*, 1905.

which was in some ways more moderate than the Government's had been.

The general discussion began on March 23rd and lasted till April 6th. The Catholics denounced the law as a law of persecution. Of the Republican Moderates the majority denied that the time was ripe for such a step, while others were in favour of the Bill, only desiring that as many concessions should be made to the Church as possible. The Premier himself held aloof. It is to be noted that throughout the whole debate he never once addressed the House. The burden of defending the Bill fell mainly on the capable shoulders of Briand, who showed himself a miracle of persuasiveness, moderation and good temper. The "urgency" of the law was voted on April 8th, and the House proceeded to discuss the clauses. A number of amendments were carried, some toning down, others aggravating, the original text. On July 3rd the Bill was passed by 341 votes to 233. Next day it was laid before the Senate. The debate began on November 9th, after the recess. No amendments were successful; and on December 6th the Law was passed. Three days later it was officially promulgated.

The main provisions of the Separation Law of 1905 [39] (which, it must be remembered, had reference not to the Catholic Church only but also to the two other religious bodies granted State " recognition " by Napoleon —viz. the Protestant and the Jewish) may be summarized as follows: (1) The Republic guarantees liberty of conscience and of public worship subject to the later provisions of the Law (Article 1) : (2) It does not recognize or subsidize any form of religion. In the budgets of the State, the departments and the communes all subventions for public worship are suppressed, except in the case of chaplaincies in public secondary schools, hospitals and prisons (2) : (3) An inventory shall be made of all ecclesiastical property, moveable and immoveable (3) : (4) Within a year of the passing of the

[39] Complete text in Debidour, ii. 577ff.

Law all the property of the *menses* and *fabriques*[40] shall be transferred to the associations to be formed under a later clause of the Law. Such associations shall conform to the general rules of the forms of religion which they concern (4). [This important concession, which was not in the original *projet*, was a definite recognition of the right of the Catholic Church to exercise its own discipline] : (5) Property which belonged to the State, departments or communes shall go back to its original owners, apart from pious endowments subsequent to the Concordat (5) : (6) In the case of two or more associations setting up rival claims to the same property, the Council of State shall decide its attribution (8) : (7) Ministers of religion of over twenty years' service are to have pensions of varying amount. Those not entitled to pensions shall have subsidies at varying rates (11) : (8) All religious edifices and the movable property therein which belong to the State, departments or communes are left gratuitously at the disposal of the associations to be formed under the Law (13) : (9) But presbyteries and seminaries are granted rent-free for only five years and episcopal palaces for only two (14) : (10) The associations formed for " the expenses, the upkeep and the public exercise of a religion " are to consist of residents in the parish, and the number of members is to vary according to the population. They are permitted to raise funds by subscriptions, collections and fees; and are allowed to distribute their surplus to other associations. Their accounts are to be inspected yearly by a Government official and their accumulated funds are limited in amount, according to their revenue (19) : (11) The dispensation of ecclesiastics from military service is maintained (39).

V

The Concordat was thus at an end. The treaty which the combined might and political acumen of Napoleon had wrung from the unwilling hands of Pius VII., and which,

[40] *Menses*, endowments of sees, chapters and cures: *fabriques*, revenues of churches.

through many changes of regime, had yoked together Church
and State in France for just over a century, was denounced
by the will of one of the high contracting parties. So far the
State was acting entirely within its competence, and the
Church could only accept the *fait accompli*. But the provisions of the Separation Law went much further than that.
It did not merely end one legal situation of the Catholic
Church within the national life : it also created another—and
that without any previous consultation with the Church itself.

It was here that the disastrous mistake of the Government
in breaking off diplomatic relations with the Holy See became
manifest. It is obvious that the civil power in France could
never afford—or even effectively contrive—to ignore the
existence of a body at once so powerful, so deeply rooted, and
so centralized as the Roman Catholic Church. The statement
in Article 2 of the Law, " The Republic does not recognize
. . . any form of religion," was quickly to be proved (at least
in its strict interpretation) a sheer legal absurdity : and indeed
it was contradicted by Article 4 of the Law itself. If the
contract between the Church and State was at an end, it was
only common sense to liquidate it formally by assigning to the
Church a new juridical status that might be understood and
accepted on both sides. Further, the authors of the Law were
perfectly willing and even anxious that the Church should
retain a legal right to the national cathedrals and parish
churches—in fact, they could conceive no other use to which
they might be put. Nor had they any wish to deprive the
Church of such endowments as it already possessed. All these
matters were clearly subjects for bargaining : but effective
bargaining was impossible in the absence of any official
channel of communication between the French Government
and the Head of the Church. It is probable that the
destroyers of the Concordat would have been glad to see the
authority of the Pope flouted by his spiritual children, and a
national Church more or less independent of Rome come into
being. It would even appear [41] that the Government, in the
face of the Pope's intractable refusal to accept the Law, used

[41] See Houtin, *Une vie de prêtre* (Eng. tr.) 230ff.

money from its secret funds to subsidize more than one schismatic movement. But the result was grotesque failure. Whether it be true or not, as Napoleon believed, that " there is not enough religion in France to make a schism," [42] the Ultramontane principle had by this time so penetrated the marrow of French Catholics that when the testing time came they ranged themselves loyally behind the Pope's decision, even though many of them would have desired it other than it was.

Thus the issue lay in the hands of Rome: and for this reason the real ruling factor of the situation was the character and mental make-up of the reigning Pontiff. Unluckily, this was precisely of the type to make a difficult situation more difficult still. It is quite possible that if Leo XIII. had had the handling of the final stages of the anticlerical offensive against the Church, Separation would never have come at all: for neither side then really wanted it. It is at least fairly certain that, if it *had* come, it would have assumed a different form. No doubt Pius X. was entirely within his rights in refusing to accept an arrangement that he had had no hand in making: but one feels that Leo XIII. (or Rampolla, if he and not Sarto had been the choice of the Conclave in 1903) would have found some means of adapting it so as to make it tolerable by both sides. The action of the Government in 1906-7 was to prove that it had a genuine desire to meet the Church half-way. The *associations cultuelles* premised by Article 18 of the Law may have been inacceptable as they stood, on the ground that to regulate the " exercise " of worship (as distinct from merely paying for its " upkeep ") was the business of the clergy, not of the laity. But it should not have been beyond the wit of man so to adjust them as to provide a satisfactory basis for the existence of the Church as a corporate, property-holding and reasonably autonomous body within the framework of the French State. Pius X., however, took the opposite line. His mind was cast in the rigid mould of the saintly bigot, and, unlike his predecessor, he had neither the ability nor the will to understand the

[42] Houtin, *op. cit.*, 234 and n.

French mentality and the French situation. He was a theocrat pure and simple. To him the bishops were merely the organs of his inspired personal will. Above all, he had a horror of the laity in any other capacity save that of the docile sheep of the Church's pasture. Ill-informed by those whose interest it was to deceive him, he may even have hoped that the Separation Law might be made a lever for overthrowing the Republic altogether, with an outraged Deity to lend a hand. Two months, therefore, after the promulgation of the Law and without previous consultation with the episcopate, he issued the Encyclical *Vehementer* [43] (February 11th, 1906), in which, after denouncing the Law as an outrage on the Divine majesty and a violation of the law of nations respecting the sanctity of treaties, he went on to declare its provisions " contrary to the constitution of the Church as founded by Jesus Christ," by which the office of the Pastors was to rule and that of the flock simply to obey.

This condemnation was a condemnation of principle only and left it still possible to decide, if the worst came to the worst, that the Law might be tolerated after all. This possibility seemed to be strengthened by the fact that a few days after the issue of his Encyclical the Pope asked the French bishops to confer and advise as to the practical line to be adopted. To the majority of them the question did not appear quite so simple as the Encyclical seemed to premise. After all, it was they who would have to work the new system, and they naturally did not wish it to be worse than was absolutely necessary. In particular, they were confronted with a financial situation of the utmost gravity. The *budget des cultes* had gone beyond recall : but at least they were anxious to save what they could from the general wreck, as well as to secure for the Church a legal right to its sacred buildings. It was no less clear to men, like them, on the spot that the hope that a sudden veering of national opinion might either destroy the Republic or compel it to retrace its steps was an illusion. If they had any doubts on the subject the course of events was soon to bring conviction. It is true that

[43] Official French translation in Debidour, ii. 588ff.

at the beginning of 1906 the taking of the Church inventories prescribed by the Law was used by the Catholic intransigents —not without the hope of influencing the Pope's action thereby—as an occasion for exciting popular disturbances in many localities, by fostering the impression that what was really intended as a means of safeguarding the Church's property was an act of spoliation.   But so slight was the impression made that early in March the comparatively moderate Rouvier ministry gave way to a new government of which the leading figures were Briand, the author of the Law, and Clémenceau, the most irreconcilable foe of the Concordat.   Even so, there was no desire on its part to push matters to extremes.   A regulation of March 16th extended from one year to two the period within which the Church might put itself in a position to secure the property that the Law permitted it to retain.   But that there was also no chance of the general principle being abandoned was made clear by the general elections of May 1906, which, by returning a Chamber even more pledged to Separation than its predecessor, proved that the majority of the nation was now convinced that the Concordat had had its day.

Impressed by these portents, the bishops were more than ever anxious to make the best of a bad job.   Their view was shared by a large number of the intelligent laity.   Twenty-three of the most distinguished of these, encouraged by the Pope's resolve to consult the bishops, had already presented a petition praying them to advise acceptance of the Law.   This petition was published without their consent in the *Figaro* of March 26th—to the rage of the intransigents, who thought that the laity should mind their own business and dubbed the signatories " *cardinaux verts*," from the green braid on the uniform of the Academy, to which half of them belonged. When the bishops met in conclave in Paris at the end of May, they decided by a majority of 72 to 2 that the *associations cultuelles* could not be admitted as they stood, but went on to accept by 48 votes to 26 a proposal by Fulbert-Petit, Archbishop of Besançon, to approve them (under the title of *associations fabriciennes*) in a slightly modified form which, there was good reason to believe, would satisfy the requirements both of French and the Canon Law. This proposal was forwarded to Rome, where it was submitted to a commission of Cardinals and found a supporter in Rampolla. [44] The Pope, however, refused to heed. In judging his attitude there is no necessity to question his sincerity and good faith. It was, in fact, strictly logical : and he did no more than to put into practice the theory of the Church as the Ultramontanes had triumphantly formulated it. The days of the " hypothesis " were over for the time being, and the " thesis " resumed its sway. Pius X. had none of Leo XIII.'s taste for accommodations : he was that dangerous person— the man of an idea. Thus, when on August 20th he issued a new Encyclical, *Gravissimo*, [45] it was only to reaffirm the total rejection of the *associations cultuelles* already intimated in its predecessor. He even declared, on the strength of the first of the two votes of the bishops in Paris, that in doing so he was only " confirming " their " almost unanimous opinion." No overt mention was made of the bishops' proposal : but it was implicitly rejected in the assertion that " it is not permissible to attempt any other kind of association that does not secure in a sure and legal fashion that the divine Constitution of the Church, the immutable rights of the Roman Pontiffs and of the bishops, as well as their authority over the kinds of property necessary to the Church, particularly over the sacred buildings, are irrevocably guaranteed."

The disallowing of the *associations cultuelles* meant that there was no one to whom the Church's property could be transferred or its buildings assigned. If the Law were strictly executed, the property would have to be sequestrated and the churches closed. At a second meeting of the bishops in September it was decided not to give up the use of the churches save under coercion. The Government for its part was averse from resorting to force. On the expiry therefore of the year's grace assigned by the Law for the formation of

[44] Renard, *Vie du Cardinal Mathieu*, 467. Mathieu was the French *Cardinal de Curie* in Rome : and his *Life* throws much light on what was happening there between 1900 and 1908.
[45] Official translation in Debidour, ii. 598ff.

associations cultuelles, Briand issued a circular to the prefects ordering that, during the extra year conceded the previous March, services might be held in the churches on the same terms as other public meetings—i.e. on condition of a *déclaration de réunion publique* as required by the Law of 1881 ; a single declaration being allowed to cover a whole year. But the Pope at once intimated to the bishops through Cardinal Richard that no such declaration must be made. The Government retorted by ordering sequestration of the Church's property, and the eviction of their occupants from episcopal palaces and seminaries. At the same time it expelled from France the unofficial agent of the Holy See in Paris, Mgr. Montagnini, whose confiscated papers revealed compromising intrigues with the parties of the opposition.

Meanwhile Briand, immediately after the issue of his circular, had presented to the Chamber a Bill designed to regularize the use of the churches by Catholics on lines similar to those laid down in that document. The Bill became law on January 2nd, 1907.[46] It began by assigning the forfeited Church property to benevolent societies : and then proceeded to enact that the faithful might continue to enjoy the use of the churches, in default of the *associations cultuelles* prescribed by the Law of 1905, either through associations formed in accordance with the Law of 1901, or through individuals making a declaration as required by the Law of 1881 ; with the proviso that ecclesiastics who failed to comply with the present law within a month should forfeit their pensions. The Pope, however, in a new Encyclical, repeated his refusal of this solution (January 6th).

Ten days later a third Assembly of the bishops decided to try a system of contracts between the prefect or *maire* on the one hand and the bishop or curé on the other. The Pope allowed the experiment to be attempted : but the bishops themselves imposed conditions that the Government was unable to accept. This scheme too, then, fell to the ground.

As the clergy continued to officiate in their churches without having made any declaration, a number of them were

[46] Text Debidour, ii. 601f.

prosecuted locally for breaking the Law. In order to get over this difficulty, the Government secured the passage of a fresh Law,[47] bearing date March 28th, 1907, modifying the Law of 1881 by abolishing the requirement of a previous declaration for public meetings. In other words, the civil power was henceforth to turn a blind eye to Catholic worship altogether.

Such was the extraordinary situation that was to persist in France for the best part of a generation—in theory at any rate. The Catholic Church was without legal status of any kind; it could hold no property; it was "literally an outlaw."[48] Of course, such a theory could not always be maintained in practice. The courts of law, when adjudicating on cases affecting religion, were compelled by the logic of facts to recognize the hierarchical organization of the Church and even its doctrinal system.[49] But to exist merely on sufferance in this way obviously meant for the Church a position not only humiliating but perilous. If at any moment the Government chose to withdraw its contemptuous toleration, it was entirely without remedy. To this was added a perpetual anxiety as to ways and means. It is true that in the first flush of enthusiasm and indignation the Catholics rallied gallantly to the Pope's appeal to make up by generous giving for the financial loss that the Church had suffered. But this generosity was not altogether maintained as time went on : and in any case it fell far short of making good the deficit. The lot of the clergy was terribly hard. They had joyfully confronted the prospect of persecution, but what they were actually called to endure was the slow, prosaic grind of indigence. Further, it was out of the question to keep the staffing of parishes up to the level made possible by the *budget des cultes,* and many curés found themselves permanently without priests. The number of recruits to the sacred ministry, too, fell off to a disastrous extent.

[47] Text *ibid.,* 603.
[48] R. E. Balfour in *Theology,* (" Vicissitudes of Catholicism in Modern France ") May-June 1932.
[49] See Bureau, *Quinze Années de Séparation,* 1921, Ch. iii.

Yet despite all these handicaps Catholicism has managed to hold up its head and even in many ways to advance. The years immediately before 1914 were marked in French intellectual circles by a revival of Catholic belief (of a type at once mystical and authoritarian) that was signalized by the return to the Church of persons of real literary eminence and specially influenced the younger generation. This turn of the tide was assisted by the Great War, even though the first manifestations of revived fervour proved transient, in France as elsewhere. In particular, the *union sacrée* in the face of the national peril rolled away for good the reproach that Catholics were " bad Frenchmen." The clergy fought and died for France with magnificent heroism : and the members of the religious congregations came back of their own free will to serve in defence of the country that had driven them from its bosom. Again, in the years succeeding the War, the menace of Bolshevism caused those threatened by it to look with new favour on a force that was essentially one of " social conservation." Concurrently with all this, the antagonism of Catholics to the Republic diminished. Pius X. had been unfavourable to *ralliement* and returned to the idea of a *parti catholique* that should take its stand strictly " *sur le terrain religieux.*" But by 1914 this had proved a failure, and under his successor the tendency was towards a *néo-ralliement*. Thus since the war the tension between the Republic and the Church has relaxed, and the old anticlericalism wears a somewhat outmoded look.

One thing, however, seems fairly clear. Whatever new *modus vivendi* may be achieved, the Concordat will never be revived : for the Catholics would not have it back if they could. Rome prizes too much the independence and authority that Separation gives her : and her French children, too, are unwilling to put their necks again under the yoke of the State. And even the State, as it looks back on the Concordatist regime, may well wonder if it really was of much use in serving the Erastian purpose with which its author created it. A professor at the Sorbonne, M. Guignebert, has said that " it was Napoleon and not the Church that was the dupe of the bargain."[50]   Certainly it is a fact beyond dispute that one of the most conspicuous effects of the Concordat was to develop and fortify that Ultramontanism which makes Catholicism " not only a system of belief but also a system of government," and for that reason causes it to be always, in principle at least, an alien in the modern State.

[50] Guignebert, *Le Problème religieux dans la France d'aujourdhui*, 1922, 15.   Also 4.

CHAPTER XIII

THE INTERNAL LIFE OF THE FRENCH CHURCH UNDER LEO XIII

A. MODERNISM

THE story told in the last few chapters has been of necessity largely concerned with the action of the Church of France in the political sphere. On this stage its rôle cannot be described as a particularly impressive or effective one. Its efforts to overthrow the Republic had been no more successful than its previous efforts to constitute the Monarchy, and only resulted in hardening the hearts of its enemies and provoking them to fresh action for its hurt. In the sphere of the Church's internal life, on the other hand, the pontificate of Leo XIII. was a time of notable developments in a number of directions. Some of these have been already dealt with in the preceding narrative—such as the gallant, if ultimately futile, attempt of the Church to maintain its schools in the teeth of those of the State, and, in particular, the efforts of an active minority to mediate between Catholicism and the rising tide of democracy. In these two concluding chapters it remains to describe briefly the movement of these years in regard to (1) the intellectual re-statement of the traditional faith, especially in the sphere of biblical exegesis, (2) the devotional life, (3) missionary enterprise abroad.

I

The Liberalism of the French " Liberal Catholics " was concerned (as we saw in an earlier chapter) with liberty in the political, not the theological sphere. The age of Montalembert and Dupanloup was a time of remarkable developments in both the historical and the physical sciences. But in these developments they and their following appear to have taken little interest—still less did they recognize a duty to attempt a reconciliation between the new knowledge and the traditional doctrine of the Church. It was not till towards the end of the century that any serious efforts towards such a reconciliation

were made among French Catholics. Even then the great mass
of the clergy was still quite content to leave things as they
were. Their fear of ecclesiastical authority, their lack of
education and intellectual interest, their isolation from the
main currents of contemporary life—above all, their dread of
making terms in any way with forces that they had been
taught to believe fundamentally anti-Christian—all these
things conspired to keep them in the old rut. But the new
ideas could not be kept permanently at arm's length, even in
a Church so reactionary in mental attitude as the Ultramon-
tanized Church of France. It was inevitable that sooner or
later the more intellectual and progressive-minded of the
French clergy should feel the influence of ideas that were " in
the air " all round them and the necessity, if they were to
retain their faith, of harmonizing it with them.

A further stimulus to a reconsideration of traditional
positions was the emergence, in the years round 1890, of a
group of idealistically-minded intellectuals known as *les néo-
chrétiens.*[1] They represented the inevitable reaction from the
self-confident optimism of nineteenth-century scientific materialism, which appeared to them to have ended in nothing but
negation and despair. " Science " had destroyed the old
solutions of the problems of human existence without putting
anything in their place : worse still, it had sapped the foundations of morality. It was the view that found its most
resounding expression in a hotly-discussed article[2] written by
Ferdinand Brunetière on what he called " the bankruptcy of
science " (1895). Academician, editor of the *Revue des
Deux Mondes* and the foremost literary critic of his time,
Brunetière was already well on the way to that conversion to

---

[1] On these see Lecanuet, *Vie de l'Église sous Léon XIII.,* 457f. Also
Rivière, *Le Modernisme dans l'Église,* 86f. Besides P. Desjardins,
Édouard Rod, Édmond Schuré and the Vicomte Melchior de Vogué
were prominently associated with the movement.

[2] *Revue des Deux Mondes* " Après une visite au Vatican," January 1st,
1895. The article provoked a vigorous reply from the eminent chemist
Berthelot in *Revue de Paris* (February 1st). Debidour, ii. 135f. D'Hulst
also criticized it as tending to " fideism." Lecanuet, *op. cit.,* 461 n. For
an account of Brunetière's mental evolution see Émile Faguet, *Ferdinand
Brunetière,* 1911 : " *voilà le permanent de Brunetière, moraliste et
traditionniste.*"

practising Catholicism which was one of the most widely advertised triumphs of the Church in the later 'nineties, and was to enthrone the panegyrist of Bossuet as a sort of minor Bossuet himself in the Catholic world of his closing years. The case was otherwise with the *néo-chrétiens*. Their spiritual odyssey was in the end to lead most of them away from the Church altogether. But in these early days they seemed to hover rather wistfully on its outskirts. They had a passionate reverence for Jesus Christ and an immense admiration for Christianity in its moral aspect. But the Christian morality, in their opinion, was encumbered by a mass of dogmas that were a legacy from the past and were in obvious contradiction with the conclusions of modern thought. Was it not possible, they asked, to separate morality from dogma and to use the mighty organization of the Church, so deeply rooted still in French hearts, for the moral renewal of the national life, without regard to differences of theological opinion? Such was the view of the leading spirit among the *néo-chrétiens,* Paul Desjardins, who founded about 1891 the non-sectarian *Union pour l'Action Morale* to give it practical effect. It is not surprising that so promising an outlook should have evoked in certain sections of the Church a desire to meet the *néo-chrétiens* half-way, and to show them that the acceptance of its faith might involve a less drastic " sacrifice of the intellect " than they had feared.

One manifestation of the new mediating tendency has been already spoken of—the movement nicknamed "Americanism." The interest of its promoters lay in the field of action rather than of thought : and its encroachments on the doctrinal preserve, so far as they existed outside the imagination of the fanatics who denounced it, were neither grave nor deliberately meant. At the same time it bore witness to a dissatisfaction with traditional ideas and methods which, in minds more daring and hands more ruthless, might issue in a demand for far-reaching doctrinal reconstruction. It is not unreasonable then to see in it a sort of mild forerunner of the " Modernism " which, already in process of gestation, was to reach its crisis stage in the course of the next decade.

II

In considering "Modernism"[3] we must beware of regarding it as a concerted and harmonious movement: still less was it a deliberate and organized conspiracy to overthrow the traditional dogmatic system of the Church. The Encyclical *Pascendi*, which was the crushing counter-stroke of the Holy See to the campaign of the Modernists, not only invented a name for them but systematized a floating and rather hetero-geneous mass of ideas into a coherent body of thought that never had any actual existence in the world of fact. The most famous Modernist of them all, M. Loisy, has said with truth that " there was never a school with a recognized head ... a homogeneous and compact group."[4] Modernism in fact was less a school than a " tendency " shared by a con-siderable body of mainly independent thinkers who sought to solve the same problems from different angles, but on not dissimilar lines. It was (at least in its earlier stages) not even a movement, but rather (to quote Dr. Lilley) " a complex of movements within the Roman communion, all alike inspired by a desire to bring the tradition of Christian faith and practice into closer relation with the intellectual habits and social aspirations of our time. These movements arose spontaneously and for the most part in entire indepen-

[3] The literature of Modernism is very extensive. A bibliography is given in Rivière, *Le Modernisme dans l'Eglise,* 1929, which also provides a comprehensive account of the movement. Loisy complains of this book that it is "written entirely in the spirit of Batiffol." It is certainly not favourable to the Modernists: but neither is it blindly traditionalist. The author admits (p. 556) that "the disavowal inflicted on" the Modernist solution of the problem of reconciling faith and reason "involves the obligation to replace it by something more adequate." There is much on the subject in Lecanuet, *La Vie de l'Église sous Léon XIII.,* Ch. vii.-xi. Lecanuet is very sympathetic to Blondel and Laberthonnière, less so to Loisy. See also Weill, *Catholicisme libéral en France,* Ch. xii. The account here given of Loisy is largely based on his own autobiographical writings (see below). See also Baudrillart, *Vie de Mgr. d'Hulst,* 2 vols., F. von Hügel's *Selected Letters* (ed. B. Holland) 1927. Houtin's books are worth reading, but should be used with caution. There is a good short account of Modernism by Dr. Lilley in Hasting's *Dictionary of Religion and Ethics.* A recent book in English is Vidler, *The Modernist Movement in the Roman Church,* 1934, but it is mainly concerned with Loisy and Tyrrell. See also Inge, *Outspoken Essays,* First series, 137ff for a criticism of the Modernist position.
[4] Loisy, *Simples réflexions,* 13.

dence of one another during the last decade of the nineteenth century." [5]

So far as France, the birthplace of the movement, is concerned, two groups in particular may be distinguished which, starting each from the consideration of a different group of problems—in the one case philosophical, in the other historical—tended in course of time to approximate, but only to approximate, to one another in some sort of synthesis of their respective conclusions.

Of these two groups, the first to get to work—though for a long time its activity excited no great attention—was that which concerned itself with the historical basis of the Christian religion. " The Modernist movement," says Loisy, " did not begin with philosophy but with ecclesiastical history and, a little later, with biblical exegesis." [6] The focus of this activity was the Institut Catholique which (as we have seen) was the fruit of the imperfectly realized attempt to found a Catholic University at Paris made possible by the " *Loi Dupanloup* " of 1875. In the early 'eighties the one bright star in a small and otherwise undistinguished group of theological professors was the future historian of the early Church, Louis Duchesne, who had become professor of ecclesiastical history in 1878, at the age of thirty-five. Duchesne's type of mind was as far as possible removed from that of the romantic and enthusiastic school of Church history represented by Montalembert. In him an incisive mind and caustic wit found their fitting accompaniment in a brilliant critical faculty which submitted the documents it worked on to a ruthless analysis, and never hesitated to surrender either hypothesis or tradition at the bidding of fact. Not the least of his many services to historical science was the work he did in exploding the legends ascribing an apostolic origin to the leading churches of ancient Gaul. These legends had been disproved by the learned French Benedictines of the seventeenth century : but the neo-Ultramontanes of the nineteenth gave them fresh currency. Before the learning and critical sagacity of Duchesne they finally

[5] Lilley (as above).
[6] Loisy, *ibid.*, 144.

disappeared beyond hope of serious revival—not, however, without strong protests from many quarters.

Duchesne has been called " the father of Modernism." The title is a misnomer except in a very limited sense. He was essentially a savant, and had in him nothing of the stuff of the heresiarch. Profoundly sceptical in many ways, he at the same time shewed a consistent determination to avoid embroiling himself seriously with the ecclesiastical higher command, while allowing himself privately much latitude of satirical comment at its expense. In his chosen sphere of Church history he believed himself to be comparatively safe. The belief was not wholly justified by the event : for he had more than one brush with authority and his great *Histoire ancienne de l'Église* was to find a place ultimately on the Index. But at least he was safer on this ground than anywhere else, and he was not disposed to quit it. We know from a letter written by him to Loisy in 1881 [7] that even at that period he was well aware of the difficulties attending the traditional Catholic interpretation of the Bible. But he did not mean to venture personally on such dangerous territory. On the other hand, he could not prevent others from applying, if they chose, his own critical principles to the sacred books. It was from him that Loisy first learned the methods that he was to apply, first to the old Testament and then to the New, with such devastating results : though we have Loisy's own word for it that he made his way entirely by himself and that Duchesne was in no sense his " guide." [8] Rather did the older man try to put a brake on the ardour of the younger when it seemed likely to lead him into compromising situations. Had Duchesne had his way, Loisy would have abandoned Biblical exegesis and confined himself to the chaste and secure pursuit of Semitic philology. "You and I," he said, "will never be *cardinaux rouges,* but we may be *cardinaux verts* " [9] (i.e. members of the French Academy)—a prophecy

[7] *Mémoires,* i. 98.
[8] *Ibid.,* 104 ; cf. 135.
[9] *Ibid.,* 164.

which in Duchesne's case was to be fulfilled. But
Loisy was made of different stuff. He, too, had no desire to
play the rôle of a party chief : his temperament was that of
the scholarly recluse. But he had chosen his path : and being
courageous and intensely stubborn he meant to stick to it
whatever the consequences. He might occasionally bend, but
he would never break. If left to go his own way, he was not
inclined to be aggressive. But when he was struck he could
give as good as, and better than, he got. His was not, perhaps,
a very amiable temper : [10] and he wielded a pen which had not
a little of the terrible biting quality of Voltaire.

Inasmuch as Loisy is easily the most striking and celebrated
among the champions of Modernism, it may be well to centre
our account of the movement in its French manifestation
around the story of his career and spiritual evolution. The
materials for this story are copious : for, in addition to the re-
trospect published by him in 1911, with the title of *Choses
passées,* he produced in 1931 three lengthy and fascinating
volumes of *Mémoires* [11] describing with a wealth of docu-
mentary matter the whole of his chequered life history.

Alfred Firmin Loisy was born in 1857 at Ambrières, a
village in the department of the Maine. In 1872 he became
a pupil at the *collège écclesiastique* at St. Dizier. He has told
us that at first the thought of the priesthood in no way
attracted him : but at sixteen, as the result of a retreat preached
at his college, he decided to embrace the ecclesiastical state.
He entered the *grand séminaire* at Châlons in October 1874.
Here, though diligent and devout, he incurred to some extent
the suspicion of the authorities, who regarded him as insuffi-
ciently deferential to ecclesiastical tradition. From 1875
onwards, indeed, he was " in a state of perpetual anguish." [12]
While remaining entirely respectful to what he was taught to
believe to be the doctrines of the Church, he was yet tor-
mented against his will by the question whether they were

[10] Loisy himself records Cardinal Mathieu's advice to him in 1901 :
" *N'écoutez jamais la mauvaise humeur.*" *Mémoires,* ii. 60.
[11] *Mémoires pour servir à l'histoire réligieuse de notre temps,* 1931.
[12] *Choses passées,* 34.

really true after all. His spiritual directors dismissed his
doubts as scruples, and he himself tried to escape from them
in the practice of a mystical piety. But the " anguish " refused to be appeased. He was ordained sub-deacon in June
1878. Thus, he writes, " the great mistake of my life was
consummated." [13]

A year later began his long connection with the Institut
Catholique of Paris. In 1878, three years after its foundation, the French bishops had decided to add to the existing
faculties a Faculty of Theology, to which they might send
specially promising students from their seminaries, with a view
to their returning thither as professors after receiving the
higher teaching afforded in this way. From the seminary of
Châlons the Bishop, Mgr. Meignan, chose Loisy, who went to
Paris in September 1878. He was not greatly impressed by
the teaching he received, and almost immediately his health
broke down. He returned to Châlons, where he was ordained
deacon and priest in 1879. He was appointed *desservant* of
two country parishes in rapid succession.

His experience as a parish priest was not of long duration.
In May 1881, in response to pressure from Duchesne, who
desired to gather round him a band of youthful workers, he
sought and obtained permission from his bishop to return to
the Institut Catholique. His own idea was to remain there
for only a short time and then, if possible, to return as professor to Châlons. But in the following November his skill in
Hebrew led to his appointment to give, as *répetiteur,* a course
of instruction in the elements of that language. This was so
successful that in May of the next year the Rector, Mgr.
d'Hulst, asked Mgr. Meignan to allow Loisy to remain
permanently in Paris, with a view to his specializing in
oriental languages and ultimately occupying a chair of Holy
Scripture. The Bishop gave consent, adding in a letter to
Loisy [14] a word of warning. " Holy Scripture," he wrote,
" needs to be studied with a great humility, a great distrust of
self and of novelties. More than one German Protestant has

[13] *Ibid.,* 46.
[14] Printed in full in *Choses passées,* 382f.

lost his faith in the searching test of a thorough study of it.
May God allow you to keep yours! "

The Bishop's words were more than a mere conventional
monition, and must be interpreted in connection with his remarkable interview with Loisy ten years later.   Of all the
French bishops Mgr. Meignan was the most conversant with
Biblical problems. [15]   At the Vatican Council he had urged
upon the Fathers the necessity of taking serious account of the
danger that threatened the traditional faith of the Church
through the developments of Biblical science outside its pale.
He himself was well read in the writings of Protestant critics
and had written extensively against them.   But, like Duchesne,
he was not unaware of the strength of their positions, and he
realized that to grant these would involve an abandonment of
tradition to which the rulers of the Church would never consent.   Thus for a critical and progressive mind like Loisy's
the scientific study of the Bible must be beset with pitfalls.
Once let him allow himself to be convinced of the cogency of
the arguments with which he would be compelled to acquaint
himself and his position in the Church would become un-
tenable.

So the Bishop believed.   But Loisy himself was of a
different opinion.   The disintegration of his belief in the
traditional Catholic position had indeed begun already : and
was to make rapid progress as his studies proceeded.   For this
the influence of Protestant critics was hardly even necessary.
When accused at a later period of having erred through
"reading the Germans," [16] he objected that his difficulties arose
from the fact that he had read the Bible.   As early as 1883
he could write in his diary, " The Church is at the present
moment an obstacle to the intellectual development of mankind " [17]—because of its blind obscurantism and resistance to
the progress of science.   Yet he did not regard it as obligatory
upon him for this reason to abandon either his priesthood or
his teaching.   It was not impossible that the Church's attitude

[15] Lecanuet, 320f.
[16] At his interview with Cardinal Richard in 1893. *Choses passées,* 151.
[17] *Ibid.,* 68.

should be changed: and meanwhile he could still believe that she was the greatest existing force for the moral education of humanity. The Catholic scholar must pursue the path of research wherever it might lead, and trust that some day and somehow the traditional theology might be altered and adapted to square with the conclusions that a scientific criticism might impose. Truth was truth wherever it came from. It was in this belief that he felt himself able to confide to his diary in 1884: "Now I am persuaded that I did well to receive Holy Orders. Now I am enrolled, I have decided to fight with courage. My only fear is that my efforts should be in vain." [18]

These views, however, Loisy kept to himself. It is true that when in 1884 he submitted a thesis on inspiration for his doctorate to a preliminary examination by Mgr. d'Hulst the latter advised him not to send it in. But d'Hulst was not without sympathy for the critical position himself: and he did not regard Loisy's divagation from the strict path of orthodoxy (so far as he was permitted to know it) as disqualifying him from teaching at the Institut Catholique. When in 1888 the professor of exegesis, M. Martin, was compelled to absent himself, Loisy was appointed as temporary substitute and again the following year. On M. Martin's death in 1890 the appointment was made permanent.

In undertaking his new functions Loisy laid down for himself an elaborate and comprehensive programme, [19] the execution of which would occupy a number of years. He himself has characterized this programme as " a conscious preparation for a veritable revolution of Biblical science in French Catholicism." [20] He was perfectly aware that such a revolution would excite opposition: but he proposed to deal with the less contentious questions first, and to trust that as time went on the gradual infiltration of the new point of view might make possible the acceptance of what was more revolutionary. [21] He believed that " orthodoxy is only un-

[18] *Mémoires*, i. 135.
[19] Set forth in *L'Enseignement biblique* in 1892. *Choses passées*, 85ff.
[20] *Mémoires*, i. 175.
[21] *Choses passées*, 91.

changeable in the imagination of those who believe in it." [22]
History proved that the doctrine of the Church, so far from
being static, had undergone a process of continuous evolution
and change in adapting itself to the prevailing ideas of succeeding ages. What had happened in the past would go on
happening in the future. Meanwhile the inevitable developments that were coming must be prepared for by a study
of the sacred books without regard to theological pre-
possessions—such a study as that of which he had learned the
method at the feet of Renan, whose lectures at the Collège de
France he had attended from 1882 to 1885 and whom he was
to hail later as " the first master of the French modernists." [23]
The texts of the Bible, he believed, were susceptible of two
meanings—the historical and the traditional—" the first being
that which belongs to them in virtue of their origin and their
own nature, the second that which has grafted itself on to
them, by the operation of faith, in the later evolution of
Judaism and Christianity. For the critical historian the first
alone is to be considered as the meaning of the Biblical text :
the second concerns the history of exegesis and of beliefs." [24]
Of the two his own concern was for the moment solely with
the first.

In addition to his lectures Loisy, stung perhaps by a rather
Rabelaisian joke of Duchesne's concerning his *infécondité*,
began about this time to produce books as well. A successful
thesis for the doctorate, based on his first course of lectures,
was published in 1890 with the title *History of the Canon of
the Old Testament*. This was followed next year by a
History of the Canon of the New Testament. In 1892 he
published in the *Revue des Réligions* a series of articles on *The
Chaldean Myths of Creation and the Deluge,* which treated
the " grandiose narratives " of Genesis as conveying " lofty
theological and moral lessons " rather than as statements of
historic fact. [25] In the same year he began a serial publica-

[22] *Mémoires*, i. 176.
[23] *Revue d'histoire et de litt. relig.* 1910, vol. i., p. 584 (quoted Rivière, 88).
[24] *Mémoires*, i. 178.
[25] *Choses passées*, 109.

tion of his lectures under the title of *L'Enseignement biblique*.

The lectures excited much interest and attracted a considerable number of the younger and more thoughtful clergy. But the enemy was on the look-out. In 1891 a short essay on *Proverbs* was denounced to Rome. A more serious incident occurred in October of the next year. M. Icard, the saintly but very traditionally-minded Superior of Saint Sulpice, forbade his students to attend any longer Loisy's lectures on Holy Scripture. (He had taken a similar step ten years before in regard to Duchesne's lectures.) Mgr. d'Hulst treated the matter lightly and continued to defend his professor. But he began to feel uncomfortable.

Loisy, too, saw the danger that threatened him. Looking round for a possible supporter of consequence, he bethought himself of Mgr. Meignan, now Archbishop of Tours and on the eve of becoming a Cardinal. An interview followed on October 24th. It was recorded more or less *verbatim* by Loisy [26] and casts a curious light on the mentality of a Prince of the Church, learned, capable and kindly, but essentially opportunist. After a preliminary discussion of the difficulties surrounding the Book of Daniel, the Archbishop expressed himself with singular frankness on the prospects of Biblical criticism in the Church. " Criticism," he said, " has never existed in the Church. The whole Catholic clergy is in a state of profound ignorance. In trying to get them out of it one runs great risks : for our theologians are ferocious : they put us on the Index for nothing. Believe me, *mon petit Loisy*, it is necessary to be very prudent. I have helped to engage you in the way of science : that is why I have a right to say to you : Take care ! *C'est un conseil de père.* If you expose yourself to danger, those who think like you will not come to your help. . . . Let us then be the advocates of tradition— *des avocats sincères, toujours sincères."* A recasting of the traditional exegesis is impossible. " In truth we are working in a closed room. I, too, have tried—very gently—to open the window a little : in all my books I have slipped in some-

---

[26] See *Choses passées,* 116ff. (*Mémoires,* i. 224ff.)

thing useful. But what one must avoid above all is to compromise oneself."

Clearly there was little hope of help in that quarter.
Actually, it was d'Hulst who was to challenge Catholic opinion
in defence of Loisy and what he believed to be Loisy's views.
But unfortunately his generous and well-meant intervention
was to bring disaster not only on his protégé but also on
himself.

The Rector of the Institut was a liberal-minded man. He
was in touch with the currents of the intellectual world of his
time, and was genuinely anxious to help souls dismayed by the
gulf between the Church and modern thought. He was no
less anxious to represent his beloved Institut as a centre of
light and leading. These motives prompted him to write an
article on Renan, [27] which appeared in the *Correspondant*
after the great critic's death and at about the same time as
Loisy's interview with Mgr. Meignan. In this he was careful
to avoid the usual orthodox tone of windy denunciation, and
asked boldly " what would have happened " if Renan in his
seminary years had received an initiation into the sacred
sciences which, instead of being " at once elementary and out-
of-date," had been of the kind now afforded by the Institut
Catholique. A further article appeared in the same organ on
January 25th, 1903, in which d'Hulst boldly tackled *La
Question biblique*. [28] He raised the issue of " the errors in the
Bible," and divided Catholic exegetists into three schools
according to their attitude in regard to them : the " traditional," the " middle " and the " broad." For the first there
can be no errors in the Bible, for it was written by God
Himself. For the last the inerrancy of Scripture related only
to the sphere of faith and morals, and therefore errors of
scientific or historical fact were immaterial. He himself
appeared to identify himself with the *école moyenne,* and it
was from this standpoint that he ventured to criticize the two
extremes. In his account of the *école large* he seems to have
imagined that he was defining the position of Loisy : and his

[27] *Correspondant,* October 25th, 1892. Quoted *Choses passées,* 113.
[28] *Choses passées,* 125f. Lecanuet, 351f.

friendly criticism of its "audacities and temerities" was largely intended for Loisy's benefit. Actually, as we know, Loisy's position was quite different. The "broad school" attitude, he says, was more or less d'Hulst's own. [29] In any case the Rector pleaded for its toleration : and this was where his crime lay in the eyes of the traditionalists.

The article created a great stir. Everyone was convinced that the *école large* represented Loisy, and that d'Hulst had written to defend him. The traditionalists were furious : and the Holy See seemed disposed to give them satisfaction by condemning d'Hulst. To prevent this the latter went to Rome, where unfortunately he was not in very good odour owing to his lack of enthusiasm for *ralliement*. Good man and honourable as he was, he quailed before the prospect of a condemnation, fearing its consequences for his Institut even more than for himself. A bargain was struck, the nature of which was revealed on his return. In a letter to the bishops-protector of the Institut [30] he recommended that, " in order that Loisy's reputation might not be injurious to it," he should be deprived of his chair of Holy Scripture and confined to his other task of teaching Hebrew. The bishops approved : and met in November to give formal effect to the proposal. But a few days before Loisy had published an article in *L'Enseigne-ment biblique* in which he boldly asserted that in view of the achieved results of criticism " it is no longer a question of knowing what errors the Bible contains but of knowing what truth it contains " and enumerated the positions that he re-garded as " *acquises à la science.*" [31] D'Hulst felt it his duty to bring the article before the bishops, who decided now that Loisy must leave the Institut Catholique altogether. [32] Loisy accepted the verdict in a letter to d'Hulst of extreme bitter-ness, which he later regarded as excessive. [33] D'Hulst's only

[29] *Mémoires*, i. 239. Cf. Lecanuet, 351.

[30] Text in *Choses passées*, 384f. Taken from Baudrillart, *Vie de Mgr. d'Hulst*, i. 484.

[31] *Choses passées*, 138f.

[32] Minute of decision in *Choses passées*, 386. Taken from Baudrillart, as above, i. 487.

[33] *Mémoires*, i. 273f.

comment in reply was, "You have thrown yourself in front of a locomotive in motion." [34]

The "locomotive" was the Encyclical *Providentissimus Deus*, [35] which appeared on November 18th, 1893. D'Hulst had known that it was imminent : and this knowledge had largely determined his recent action. The Encyclical was not a very helpful document. It declared that " Divine inspiration in itself excludes all error " in the Bible—to deny this is " to make God Himself the author of error." The position of the *école large,* confining the scope of inspiration to faith and morals, is rejected as " false." It was clear that, however ready to move with the times Leo XIII. might be in the matter of politics, in the intellectual sphere his attitude was simply that of Canute. Loisy wrote to the Pope expressing " submission " to his rulings [36] and informed Cardinal Richard that *L'Enseignement biblique* would not appear again.

Driven from the Institut, Loisy found employment with some difficulty as chaplain of a convent school for girls at Neuilly. " Events have proved you right," he wrote to Cardinal Meignan. " There is nothing to be done " to change the system of apologetic. [37] Certainly Rome seemed at no pains to belie his pessimism. In January 1897, a decree of the Congregation of the Index declared that it was not permitted to question the text of the " three heavenly witnesses " in 1 John [38]—a palpable interpolation. Next year the Pope in a letter to the Franciscan General [39] issued a fresh warning against " new opinions," and on September 8th, 1898, in an Encyclical to the French clergy, [40] called attention to the instructions given in the Encyclical *Providentissimus* and denounced those writers who " themselves made breaches in the walls of the city they were charged to defend." The traditionalists were in high feather : and when the exceed-

[34] *Choses passées,* 146.
[35] Analysed in Lecanuet, 356ff.
[36] Text of letter in *Choses passées,* 388f.
[37] *Mémoires,* i. 326.
[38] Lecanuet, 362. He calls it " *décret malheureux qu'on a vivement regretté depuis lors.*"
[39] Quoted *ibid.,* 366.
[40] Relevant extract in *Choses passées,* 391.

ingly moderate Père Lagrange, head of the Dominican school of biblical antiquities at Jerusalem and editor of the *Revue biblique,* ventured, at the Catholic Scientific Congress at Fribourg in 1898, to exhort Catholic scholars to " go forward but to go forward with respect," the Archbishop of Jerusalem promptly denounced him to Rome. [41] In the face of this situation, the more progressive Catholic critics could only find comfort in explaining the Encyclical *Providentissimus* away, or hoping that in time the papal rulings might undergo revision.

Apart from a few reviews of books, Loisy kept silence at first altogether. But from 1896 onwards he resumed his literary activity to some extent, especially in the *Revue d'histoire et de littérature réligieuses,* founded by him to carry on the work of *L'Enseignement biblique.* In his articles he generally adopted the prudent disguise of such pseudonyms as " Firmin," " Desprez," and " Simon."

These occasional articles, however, were very far from being Loisy's chief occupation in these years. It was then that he pursued the researches that found their fruit in the large exegetical works on the Gospels published during the next decade. Even more important was the intellectual travail by which he sought to work out for himself a new philosophy of Catholicism, in accordance with what he believed to be the achieved results of criticism in regard to the Bible and Church history. The beautiful piety of his Dominican nuns at Neuilly seemed to him to have its source in the fact that they thought " religiously " and not " theologically." Further, one of his duties was to teach the girls their catechism : and this led him to " meditate and study " it. [42] Gradually the idea formed itself in his mind of a book that would supply " a philosophic and historical interpretation of Catholicism which would be at once its apology and the discreet programme of the reforms that it would have to effect in itself in order to perform its mission to the contemporary world." [43] This book was never

[41] Lecanuet, 363.
[42] *Choses passées,* 162, 166.
[43] *Ibid.,* 170.

to be published as a whole : but parts of it appeared in the form of articles in reviews, and its leading ideas inspired the famous *L'Évangile et l'Église.*

III

Loisy's *livre inédit* [44] is not only interesting in itself but even more as supplying a point of junction between the two streams of tendency which (as we have seen) went to create what is called " Modernism." While he and others were seeking to apply the methods of historical criticism to the Bible and the early history of the Church, another group had been attempting to evolve a new philosophy of the Christian religion. The two groups, though distinct, were not without relations with one another ; the gifted and attractive Abbé Marcel Hébert in particular serving as a link between them.

One of the first acts of Leo XIII. on becoming Pope had been to issue the Encyclical *Aeterni Patris* (August 4th, 1879) in which he expounded the need of a Christian philosophy that " would engender, nourish, defend and fortify the faith." [45] For this purpose he strongly recommended the scholasticism of St. Thomas Aquinas, and urged that it should be made the basis of clerical training. This aim he consistently pursued throughout his pontificate. The result was seen in a " neo-Thomist" movement that found expression in two rival schools —the Roman school, which treated philosophy exclusively as " the handmaid of theology," and the more liberal school of Louvain, which sought rather to find in St. Thomas a point of contact between religion and science. But to minds familiar with modern philosophical speculation this harking back to the thirteenth century appeared unsatisfactory. In the 'eighties Ollé-Laprune [46] sought to justify Christianity by showing " its conformity with the deepest aspirations of human nature." His ideas were further developed by his brilliant pupil Maurice Blondel, who in 1893 sustained at the Sorbonne a thesis called

---

[44] For an account of this see *Choses passées,* 174—206, *Mémoires,* i. 445ff.
[45] On this and what follows see Lecanuet, 466ff.
[46] On Ollé-Laprune, Blondel and Laberthonnière and their " new apologetic " see Lecanuet, 497ff. Also Rivière, 118ff.

" *L'Action: Essai d'une critique de la vie et d'une science de la pratique.*" Its positions were expanded in a *Lettre sur l'Apologétique* published in 1896 in the *Annales de Philosophie chrétienne,* a review which was to serve as the main organ of the new ideas. According to Blondel the fault of the traditional Christian philosophy had been to overstress the idea of God as " transcendent," and to represent the supernatural exclusively as something imposed on man from outside. Whereas the truth is that the nature of man in itself postulates the supernatural. Religion is not (as its enemies affirm) an enslavement of man, but the only means of his self-realization. It is this in virtue of the Divine " immanence," through which the divine within him reaches forth to the divine outside him and in the latter finds its predestined complement. The first step, then, towards God is to will to have Him : and this will must find expression in *action*.

Blondel's views were to a large extent shared by Georges Fonségrive, editor of the extremely able Liberal Catholic review called *La Quinzaine*.[47] But his most ardent defender and follower was a distinguished young Oratorian, Père Laberthonnière. In an essay entitled *Le Problème réligieux,* Laberthonnière not only reaffirmed the " method of immanence " in the philosophical sphere but went on to apply it to the theological ideas of grace and revelation. " Faith " is the active response of the soul to God, whereby it surrenders itself to His working and is able to receive what He wills to bestow. In a later work Laberthonnière expanded this idea into the theory of *Le Dogmatisme moral* which gives its name to his essay. Following the lines laid down by Newman before him, he emphasized the part played by the will in the achieving of religious certitude. Such certitude, he says, " is moral in the sense that it is our own work—a work which we accomplish with the help of God and of others, but for which our own action is indispensable."[48] Truth, in fact, is not static, but dynamic. It is no mere matter of accepting a number of in-

---

[47] The *Quinzaine* terminated its existence in 1907 as a result of its publication of Le Roy's article on *Qu'est ce qu'est un dogme?* (*v. infra,* 315).

[48] Quoted by Lecanuet, 530.

tellectual concepts from outside, but is achieved in the process of living. The true Christian philosophy is the ever-developing product of human experience in its totality—a " philosophy of action."

Here we have already laid down two leading ideas which were to play a preponderant part in the evolution of the Modernist position—the " method of immanence " (by many exaggerated into a denial of the Divine transcendence altogether) and the important place assigned to the will in the search for truth. To these, in Loisy's working out of his new " interpretation of Catholicism," was added a third. Soon after going to Neuilly he had begun a careful study of the writings of Newman, which had been recommended to him by his friend Baron Friedrich von Hügel. [49] In them, in addition to the insistence on the " will to believe," he found confirmation of his own view of Christian doctrine as a thing not fixed and unchangeable from the beginning but the result of a continual process of " development." In his view, however, Newman had only given a partial application to this principle, in confining it to the elaboration of the Church's existing system of faith and worship. He himself was prepared to extend it to cover the whole field of man's religious history—backwards to the divine revelation in both Testaments of the Bible and forwards to the incessant " reinterpretations " which the faith must undergo if it was not to be left behind by the march of humanity. [50] In envisaging these latter he freely adopted the method of explaining the dogmas of religion in a " symbolical " sense which his friend Marcel Hébert had worked out as he found himself less and less able to accept those dogmas literally. [51] In the Catholicism of the future men must exchange the " letter " for the " spirit," and penetrate behind the inherited formula to the spiritual truth that it enshrines.

Loisy's chaplaincy at Neuilly came abruptly to an end in September 1899 in consequence of a severe attack of hæmorrhage which nearly terminated fatally. With the help of his

[49] *Choses passées,* 164.   [50] *Mémoires,* i. 451.   [51] Rivière, 143.

good friend Mgr. Mignot, Bishop of Fréjus (one of the two French bishops who really sympathized with the new ideas) [52] he obtained from the Pope an "indult" permitting him to have a private chapel. Immediately afterwards he took up his residence at Bellevue, not far from Paris. Here he resumed his studies and his writings of articles for reviews.

By this time there were grave signs of trouble ahead. The condemnation of "Americanism" by Leo XIII. in January 1899 was of no good augury for the progressive school of Catholic thought. At the end of the same year Mgr. Batiffol, Rector of the Institut Catholique of Toulouse, publicly denounced the various types of false doctrine that were gaining a hold in the Church, with special reference to those who paid excessive heed to the findings of Protestant scholars and those who resolved its historic faith into "a purely subjective symbolism." [53] The hand of authority fell before long on Loisy himself. The first of a series of articles (signed "Firmin") on *The Religion of Israel* excited the disapproval of Cardinal Richard, who forbade the publication of the remainder [54] (October 1900). Loisy retorted by declaring that he would no longer accept a small pension from the diocesan funds given to him on the ground of his ill-health. [55]

The gesture was a sign that he did not propose to lie down quietly under the censure inflicted on him. Not only did he decide to abandon henceforth the use of pseudonyms, but he proceeded without delay to find for himself a position that would at the same time make him financially independent of the Church and give him a status in the lay world of learning. In November 1900 he gave his first lecture as *conférencier libre* at the École des Hautes Études before a numerous assembly, including not a few ecclesiastics. The subject of his first course was "The Babylonian Myths and the first

---

[52] On this admirable and liberally-minded prelate see an obituary article by his friend, Baron Friedrich von Hügel, in *Contemporary Review*, May 1918. The other bishop was Mgr. Lacroix of Tarentaise (resigned 1907).

[53] *Mémoires*, i. 534 n.

[54] The Cardinal's letter (dated October 23rd) is printed in *Choses passées*, 392.

[55] Loisy's letter printed *ibid.*, 220.

chapters of Genesis." In an interview with Cardinal Richard, the latter warned him against the " perils " of his new surroundings and the temptation to yield to " subjective hypotheses." But Loisy was quite unmoved. " This very sincere kindness," he wrote afterwards, " as of Victor Hugo's Torquemada, who burned people out of charity, left on me the most deadly moral impression I have ever felt in my life." [56] Soon after he published as a pamphlet the articles on *The Religion of Israel*, which had incurred the Cardinal's condemnation. The lectures on Genesis were published in book form at the end of the year; by which time Loisy had begun to lecture on a riskier subject still—the Gospels.

Meanwhile the authorities were on the watch. In April, the students of the Institut Catholique were forbidden to attend Loisy's lectures : and about the same time Cardinal Richard denounced him to Rome. No action, however, was taken for the moment. It appeared that Rome proposed to entrust the consideration of the whole " Biblical question " to a permanent international commission appointed for the purpose.

Early in 1902 Loisy had the curious experience of being nominated as a bishop. The Prince of Monaco proposed him to the Pope for that see along with the Abbé Klein and another—" *une trinité de suspects.*" [57] Loisy accepted nomination on the ground that as a bishop he might be better able to serve the cause of the reconciliation of Catholicism and science. [58] But it hardly needs to be said that Rome would not hear of the idea. A renewal of the same nomination later, and another proposal for a French see by M. Combes' Government, had no better result.

The year 1902 saw several notable events in the history of French Modernism. In March, Albert Houtin [59] published

[56] *Mémoires,* ii. 19.
[57] *Mémoires,* ii. 93.
[58] *Choses passées,* 232.
[59] Rivière, 156f. Houtin has told the story of his life in *Une vie de prêtre* [Eng. tr. *The Life of a Priest,* 1927]. Born in 1867 and ordained priest in 1890, he became professor of history at the *petit séminaire* of Angers in 1894—a post which he resigned in 1901 on account of differences with his superiors concerning an essay of his on the early history

his treatise on *La Question biblique chez les catholiques de France au XIXme siècle.* In this the futility of the attempts of Catholic apologists in the nineteenth century to meet the critical position were shown up in caustic fashion. The book was widely read. A few months later Marcel Hébert [60] took the step that marked his final cutting adrift from Catholicism. For some time he had privately circulated his *Souvenirs d'Assise,* giving a drastic application to his " symbolic " interpretation of religious dogmas. The book came to the notice of the ecclesiastical authorities : and Hébert was already threatened with deprivation when in July 1902 he wrote an article called *Le dernier idole*—the " idol " being the conception of God as personal! The scandal was great : but as Hébert was by this time virtually outside the Church it was not thought necessary to take overt action against him. He went to Brussels, where he became an active worker in the cause of Socialism. He died at Paris in 1916.

The most significant event of the year, however, was the appearance in November of the most celebrated of all Modernist writings—Loisy's own *L'Évangile et l'Église.* [61] This was in form a reply to the equally celebrated work of Adolf Harnack, *Das Wesen des Christenthums*—the manifesto *par excellence* of German Liberal Protestantism. According to Harnack, the essential message of Jesus was trust in God as Father. This, and this only, was " the Gospel " : and the whole elaborate apparatus of the Catholic Church, with its hierarchy, its cultus, its dogmatic system, is nothing more than the burying of this Gospel under the steadily increasing weight of a vast mass of alien accretions derived from pagan sources, Hellenic and Roman. To meet this charge it was necessary to prove that the Church, so far from being a distortion, was

of the diocese of Angers (cf. Duchesne, *supra*). He then took up his abode in Paris. His autobiography is a brilliant and terrible indictment of the Catholic system : but it should be read with great caution. In his preface to the Eng. tr. Sir J. G. Frazer speaks of Houtin as " a saint who disbelieved in God." Loisy, *Mémoires,* iii. 503f. paints a very different picture. In any case Houtin's qualification for sainthood was hardly his charity.

[60] See Rivière, 140ff. : also Houtin, *Un prêtre symboliste : Marcel Hébert,* 1925.
[61] For an account of this see Rivière, 158ff.

really a legitimate and necessary development, of the Gospel of Jesus. This is what Loisy, in his own fashion, proposed to do. To begin with, he maintained that Harnack's idea of " the Gospel " was wrong. Its essence really lay in the proclamation of the Kingdom of God, with the accompanying conception of Jesus as Messiah. Both Kingdom and Messiahship were conceived by Jesus in a purely eschatological sense. They represented a body of characteristically Jewish aspirations, and were by no means the initiation of a new world-order designed to give to these practical effect. Jesus was a dreamer, whose life ended in apparent failure. But what Jesus could not do for Himself the Church had done for Him. " Jesus announced the Kingdom, and it is the Church that has come." [62] His life and teaching " needed to be interpreted " [63]—as they have been. In particular, the doctrine of His Divinity " was the sole suitable method of translating for the Greek mind the idea of the Messiah." [64] The whole Catholic system, in a word, is simply a development—a development made possible and necessary by the determination of the Church to realize in fact the idea bequeathed to it by Jesus. " The Church may say that in order to be at all periods what Jesus wished the society of His friends to be, it must have been what it has been : for it has been what it needed to be to save the Gospel by saving itself." [65] In the course of this development its formulæ of faith and worship have undergone many changes according to the prevailing ideas of the periods in which these changes occurred. Thus in approaching them it is necessary " to distinguish between the material sense of the formula and its properly religious and Christian significance." [66] For " Christianity has not escaped the necessity of the symbol, which is the normal form of cultus as of religious knowledge." [67]

In many quarters the book was at first favourably received,

[62] Loisy, L'Évangile et l'Église, 111.
[63] Ibid., 128.
[64] Ibid., 140.
[65] Ibid., 94.
[66] Ibid., 164.
[67] Ibid., 204.

the author's subtle and carefully balanced presentation of his argument serving to mask its essentially destructive nature. Both Mignot and von Hügel were delighted. But it was not long before violent attacks were directed against it. [68]   On January 17th, 1903, Cardinal Richard condemned it as " of a nature to trouble gravely the faith of believers " : [69]   and a number of bishops associated themselves with the condemnation. Houtin's *Question biblique* was condemned a month later. Loisy at once informed the Cardinal that he " condemned all the errors that may have been deducted from my book by those who interpret it from a point of view quite different from that from which I have composed it." [70]   On the strength of this the Paris *Semaine Religieuse* informed its readers that Loisy had submitted!

In view of the controversy excited by *L'Évangile et l'Église,* both von Hügel and Mignot (since 1899 Archbishop of Albi) pressed Loisy to write a pamphlet further explaining his position. Loisy was more than willing to do so: and the result was the volume, *Autour d'un petit livre* [71] (1903). Unfortunately, so far from mitigating the audacities of its predecessor, it made them worse. It assumed the form of a series of seven letters, each addressed to a person whose position was stated, but not his name—though it was fairly obvious who the persons were. E.g. the " Cardinal " to whom Letter II. (on the " Biblical question ") was directed was the eminent Academician, Cardinal Perraud of Autun. [72] The difficulties arising from the alleged lack of a historical basis for the affirmations of the Christian creed were got over by establishing a distinction between " fact " and " faith," and

[68] The first shot was fired by the Abbé Gayraud in the *Univers*. Most of the Catholic democrats were favourable to Modernism, but Gayraud was an exception.
[69] Text in *Choses passées,* 392.
[70] Letter printed *ibid.,* 251.
[71] See *Choses passées,* 259ff ; also Rivière, 175ff.
[72] The complete list is as follows: (1) *Un curé-doyen:* Abbé Ludot (Loisy's old professor of philosophy at Châlons). (2) *Un cardinal:* Cardinal Perraud. (3) *Un evêque:* Mgr. Le Camus of La Rochelle. (4) *Un archévêque:* Mgr. Mignot of Albi. (5) *Un apologiste catholique:* Abbé Félix Klein. (6) *Un jeune savant:* M. Fr. Thureau-Dangin. (7) *Un supérieur de séminaire:* M. Monier of Saint Sulpice. *Choses passées,* 260ff.

the " symbolical " or " relative " character of religious truth was again emphasized. In Loisy's large scale commentary on the *Fourth Gospel*, published at the same time as *Autour*, these ideas were freely applied to the interpretation of the Gospel narrative, which was treated as " a product of Christian mysticism," [73] and not as a genuine history of the life and teaching of Jesus.

By this time Leo XIII. had died, and Pius X. reigned in his stead. The first Encyclical of the new Pope (October 1903) was not promising for the Modernists. It bade the faithful beware of " the insidious manœuvres of a certain new science which decks itself with the mask of truth." [74] In this auspicious environment Cardinal Richard [75] (with Cardinal Perraud in active support) renewed his efforts to secure the condemnation at Rome of what had come to be called " Loisyism." Despite Mignot's efforts to avert this, the Congregation of the Holy Office put five of Loisy's books (including the last three) on the Index (December 16th). [76] At the same time the Congregation of the Index inflicted a similar stigma on Houtin's *Question biblique*.

Informed of his condemnation, Loisy declined to give more than a purely formal " adhesion " to it. [77] Cardinal Richard and the Holy See combined to bring further pressure to bear upon him, but without seriously modifying his attitude. Had this attitude been maintained the result must have been immediate excommunication. But Loisy shrank from incurring the final blow, which, added to the strain of the last months, would, he believed, break down his health altogether and render him incapable of work. He feared, moreover, that deliberately to cut himself off from the Church would be construed as a " desertion " of those who had followed him hitherto. [78] His first idea was to let the blow fall and make his explanations afterwards. But his friends persuaded him

[73] *Mémoires*, ii. 257.
[74] Loisy, *Mémoires*, ii. 265.
[75] See his letter to Pius X. in Clément, *Cardinal Richard*, 400.
[76] Text of decree in *Choses passées*, 393f.
[77] Letter printed in *Choses passées*, 277. " *Mon adhésion . . . est d'ordre purement disciplinaire.*"
[78] *Ibid.*, 288f.

THE CHURCH UNDER LEO. XIII.

that it would be better to make the explanations first. On February 28th, 1904, therefore, he wrote a personal letter [79] to the Pope declaring that, " *autant qu'il est en moi*," he submitted to the condemnation. " It is not in my power," he added, " to destroy the results of my labours." The Pope's reply was communicated to the Cardinal, who on March 12th requested Loisy's presence to hear it. The papal letter proved to be uncompromising, and the interview was stormy. But on his return home Loisy's powers of resistance suddenly broke. He sat down and wrote to the Cardinal as follows : " I declare to your Eminence that from a spirit of obedience to the Holy See I condemn the errors that the Holy Office has condemned in my writings." [80]

Of this letter Loisy was to say later that he wished it had never been written. [81] It was obviously insincere, and it only postponed a *dénouement* that was inevitable. Rome was under no illusion as to the worth of the " submission," but was prepared to hold her hand for the moment. The Pope is said to have remarked : " Loisy wishes to pose as a martyr, but I don't mean to make him one." [82] As for Loisy himself, at least he showed no desire to take unfair advantage of his respite. He gave up his lectures immediately, and retired into the country to live the life of a recluse, first at Garnay, then at Ceffonds near his family. Here he continued his Biblical studies and for a time almost entirely ceased to write.

But if its major prophet had thus withdrawn into the background, Modernism did not cease to make headway. In France, Laberthonnière and Blondel further developed their positions : and Edouard Le Roy in his article, *Qu'est ce qu'est un dogme?* republished later in the volume *Dogme et critique* (condemned in 1907), propounded a conception of dogma which found its value mainly in its " practical meaning " as a " rule of conduct." [83] A very similar view received expression

---

[79] Text in *ibid.*, 292.
[80] *Ibid.*, 299. Text of the Pope's letter in Clément, 405.
[81] *Ibid.*
[82] *Mémoires*, ii. 388.
[83] See Rivière, 248ff.

in England in the writings of the ex-Jesuit, George Tyrrell,[84] which at this period began to enjoy also a wide circulation on the Continent. Houtin, by this time an ecclesiastical Ishmael, published a continuation of his earlier work in *La Question biblique au XXme siècle* (1906), which was in its turn condemned.[85] Much scandal was caused by the appearance in the *Revue d'histoire et de littérature réligieuses* of two pseudonymous series of articles—one (signed " Dupin ") on the development of the doctrine of the Trinity (1906), the other (signed " Herzog ") on that of the doctrine of the Blessed Virgin (1907). The authorship of these articles was hotly discussed : and they were widely, though wrongly, ascribed to Loisy. It was only almost a generation later that the veil of secrecy was torn away, and they were proved to be the work of the Abbé Joseph Turmel.[86] In Italy, too, the movement obtained a wider extension still : and here it was specially formidable through its association with the Catholic democratic movement led by Don Romolo Murri.[87]

By this time Rome was seriously alarmed. Her quarrel with the French Government about the Law of Separation preoccupied her for the time being. But it was well understood that as soon as this question was liquidated she would grapple in earnest with the Modernist peril. Meanwhile, the Biblical Commission had got to work and was issuing a series of decisions that drove critical exegetists within and without the Church to despair. One of these (dated June 27th, 1906) declared that Moses wrote the entire Pentateuch, while conceding that (as Loisy puts it) he might have employed a number of secretaries.[88]

The evident hopelessness of the cause for which he had battled, coupled with disgust at Pius X.'s attitude in connec-

[84] See Rivière, 192ff.
[85] *Ibid.*, 233.
[86] Turmel persistently denied the authorship, despite the Abbé Louis Saltet's ingenious and pertinacious campaign to convict him of it. But at last he was compelled to own up and was excommunicated. See Loisy, *Mémoires*, iii. 544 n. Also Sartiaux, *Joseph Turmel*.
[87] Rivière, 90f., 280f.
[88] *Mémoires*, ii. 496.

tion with the Law of Separation,[89] destroyed any lingering attachment in Loisy for Catholicism.   At the end of 1906 the last link that bound him to his old life was severed by Rome's refusal to renew his " indult." [90]   He said Mass for the last time on November 1st.   But he was determined not to leave the Church of his own accord.   He would go when he was driven out, and not before. [91]

He had not very long to wait.   On July 4th, 1907, the decree *Lamentabili* [92] condemned sixty-four propositions, of which the majority were taken more or less from Loisy's own works.   This was followed on September 8th by the Encyclical *Pascendi,* [93] defining " Modernism " and condemning it in all its manifestations as not merely a heresy but as " the summing up and *suc véneaux* of all heresies."

In the following January the Bishop of Langres, at Merry del Val's behest, summoned Loisy to accept these acts of the Holy See.   He declined to do so, and a few days later published his extremely subversive commentary on the *Synoptic Gospels* and also a volume of *Simples Réflexions,* in which he defiantly charged Rome with misrepresentation.   On February 14th the new Archbishop of Paris, Mgr. Amette, forbade the reading of Loisy's book " on pain of excommunication specially reserved to the Sovereign Pontiff." [94]   A second summons from Langres followed on February 22nd, to be again met with a refusal.   On March 7th, therefore, a decree of the Holy Inquisition [95] imposed on Loisy the gravest penalty the Church has now power to inflict—major excommunication *nominatim ac personaliter.*   The blow had come at last :   and " my first impression," he wrote later, " was that

[89] *Choses passées,* 323.   Loisy published a number of anonymous articles on the subject, *ibid.,* 324ff.   Also *Mémoires,* ii. 442f.
[90] For the circumstances of this refusal see *Choses passées,* 317ff.
[91] Entry in Loisy's diary, November 25th, 1905, *ibid.,* 311.
[92] Analysed in Rivière, 333ff.
[93] Rivière, 349ff.   The Encyclical is criticized in *Choses passées,* 352f. " *Cette encyclique* " (says Loisy) " *denonçait . . . le système moderniste qu'en même temps elle inventait.*"
[94] Text in *Choses passées,* 395f.
[95] Printed *ibid.,* 397.

of an infinite relief." [96] His only regret was that he had not gone to meet it four years before.

The excommunication of Loisy meant the virtual end of Modernism so far as France was concerned. The mass of his followers made haste to effect their peace with the Church: others, like Houtin and Loisy himself, ultimately abandoned Christianity altogether. Theological reaction had triumphed all along the line: and even so moderate a critic as Batiffol, for all his past fulminations against heresy, found himself among its victims. The Italian Modernists did not succumb so easily. For some time still they were to defy the thunders of the Vatican. But Rome was inexorable: and the "Black Terror" of the next few years, crowned by the imposition of the anti-Modernist oath in 1910, stamped out the remnants of the "heresy," or at least drove them effectively underground.

---

[96] *Choses passées*, 367.

CHAPTER XIV

B. Devotional Life and Missionary Effort

I

It is a recurrent source of difficulty in the life of the Church that the intellectual and devotional sides of religion seldom appeal equally to the same persons. This division of interest is illustrated by the history of the Church in France in the period under review. It was a real misfortune that the task of stimulating the practice of the devout life was so largely in the hands of those who, however zealous and good they might be, were obscurantist and uncritical in their outlook, and inclined to judge the value of a devotional method chiefly by its capacity to " work." The result was to give a turn to popular piety that was not always healthy or immune from the charge of superstition. It is to be feared, too, that not infrequently the zealous pushing of a devotional practice was to a large extent dictated by its power to transfer money from the pockets of the faithful to the coffers of the Church.

Further, there was a real danger that the practice of the devout life should come to be regarded as consisting in the multiplication of *petites dévotions,* rather than in the cultivation of the graces of the Christian character. This danger was specially present in the case of the better classes of society, who readily availed themselves of the " religion made easy " which their spiritual guides were not always unwilling to provide for their benefit, as the only way to keep them up to some measure of religious practice at all. It was of such superficial and sentimental piety that Mgr. d'Hulst was thinking when he wrote : " A great deal is made to-day of a return of the ruling classes to the practice of the Christian life. But this ' Christian life '—what does it amount to but an external profession that binds to nothing and profits nothing ? A person is *bien pensant,* but he neither knows nor studies the Church's doctrine. He approaches the sacraments, but he does not reform his life and does no honour to what he receives. There are more Christians, you say. But there is also less Christianity." [1]

Yet whatever these defects and drawbacks may have been, the age was marked by not a little devotional fervour. The steadily growing hostility of the world outside to revealed religion was regarded by earnest Catholics as a challenge to a more ardent piety in themselves. Devotion to our Lord was fostered by the cultus of the Sacred Heart. This, after a period of decline in the frosty air of the eighteenth century, had been revived in the nineteenth, and had rapidly won a great success in the country of its origin. " The devotion to the Sacred Heart of Jesus," says Père Lecanuet, " dominates the whole of the century." [2] Its close connection with the cause of the Monarchy has been already spoken of : and for this reason it achieved perhaps its maximum significance at the time when the hopes of a monarchical revival were at their brightest during the 'seventies. But in the succeeding two decades it continued to flourish. In particular the liability created by the *Vœu national* of 1871 to build a great basilica on Montmartre in honour of the Sacred Heart was bravely liquidated. The gigantic building on the northern heights of Paris rose steadily from its foundations. The apse was consecrated in 1886, and five years later the whole edifice was ready for worship. The huge dome was completed in 1899. The basilica became the centre of a vast organization for prayer and pious activities all over France.

The pontificate of Leo XIII. also witnessed a great development of the cultus of the Blessed Sacrament. The Pope himself sedulously encouraged it : and a number of new congregations came into existence with the express aim of promoting it. The habit of frequent communion underwent a marked extension : and the practice of perpetual adoration in all the churches of a diocese in succession throughout the

---

[1] Quoted in Baunard, *Un siècle de l'Église de France,* 489.
[2] Lecanuet, *La Vie de l'Église sous Léon XIII.,* 123.

year made steady progress. A further impetus was given by the Eucharistic Congresses held annually at different centres all over the world. The credit of initiating these belongs to a pious Frenchwoman, Mlle. Tamisier,[3] who, after many failures and rebuffs, had the satisfaction of seeing the first Congress held at Lille in 1881. Henceforth they were to assemble every year on an ever-increasing scale of size and magnificence. Between 1882 and 1904 nine were held on French soil.

It was, however, the cultus of the Blessed Virgin that more than any other supplied the mould of popular piety. An Ultramontane writer has styled the nineteenth century " the century of Mary." [4] Her cultus, popular in France from the early Middle Ages, received a marked impetus from the solemn promulgation of the doctrine of her Immaculate Conception by Pius IX. in 1854. Four years later her alleged appearance to Bernadette Soubirous at Lourdes initiated a vast pilgrimage movement to the Pyrenean sanctuary, which increased steadily in volume from year to year. The healing waters of Lourdes attracted the sick and their friends from all parts of the world. During the twenty-five years of Leo XIII.'s pontificate 3,500 organized pilgrimages brought a total of over three million pilgrims to Lourdes, without counting the vast number of isolated pilgrims.[5] The Pope himself professed a special devotion to our Lady; and addressed numerous Encyclicals to the faithful exhorting them to a diligent use of the rosary in her honour. The great organization for women and girls called *Enfants de Marie* covered the whole of France: and innumerable other congregations and confraternities bore her name.

The business of the historian is to record and not to criticize these manifestations. Yet it is not denied by French Catholics themselves[6] that the popular devotion of the time was often mingled with much superstition and credulity. The grotesque episode connected with the name of " Diana Vaughan "

---

[3] *Ibid.*, 136.
[4] Baunard, *op. cit.*, 222.
[5] Lecanuet, 142.
[6] E.g. Baunard, 491.

showed how far this credulity could go.[7]   An anticlerical
scribbler, calling himself Léo Taxil, had won a certain
notoriety in the early 'eighties by a series of scabrous attacks
on the Church, of which the title of one, *The Secret Loves
of Pius IX.*, may give the measure.   In 1885 he professed
himself a convert to Catholicism, and proceeded to give a
gage of his sincerity in a new campaign of defamation,
directed this time against Freemasonry.   At length in 1893 he
announced the publication in monthly instalments of a work
called *Le Diable au XIXme siècle*.   In this he assumed the
rôle of " Dr. Bataille," who, though a devout Catholic, had
allowed himself to be initiated into Masonic organizations all
over the world, with the object of worming out their inner-
most secrets.   With a wealth of lurid detail borrowed from
the records of magic and sorcery in all ages, he described the
essentially Satanistic character of the Masonic cult.   The more
credulous Catholic public fell with zest on a testimony so
gratifying to its prejudices.   Emboldened by this, the
egregious Taxil proceeded to invent another character, this
time a woman, called " Diana Vaughan."   She was represented as a woman of great beauty and intelligence, who
had seen Lucifer in person, and had been put by him under
the direction of one of his satellites.   During two years she set
forth serially her experiences, first as a Satanist, then as a
Catholic convert.   Her great enemy was a Sophia Walder,
who was said to have married a demon called Bitru, and
borne to him a daughter who was the grandmother of Antichrist !   The clergy in general treated these " revelations "
with the contempt they deserved : but the *Croix* vouched for
the genuineness of " Diana Vaughan," and produced letters
from Mgr. Fava, Bishop of Grenoble, and the secretary to a
Roman Cardinal in support of this view.[8]   Léo Taxil quickly
became the idol of an enthusiastic following, which compared
him to St. Augustine and St. Thomas Aquinas.   At last he
offered to confute his critics by producing " Diana Vaughan "

---

[7] On what follows see Lecanuet, *op. cit.*, 159ff.   Also Debidour, i.
376 n., ii. 178 n.
[8] *La Croix*, November 11th, 1896.

in person in a public hall in Paris on April 19th, 1897. Before a large crowd there appeared, not the lovely "Diana Vaughan" but a bald and bearded man—Léo Taxil himself, who declared that he had never really been converted at all, but had merely been playing a trick on the credulity of Catholics.

The incident casts a curious light on the mentality of the " Catholic underworld " of the time, and was, of course, exploited to the full by the enemies of the Church. But it would be a grave injustice to regard it as more than a very partial manifestation, or one that cannot be easily parallelled in other religious communions. The age that produced the fatuous dupes of Léo Taxil also produced many characters of the finest Christian temper of both sexes, and in every degree of education and social condition. It also witnessed much lavish giving for charitable purposes. The Society of S. Vincent de Paul is specially worthy of mention for the generosity of its members, not only in cash, but in personal service as well. The amount expended by the French section of it in 1898 was nearly 3 million francs.[9] The numerous nursing congregations, again, were indefatigable in their devotion to the sick and poor—not least the " Little Sisters of the Poor," who provided homes for the aged and indigent, and supported them entirely by begging. If Catholics were for the most part over-inclined to believe that " charity " might absolve them from the duty of helping to build up a juster social order, at least the demands of " charity " were gallantly met.

II

The French are notoriously bad colonists in the sense that they find it hard to settle permanently anywhere but in their own country. A Frenchman may be ready to go abroad to " make his pile," but when the object is achieved he comes home again. This national trait would lead us to expect that French Catholics would be at least lukewarm missionaries. In point of fact the reverse is the case. No Catholic nation has so honourable a record in the mission field.[10] The greatest of

[9] Baunard, op. cit., 275.
[10] On French Catholic missions see Lecanuet, Les premières années du Pontificat de Léon XIII., Ch. vi. Also Baunard, op. cit., Ch. xix.

Catholic missionary societies, the *Propagation de la Foi,* is of French origin. It was founded at Lyons in 1822. Of its annual income nearly two-thirds at this period came from France—in 1898 over four million francs out of a total of 6,700,000. [11] And this society was only the chief of many smaller ones. Nor was the French Church less lavish of its sons and daughters than of its money. After the " dead season " of the eighteenth century, the nineteenth fully revived the glories of the seventeenth, when French missionaries covered the globe from America in the far West to China and Japan in the far East. Now as always, it was the Religious Orders that supplied the *militia Christi* in heathen lands. Besides the older Orders—the Jesuits, Dominicans, etc. with the French *Congrégation des Missions Etrangères* founded in the seventeenth century—a number of new congregations came into existence for the purpose—notably the *Congrégation du Saint Esprit,* and the famous " *Pères Blancs* " of North Africa. The work of the clerical congregations was assisted and stabilized by that of the lay teaching orders : and the devotion of the female congregations equalled that of the men, while their numbers were far greater. At the beginning of the twentieth century there were 70,000 Catholic missionaries of both sexes all over the world, of whom 17,000 odd were men. Two-thirds of the priests came from France, and four-fifths of the teaching brothers and the nuns. Further, out of 119 martyrs for the faith within a century ninety-five were French. [12] Fearless, enterprising and intensely self-sacrificing in themselves, and (as we have seen) regarded with a favourable eye even by the anticlerical rulers of France on account of the services rendered by them to French interests, the French missionaries of the later nineteenth century were able to add a new and glorious page to the tale of the " *gesta Dei per Francos.*"

The story of their achievements cannot be told at length here. It must suffice to mention briefly some of its outstanding features. The greatest missionary figure of the time,

[11] Baunard, 428.
[12] Baunard, 433.

not only in France but in the Catholic world generally, was Cardinal Lavigerie. [13] At once passionately French and passionately Catholic, he deliberately set himself in his work in North Africa to forward the interests of his country not less than those of his Church. It was to him that the establishment of the French power in Tunis was largely due. Made Archbishop of Algiers in 1866, he set up a missionary centre at Carthage in 1875 as a means of spreading, not only the religion, but the language and the political influence of France. At this time both France and Italy were casting covetous eyes on Tunis, and in 1877 Lavigerie made a league with the French Consul-General, M. Roustan, to win it for France. He founded the College of S. Louis at Tunis, bought a considerable amount of property, and distributed lavish alms to the native population. Jules Ferry watched these developments with approval, and in 1881 felt strong enough to send an army to occupy the northern part of Tunisia. Lavigerie acted as adviser to the military authorities, but was at the same time careful to intervene on behalf of the natives when they were harshly treated. He at once threw himself with enthusiasm into the task of organizing the ecclesiastical life of the new protectorate. Cathedrals were begun at Tunis and Carthage. Churches, schools and hospitals were multiplied, and carried on their evangelistic and civilizing work through the agency of Lavigerie's own *Pères Blancs* and *Sœurs Africaines* and of other religious congregations. [14] But above all, Lavigerie desired to restore the ancient glories of Carthage —to make it at once the ecclesiastical metropolis of North Africa, the capital of France's African empire, and a radiant centre of religion and civilization for the whole vast continent. In 1884, Leo XIII. issued a bull restoring the ancient primatial See of Carthage : and Lavigerie, already a Cardinal

[13] On Lavigerie's life and work see Baunard, *Le Cardinal Lavigerie*, 2 vols., 1896. Also Lecanuet, *op. cit.*, 223ff.
[14] Lavigerie's work would appear to have had a commercial side which is less attractive. This struck Archbishop Benson when he visited Carthage in 1892. See an interesting note in his diary : A. C. Benson, *Life of Archbishop Benson*, ii. 418. Lavigerie was decidedly a man of " both worlds." Debidour's portrait of him is vitriolic : but it may contain a substratum of truth.

for two years, became its first occupant. The cathedral of Carthage was consecrated in 1890. In order to obtain the money for all these vast undertakings Lavigerie went begging all over France, and even succeeded for a time in extracting a substantial grant from the French treasury.

The Cardinal's schemes were by no means confined to Algeria and Tunis. He dreamed of winning the whole of Central Africa for Christ and for France. The mysteries of "darkest Africa" had recently been revealed through the efforts of intrepid explorers : and at the conference of Berlin in 1884 the Powers had partitioned it into zones of influence among themselves, France receiving its northern portion. Already Lavigerie's *Pères Blancs* had sought to evangelize both the Soudan and Equatorial Africa. Their assault on the first was a failure, for the missionaries were all massacred : but in the case of the second they were more successful. Two centres were formed, the one near Lake Tanganyika (1878), the other near Lake Nyanza (1879). The latter was to pass through a baptism of blood and fire when the accession of the infamous King Mwanga in 1883 gave the signal for the outbreak of a fearful persecution that wiped out a large number of converts. However, the English protectorate in time restored peace and religious freedom, and the Roman Catholics have a full share in the prosperity of the various Christian missions in Uganda. In the Soudan missionary enterprise was resumed after the French capture of Timbuctoo in 1894.

The account of Lavigerie's missionary work would not be complete without some mention of the passionate campaign against slavery undertaken by him from 1885 onwards. The experience of his *Pères Blancs* in Central Africa had revealed to him the full horror of the evil : and his advancing years (he was now sixty-four) did not prevent him from raising his voice in the chief cities of Europe in a successful attempt to rouse the conscience of the civilized world against it. His activity in this direction won him the admiration, not of Catholics only, but of Christians of all communions.

While the *Pères Blancs* were evangelizing the north and centre of Africa, the *Pères du Saint Esprit* founded a flourishing mission at Zanzibar, and from thence penetrated into the interior. The same congregation did still more striking work on the west coast—in Senegal, Dahomey, Sierra Leone and especially French Congo—the last the scene of the heroic labours of Père Augouard, made bishop in 1890. By 1901 no less than 612 of its members had laid down their lives for the cause of Christ. In Madagascar the Jesuits had been at work since the 'forties. The political vicissitudes of the island caused them to be expelled more than once : but in 1896 Madagascar finally became a French colony, and in the succeeding years the French missionary work there underwent a notable expansion.

In the East, where France had enjoyed for centuries a protectorate of Christian interests, her missionaries laboured zealously but with varying fortunes. The Jesuits founded their great university at Beyrout in 1880 with the support of the French Government : and French religious of various orders were at work in Palestine and Syria, Armenia and Persia—as also in British India. It was, however, further east still—in the great peninsula of Indo-China—that the story of French missionary endeavour reached its highest point of heroism and of tragedy. Here especially the cause of Catholic missions had come to be closely involved with that of French expansion, and the spirit of national independence was continually liable to vent itself in ferocious attacks on the missionaries (who were not always discreet) and their native converts. The Church in Annam—the field *par excellence* of the *Pères des Missions Etrangères*—had undergone a terrible persecution in 1830. In the following decades persecution went on intermittently till 1874, when a French expedition compelled the Emperor Tu-Duc—" the Annamite Nero "—to accept the French protectorate. Tu-Duc, however, tried to play off China against France : and in 1882 the latter was compelled to begin a war, which after several years of mingled success and disaster, succeeded in bringing about the final conquest of the country. During these years the fury of the Annamite authorities fell again and again on the French mission stations. The worst persecution was the so-called

"Annamite Vespers" of 1885-6. It is estimated that in this period fifty priests, French and native, and over 50,000 native Christians helped with their life-blood to pay the price of the French triumph, while the French administration stood by with folded hands. At the funeral of the anticlerical Paul Bert, who died as Governor-General of Cochin-China in 1886, a few weeks after pontificating in an Annamite temple and sacrificing incense to its idols, a golden statue of Buddha was carried in procession.[15] None the less, the French conquest brought peace and prosperity to the Church. Between 1886 and 1907 the number of Christians rose from 350,000 to 800,000.[16]

The story of French missions in China is not dissimilar. Here, as elsewhere, France regarded them as a primary instrument of her own secular policy—and all the more because of her traditional privilege of protecting Catholic interests in the Far East. This privilege was seriously threatened when Leo. XIII. proposed in 1886 to deal directly with China through a Nuncio at Peking: but the French Government protested so strongly that he was obliged to abandon the idea. An attempt the following year to transfer the French protectorate to Germany was rejected by him.[17] The result of this close connection between religious and national interests was seen in sporadic persecutions, which became general at the time of the great "Boxer" rebellion in 1900 for the final ousting of the "Western devils" from the Celestial Empire. Some seven or eight thousand Christians are said to have perished in the course of this: and the Christians besieged in Peking were only saved from extermination by the capture of the city by the joint forces of the Powers.

One more field cultivated by the labours of French missionaries remains to be mentioned—a field made illustrious for all time by the noblest name of them all—the incomparable Father Damien. Damien Deveuster was not indeed French

[15] Lecanuet, *op. cit.*, 271 and n.
[16] *Ibid.*
[17] See Lecanuet, 277ff.

but Belgian by birth : but he belonged to a French order and worked under French auspices. The *Pères de Picpus* had been labouring in the Sandwich Isles since 1827. Here Damien joined them in 1864, and in 1873 devoted himself to the care of the lepers isolated in the island of Molokai. The story of his heroic ministry is so well known that it is unnecessary to retell it here. Stricken with leprosy himself in 1885, he died, his flesh eaten away to the bone, in 1889.

The writer of this book has had much to tell of the follies and frailties with which the Catholic name may be associated. In the heroisms of this last chapter, and supremely in the story of Father Damien, we may see the other side of the medal—that capacity for limitless self-sacrifice which perhaps no other Christian body is able to evoke in the same degree as the great and august communion of Rome, and which is the real secret of her abiding power.

EPILOGUE

It has been rather cynically remarked that " the pontificates of Popes who have been distinguished for personal holiness have been uniformly disastrous for the Church." This certainly seems to be true in the case of Pius X. His defenders are in the habit of alleging that the Church in his time was in " a state of siege," and that his uncompromising refusal to parley with the enemy without and his court-martial methods within were the necessary conditions of her salvation. But to an impartial observer the " besieged fortress " conception of the relation of the Church to the world is one that seems to be open to grave objections. On the Ultramontane theory that the Church is always right and needs no instruction from any quarter save her own past, it may be the natural and necessary view to take. But to those who believe that " God fulfils Himself in many ways," it would appear that even the Church may have something to learn from the travail of human thought and experience. Nor is it wise to forget that to meet one's enemy with defiance and contempt may often be simply to harden his heart and redouble his violence. It may be a mistake to regard Leo XIII. as in any real sense a " liberal " pontiff. Intellectually, he belonged to the old order, and, like most men, he became less accessible to new lights as he grew older. He believed with all his heart in the absolute power of the Pope over the Church, as finally vindicated by his predecessor : and he was not less determined to exercise it, in his own way, to the full. He was, too, rather a diplomat perhaps than a real statesman : his policy was largely dictated by the expediency of the moment. But at least he took no delight in pushing issues to extremes, and preferred, when he could, to " agree with his adversary quickly." It is even possible to hold that in his time the papal autocracy was of positive advantage to the Church : for without his restraining hand the French part of it might well have dashed itself to pieces. Unfortunately the reign of his .successor was to exhibit the Ultramontane principle in a less favourable light. The elements in Catholicism which the moderation of Leo XIII. had held in check were to ascend the papal throne itself under Pius X. ; with the result that by the end of the first decade of the twentieth century the Church in France presented a sorry spectacle to all save the blind votaries of tradition.

The value of the Concordat is matter for debate. It gave the Church a recognized place in the national life and kept it supplied with the sinews of war for its pastoral work. On the other hand, the Liberal Catholics in 1905 were, generally speaking, in favour of Separation, as likely to give the Church a greater freedom of action, and to increase at once the self-respect of the clergy and the self-reliance of the laity. But they regarded the *associations cultuelles* as a vital part of the new order and were strongly in favour of their adoption. [1] Those who regretted the passing of the Concordat were of the same opinion now that that passing was an accomplished fact. Pius X., however, seemed determined to disappoint all but his fanatical partisans. He had already done all he could to hasten the coming of Separation. He now refused to en-dorse, even in modified form, an arrangement which would not only have preserved to the Church a remnant of its resources, but held out the promise of bringing clergy and laity together in a fruitful collaboration, and so breaking down the " wall of ice " between them that had had such unfortunate results.

His handling of the problem created by the rise of Modernism was not less disastrous. It cannot be denied that the position of many of the Modernists (and of Loisy in par-ticular) was quite incompatible with any conception of Chris-tianity as a religion resting on a historic Divine revelation : and it is improbable that those holding it could in any case have remained permanently within the Church. But here again the blind refusal of Rome to entertain even the most solidly-established conclusions of scientific criticism tended to drive

[1] Weill, 237.

men to extremes : while the anti-Modernist " Terror " struck
not only at views fundamentally inconsistent with Christianity,
but also at the whole of the intellectual life of the Church.

Finally, it was at the hand of Pius X. that the Christian
democratic movement, which, encouraged by his predecessor,
had held out such fair hopes in the 'nineties, received its deathblow. As reactionary in politics as in religion, the Pope
showed himself not simply indifferent but hostile to those
forces in the modern world that were making for the setting up
of a new and juster social order. His condemnation of the
Sillon in 1910 (largely at the bidding of the *Action Française*!)
has been not unjustly described by Loisy as " the most
odious act of his pontificate." [2]

Yet in the face of all these fatal mistakes the Church of
France stood helpless. For over half a century it had progressively surrendered its destinies into the hands of an ecclesiastical despot : and now it was reaping what it had sown.
Well might Mgr. Mignot say in the bitterness of his spirit when
the Pope flouted the wishes of the French episcopate at the
time of the passing of the Separation Law : " This is what
Dom Guéranger, Cardinal Pie and Louis Veuillot have
brought us to. They wanted an infallible Pope. They have
got one." [3]

[2] *Mémoires,* iii. 194.
[3] Houtin, *Une vie de prêtre* [English translation] 235.

INDEX

DATE	
AP 27 '87	
GAYLORD	